READING REVELATION

To my wife Paula, my daughter Jennifer,
and my sons Joe and Stephen

Reading Revelation

A Literary and Theological Commentary
Revised Edition

Joseph L. Trafton

SMYTH&HELWYS
PUBLISHING, INCORPORATED · MACON, GEORGIA

Smyth & Helwys Publishing, Inc.
6316 Peake Road
Macon, Georgia 31210-3960
1-800-747-3016

Trafton, Joseph L.

The paper used in this publication meets the minimum
requirements of American National Standard for Information
Sciences—Permanence of Paper for Printed Library Materials.
ANSI Z39.48–1984   (alk. paper)

Library of Congress Cataloging-in-Publication Data

Trafton, Joseph L.
Reading Revelation: a literary and theological commentary / by Joseph L. Trafton.
    p. cm.
    Includes bibliographical references and index.
    ISBN 1-57312-289-0 (pbk. : alk. paper)
    1. Bible. N.T. Revelation—Commentaries.
    I. Title.

BS2825.53.T73 2005

228'.07--dc22   2004028125

Disclaimer of Liability: With respect to statements of opinion or fact available in this work of nonfiction,
Smyth & Helwys Publishing Inc. nor any of its employees, makes any warranty, express or implied, or
assumes any legal liability or responsibility for the accuracy or completeness of any information disclosed,
or represents that its use would not infringe privately-owned rights.

Contents

John's Second "In the Spirit" Experience (4:1–11:19)

Three Signs in Heaven (12:1–16:21)

John's Third "In the Spirit" Experience (17:1–20:15)

Editor's Foreword

"Reading the New Testament" is a commentary series that aims to present cutting-edge research in popular form that is accessible to upper-level undergraduates, seminarians, seminary-educated pastors, and educated laypeople, as well as to graduate students and professors. The volumes in this series do not follow the word-by-word, phrase-by-phrase, verse-by-verse method of traditional commentaries. Rather they are concerned to understand large thought units and their relationship to an author's thought as a whole. The focus is on a close reading of the final form of the text. The aim is to make one feel at home in the biblical text itself. The approach of these volumes involves a concern both for *how* an author communicates and *what* the religious point of the text is. Care is taken to relate both the *how* and the *what* of the text to its milieu: Christian (New Testament and noncanonical), Jewish (scriptural and postbiblical), and Greco-Roman. This enables both the communication strategies and the religious message of the text to be clarified against a range of historical and cultural possibilities. Moreover, a section of commentary on a large thought unit will often contain a brief excursus on some topic raised by the material in the unit, sometimes sketching Old Testament, postbiblical Jewish, Greco-Roman, New Testament, and noncanonical Christian views on the subject. Throughout, the basic concern is to treat the New Testament texts as religious documents whose religious message needs to be set forth with compelling clarity. All other concerns are subordinated to this. It is the hope of all participants in this project that our efforts at exposition will enable the New Testament to be understood better and communicated more competently.

—Charles H. Talbert,
General Editor

Author's Preface

Upon learning that I had accepted an invitation to write a commentary on the book of Revelation, a friend of mine asked bluntly, "Are you crazy or just plain stupid?" I answered, "Yes." Anyone who would seek to understand this strange book and then explain it to others must certainly be devoid of basic sensibilities. Indeed, whether trying to solve the book's structure or make sense of its imagery, you constantly get the feeling of trying to hold a live fish in your bare hands: every time you think you have it, it slips out. It would be easy enough, of course, to pretend to have everything all figured out—to draw up impressive-looking charts, pluck Scriptures blithely from here and there, and tie everything in with current world events (especially those relating to Israel!), thus demonstrating (1) one's stature as an expert in "prophecy" and (2) that we are living in "the last days." But doing so, in my view, would be perpetrating an incorrect view of the book that has become so entrenched in many Christian circles that it has been afforded the same honor as, say, the doctrine of the Trinity, if not a higher one. To propose a distinctly different understanding of the book invites disbelief and knee-jerk criticism; hence, my friend's question is appropriate on several levels.

If there is one trait I would add to my friend's question as essential for the interpreter of this book, it would be humility. As I often tell my students when discussing Revelation, "I know enough to know that I don't know enough." To claim otherwise about this book only validates my point. But if we approach it with genuine humility, setting aside preconceived notions about what it is "supposed" to mean and simply *listen* to it, then we can begin to sense something of its enormous power and beauty. Whether or not my interpretation of the book is correct at every (or any!) point is not important; if I can help the reader take that first and all-important step of learning to listen to what John has written, then I have succeeded.

I am grateful to Charles Talbert, who invited me to write the commentary and has demonstrated enormous patience in awaiting its completion.

Special thanks also go to J. Ramsey Michaels, who introduced me to the study of the book of Revelation and directed my master's thesis on it many years ago; Robert H. Mounce, who not only wrote a marvelous commentary on Revelation but also secured my teaching position for me at Western Kentucky University; James H. Charlesworth, who gave me the tools for understanding Revelation in its larger Jewish context; Michael Card, who sent me a prerelease copy of his musical interpretation of Revelation, *Unveiled Hope*, with its hauntingly beautiful song "The New Jerusalem"; Ryan Stokes, who shared with me his identification of a chiastic use of "conquer" throughout the book; and three classes of "book of Revelation" students at Western Kentucky University, who helped me work through many of the ideas contained in this commentary. My daughter Jennifer and my sons Joe and Stephen—all creative artists—have helped their father begin the journey of learning to appreciate the artistic character of the book; Jennifer also proofread the entire manuscript and made numerous editorial suggestions. Finally, there is no way I could have ever completed this commentary without the unfailing love and encouragement of my wife Paula.

Introduction

A beast with ten horns and seven heads, one of which features a fatal wound that has been healed. A woman clothed with the sun, with the moon under her feet and a crown of twelve stars on her head. Two "witnesses" with fire coming out of their mouths and devouring their enemies. An army of locusts with human-like faces and tails and stingers like scorpions. A white horse ridden by one who is dressed in a robe dipped in blood and has a sharp sword coming out of his mouth. A blazing mountain thrown into the sea that turns a third of it to blood. An enormous red dragon hurled down from heaven. A city of pure gold with twelve gates, each made of a single pearl. Seven seals. Seven trumpets. Seven bowls. The mark of the beast. Armageddon. 1,000 years. 144,000. 666.

Is it any wonder that the book of Revelation tends to elicit two almost diametrically opposed responses from its readers? On the one hand are those who become fascinated with it; they approach the book, it often seems, as if it were the ultimate jigsaw puzzle and vow not to rest until they have fit together every last piece. On the other hand are those who throw up their hands in despair of ever finding any meaning in the book; they are convinced that any effort to do so is doomed to failure.

Is there a middle ground? Is it possible to read Revelation in such a manner that one can indeed make sense out of it, even if many details remain elusive? This commentary will attempt to guide the reader through such a reading of this puzzling book. I will even go so far as to suggest that finding the proper approach to reading Revelation is not all that difficult, provided that we are willing to take to heart the book's claim.

"The words of the prophecy":
Finding a Starting Point for Reading Revelation

The starting point for understanding any piece of writing is recognizing what it claims about itself. If we read a newspaper editorial as merely a presentation of facts or a biography of a great woman as fiction or a science fiction novel as a representation of the universe as it really is, then we will misread it.

The same is true for Revelation. Our starting point must be to try to determine what sort of book it claims to be. To our delight we learn at the outset that the author calls his book "prophecy" (1:3). But therein lies the problem. Modern culture equates prophecy with prediction. To say that Revelation is prophecy, then, suggests to many readers that it is a book that predicts the future. Hence, readers typically interpret the book against modern events in order to see if its "prophecies" are being fulfilled in the world today.

But to do so is to misunderstand the meaning of "prophecy" in the ancient world. In the Old Testament, prophecy involved communicating a message from God. In Deut 18:18 God tells Moses, "I will raise up for them a prophet like you from among their brethren; and I will put my words in his mouth, and he shall speak to them all that I command him." The prophet speaks God's message. Similarly, when appointing Aaron as Moses' spokesman in Exod 7:1-2, God says to Moses, "See, I make you as God to Pharaoh; and Aaron your brother shall be your prophet. You shall speak all that I command you; and Aaron your brother shall tell Pharaoh to let the people of Israel go out of his land." The Old Testament prophets served as spokespeople for God, relaying his word to the Israelites. To be sure, God's message could include predictions (e.g., Jeremiah's prediction of the fall of Jerusalem), but such predictions were part of a larger message designed for the present situation (e.g., Jeremiah's critique of faithless Israel).

That prophecy is the communication of a message from God for the present situation is also the understanding of the New Testament. Paul characterizes prophecy (a manifestation of the Spirit—1 Cor 12:7, 10) as speaking to people "for their upbuilding and encouragement and consolation" (1 Cor 14:3). When the disciples speak in tongues on the day of Pentecost—an event accompanied by a citation of Joel 2:28-32 in which "prophesying" is mentioned twice (Acts 2:17, 18)—such speaking signifies the present activity of the Holy Spirit as the disciples tell their listeners of "the mighty works of God" (Acts 2:11). Even in the case of Agabus's prophecy, which predicts Paul's arrest in Jerusalem, the focus is on the fact that it is a message from the Holy Spirit (Acts 21:10-11). The fact that it is a prediction does not make it any less relevant to the immediate concern of Paul, the one to whom it was given. Paul could have chosen to break off his trip to Jerusalem had he been so inclined.

John's claim that his book is prophecy is consistent with this background. The opening word of the book, *apokalupsis* (from which comes the oft-used designation "the Apocalypse") identifies it as a "revelation," which invokes the notion of uncovering something that is hidden. Hence, by speaking of a "revelation of Jesus Christ," John claims that the contents of the book are not his own ideas; rather, they have been given to him by Jesus Christ, who, in turn, received them from God (1:1). Furthermore, he understands that he has been commissioned to pass along this revelation to other Christians, specifically the seven churches of the province of Asia (1:1, 11). This identification of the book as a revelation, therefore, confirms its place within the classic understanding of prophecy.

The starting point for understanding the book, then, will be to take seriously the book's claim to be prophecy—i.e., to see it as a message that, according to its author, has been given to him by God to pass along to a specific group of Christians in his day. A proper approach to Revelation as prophecy will help us focus our attention on what it claims to be: a book for first-century Christians. While this approach will not discount altogether the possibility that the book contains predictions, it will enable us to keep such predictions in their proper perspective when we encounter them.

"The seven churches that are in Asia":
Reading Revelation in Its Historical Context

If we are going to understand Revelation as prophecy, we must begin by situating the book within its proper historical context. Who wrote it, and under what circumstances did he write? Even more importantly, just who were these seven churches of Asia, and why did they need a prophecy from God?

The author of Revelation identifies himself as "John" (1:1, 4, 9; 22:8). Early Christian writers (e.g., Justin, *Dialogue with Trypho* 81.4; Irenaeus, *Against Heresies* 4.20.11) frequently understood the author to be the Apostle John, the brother of James, the son of Zebedee, one of the twelve disciples of Jesus—an identification that has become the "traditional" understanding among many Christians. Yet the author provides the reader with none of these specifics; he simply calls himself "John." Indeed, the fourth century church historian Eusebius suggested, on the basis of a quotation from the early second century bishop Papias of Hierapolis (*Ecclesiastical History*

3.39.2-4), that there were *two* Johns in the first century church, the Apostle John and John the Elder, the latter being the author of Revelation (*Ecclesiastical History* 3.39.6). A few early Christians (cf. Eusebius, *Ecclesiastical History* 7.25.2) even argued that the book was not penned by anyone named John at all but rather by the heretic Cerinthus. We need not press the point here. Although the author apparently expected his readers to know who he was, he did not base the authority of his book upon his own stature or upon any alleged relationship with the earthly Jesus but rather upon the revelation that had been given to him. While we cannot dismiss the Apostle John from consideration, the question of who wrote Revelation ultimately bears little relevance for understanding the book. We shall simply call the author by the name he uses for himself: John.

A related question is whether this "John" also authored the Gospel and letters of John in the New Testament. A positive answer here would be relevant to the interpretation of Revelation, because we would then have a larger corpus of literature by the same author within which we could read it. Once again, the testimony of the early church is not uniform. While some (e.g., Jerome, *Lives of Illustrious Men* 9) believed that the same author—namely the Apostle John—wrote all five books, others (e.g., Dionysius of Alexandria, according to Eusebius, *Ecclesiastical History* 7.25.6-27) argued that the Gospel and Revelation came from different writers. Modern scholarship is divided over whether even the Gospel and letters of John come from a single author (or two or three or even a "Johannine school"), much less Revelation! From earliest times, significant linguistic, stylistic, and theological differences between Revelation on the one hand and the Gospel and letters of John on the other have been noted. While this does not prove different authorship, and while there are indeed *some* conceptual parallels (e.g., Jesus as the Word: John 1:1; 1 John 1:1; Rev 19:13), there is no compelling reason to argue for the probability of common authorship of the five books. Indeed, in 2 John and 3 John the author identifies himself simply as "the elder" (2 John 1; 3 John 1), and in 1 John he never identifies himself at all; the Gospel of John relates its contents to "the disciple whom Jesus loved" (John 21:20-24; cf. John 19:35), who is otherwise unnamed. Only in Revelation does the author call himself "John." Hence, we should not give a privileged position to the Gospel and letters of John when we read Revelation.

John claims to have received the revelation while on the island of Patmos (1:9). Patmos is a small, rocky island about ten miles long and five miles wide off the southwest coast of modern Turkey (cf. Pliny, *Natural History* 4.12.23). The Romans often used such islands as places to exile certain kinds of prisoners, though there is no concrete evidence that they used Patmos in this manner. That he is on Patmos "on account of the word of God and the witness of Jesus" (1:9) is probably an indication that John is in exile, though the specific details of his exile are not known. Certainly some early church fathers (e.g., Clement of Alexandria, *Who Is the Rich Man Who Will Be Saved?* 42; Eusebius, *Ecclesiastical History* 3.18.1) understood John's plight in this way.

Revelation is usually dated either in the late 60s or in the mid-90s AD. Arguments for the early date generally center on the following considerations: (1) the angel's command to John in 11:1-2 to measure the Temple would make sense only if the Jewish Temple in Jerusalem were still standing—the Romans destroyed it in AD 70; (2) a number of features of the book, including the number 666 in 13:18, point to the Emperor Nero, who committed suicide in AD 68; and (3) the interpretation in 17:10-11 of the seven heads of the beast, which identifies them as seven kings, five of whom have "fallen," logically puts the writing of the book in the time of the sixth Roman emperor, Galba, who ruled briefly in AD 68–69. None of these arguments is persuasive, as the commentary will show.

Most scholars date the book to the end of the reign of the Emperor Domitian (AD 81–96), a position already held by the second century bishop Irenaeus (*Against Heresies* 5.30.3). This dating of the book rests on its supposed connection with a persecution of Christians carried out by Emperor Domitian late in his reign, which we will examine further below. But other arguments also suggest a date later rather than earlier. For example, the churches of Ephesus, Sardis, and Laodicea, all founded in the early 50s, have been in existence long enough to have suffered serious spiritual decline (2:4; 3:1, 15-16). In addition, the church at Laodicea, a city that suffered a devastating earthquake in AD 60, has had time to recover to the point that it boasts of being rich and self-sufficient (3:17). Finally, Polycarp, the bishop of Smyrna in the middle of the second century, observes that the church at Smyrna did not come into existence until after the time of Paul (Polycarp, *Philippians* 11.3), who died in the mid-60s. Our working hypothesis will be that a later date, probably during the reign of Domitian, is the most likely setting for Revelation.

John's intended readers are "the seven churches" in the Roman province of "Asia" (1:4). These seven churches are further identified as being located in Ephesus, Smyrna, Pergamum, Sardis, Thyatira, Philadelphia, and Laodicea (1:11). Precisely why these seven churches are singled out is unclear. They were not the only churches in Asia; there were also churches in Colossae (Col 1:2), Hierapolis (Col 4:13), and Troas (Acts 20:4-7; cf. 2 Cor 2:12-13). It is possible that these cities served as Roman postal distribution centers and, in turn, communication centers for the various churches in Asia—e.g., information received at Laodicea could be easily dispatched to Colossae and Hierapolis (cf. Col 4:16). If the book was to be delivered to these other churches, then the "seven" here would be symbolic—i.e., the "seven" churches represent the church (in Asia) in its entirety. Be that as it may, the cities form, in the order listed, a rough circle. Even among the seven churches alone, a book delivered from one church to the next could reasonably be expected to follow this route, beginning with the port city of Ephesus before finally reaching the inland Laodicea. John has put his prophecy in the form of a letter (1:4) and has sent it to be circulated among the seven churches.

Early Christian tradition (e.g., Tertullian, *Apology* 5.4; Eusebius, *Ecclesiastical History* 3.17-20) held that the Emperor Domitian engaged in a severe persecution of Christians toward the end of his reign. Indeed, contemporary Roman writers (e.g., Pliny the Younger, Tacitus, Suetonius; cf. Dio Cassius) vilified Domitian as a brutal tyrant. In recent years the accuracy of this portrayal of Domitian has been called into question (see especially L. L. Thompson, *The Book of Revelation: Apocalypse and Empire* [New York: Oxford University Press, 1990]). A widespread, systematic persecution of Christians by Domitian seems unlikely. Yet we must not let Domitian off the hook altogether. Archaeological evidence indicates that during his reign the promotion of emperor worship in Asia increased (see especially S. J. Friesen, *Imperial Cults and the Apocalypse of John: Reading Revelation in the Ruins* [New York: Oxford, 2001]). This could have led to sporadic, if not necessarily systematic, clashes between the Roman authorities and the Christians.

Prior to the development of emperor worship, Hellenistic cities sometimes built temples to Roma, the patron goddess of Rome. At Smyrna, for example, such a temple was erected in 193 BC, at Pergamum in 98 BC, and at Ephesus in 29 BC. Emperor worship itself began when the assassinated Julius Caesar was formally deified by the Roman Senate (42 BC) and became institutionalized when the first Roman emperor, Augustus, was deified by the Senate in 12 BC. The first Asian cities permitted to build a temple to the emperor were Pergamum (29 BC—to Augustus), Smyrna (AD 26—to Tiberius), and Ephesus (AD 90—to the Flavian emperors [Vespasian, Titus, and Domitian]). The erection of the latter temple undoubtedly provided an additional stimulus to emperor worship in the province. The dilemma for Christians would be readily apparent: can participation in emperor worship be reconciled with commitment to Jesus Christ? Is it anything more than a "civic duty"? On the other hand, should Christians avoid it, thus leaving themselves vulnerable to whatever consequences the local authorities might choose to enact? We must not overstate the notion of Roman persecution of Christians as a backdrop against which to read Revelation, but neither must we underestimate the daily struggles Asian Christians would encounter in the face of emperor worship, with its inevitable interconnection with the city of Rome itself. Certainly it is *one* feature that stands behind the book, as we shall see.

An interesting sidelight to the issue of persecution is that in the letters to Smyrna the instigators of persecution seem to be Jews (2:9-10; cf. 3:9). There are a couple of possible explanations for such activity. One is that some Jews might have been informing the local authorities of Christian nonparticipation in emperor worship. Another is that certain Jews might have been pointing out to the authorities that despite the apparent similarities between the two groups, the Christians were not, in fact, Jews, and hence were not exempt from emperor worship, as were the Jews. Neither case requires a deliberate, systematic persecution of Christians.

Understanding the problem of emperor worship in terms of daily tensions, rather than of systematic persecution, opens up the wider issue of Christian assimilation into the surrounding culture. The letters to the seven churches, in particular, provide evidence that Christians were grappling with this issue. The letters to the churches at Pergamum (2:24) and at Thyatira (2:20), for example, warn against eating food sacrificed to idols and against sexual immorality, which may well point to the activities of trade guilds, an important part of economic life in the province of Asia. Indeed, the lament over the fall of Babylon (18:1-19) focuses less on Babylon (Rome) as a persecutor of God's people than as a center of world trade.

The issue of assimilation raises, in turn, the question of who was encouraging the Christians to accommodate themselves to the culture. Though the pressures to do so would undoubtedly have been in place without any instigation as such, one of the striking features of the letters to the seven churches is the mention at several points of false teachers *within* the churches. The Ephesian Christians have rejected the false apostles (2:2) and the Nicolaitans (2:6), while some at Pergamum hold to the teachings of the latter group (2:15) and eat food sacrificed to idols and engage in sexual immorality (2:14). The church at Thyatira tolerates a self-styled "prophet" who "misleads" Christians into sexual immorality and the eating of food sacrificed to idols (2:20). The latter examples indicate that there were those in the churches who promoted cultural assimilation, perhaps for reasons (e.g., economic, civic) that seemed to them perfectly reasonable.

One final observation concerning the historical situation of the seven churches is necessary: their Christian commitment was not what it once was.

The church at Ephesus has forsaken its first love (2:4); the church at Sardis, despite its glowing reputation, is dead (3:1); the church at Laodicea is luke-warm and arrogant (3:15-17). The extent to which these problems are bound up with the preceding considerations is unknown and, in a sense, moot: the churches cannot get themselves off the hook by blaming others for their shortcomings.

An overall assessment of the situation of the seven churches in John's day is not a pretty sight. Pressures to accommodate themselves to the surrounding culture, including emperor worship, were strong; church leaders were divided in their counsel; vibrant commitment to Christ had waned. One might even dare to suggest that the seven churches were in dire need of a prophecy from God.

"I was . . . I was . . . I heard . . . I turned . . . I saw": Reading Revelation as a Literary Work

We have examined John's claim that his book is prophecy, as well as the situation of the seven churches of Asia to which, according to John, the prophecy is to be sent. But there remain some unanswered questions. How was the book composed? Was it written in a single sitting—i.e., did John simply write down the visions as he saw them and then put his pen down when they ended? Indeed, did he have visions at all? Or does the book give evidence of being a more "literary" composition? Does it have any particular organizational structure? And what about the bizarre images in the book? Are they to be understood literally or figuratively? How does one go about making sense of the book's imagery?

There are passages in Revelation that seem to suggest John recorded his visions as they happened. Two initial commands for John to "write" what he sees (1:11, 19) are followed, seven times, by a command to write a message to one of the seven churches (2:1, 8, 12, 18; 3:1, 7, 14). One can easily get the impression from chapters 2 and 3 that John is simply taking down dictation. Similar dictation is found in the beatitudes of 14:13 and 19:9. That John is writing during his actual visionary experience seems to be confirmed in 10:4, where he is about to write what the seven thunders said but is prohibited from doing so by a voice from heaven. A final command to write (21:5) seems to repeat the initial commands. We can imagine a situation, then, in which John, on the island of Patmos, entered into a visionary experience throughout which he was constantly writing—sometimes simply recording dictation and at other times describing what he saw and heard. When the experience was over, the book was complete.

This rather simple and indeed obvious approach to the composition of the book does not explain everything, however. Minimally, the first eight verses of the book—*before* John begins to recount his experience—must have been written *after* his experience. Furthermore, when he does recount his experience, the verbs are in the *past* (Greek aorist) tense: "I was . . . I was . . . I heard . . . I turned . . . I saw . . ." (1:9, 10, 12), indicating that John recorded the circumstances under which he received the revelation *after* the fact, perhaps even after having left Patmos. Or consider the second trumpet (8:8-9). How does John know that a third of the living creatures in the sea died? He does not record anyone telling him the number. Did he *count* them? Or consider the binding of Satan (20:1-3). How does John know that Satan was bound for 1,000 years and that he is to be set free at the end of that period? Does his vision actually *last* for 1,000 years? Again, no one tells him these things.

To raise such questions is not to make light of John's claim to have had a visionary experience. The point is that there is more to the composition of Revelation than simply a person transcribing dictation and recording a series of visions as they happened. It is clear that the book found its final form *after* John's experience on the island of Patmos. In addition, the book gives indication that John has added material that he did not see or hear at the time—i.e., that he has *thought about* his experience. We might note that it is not unusual for scholars to suggest that Revelation is in fact a "literary fiction," that John did not actually experience visions; rather, visions are the device he chose to organize the ideas he wished to communicate to his readers. But unless one begins with the assumption that visions do not happen, there is no reason to deny John's claim to have experienced them. What is important is that the reader recognize that Revelation is a *literary* presentation of John's experience.

If Revelation is a literary presentation, then one might ask if it demonstrates a particular organizational structure of which the reader should be aware. Two qualifications are necessary here. First, it is easy to overestimate the importance of determining the "correct" structure of a book, as if the author had everything all neatly planned and finding it will somehow make everything about the book instantaneously clear for the reader. Readers read a book from its beginning to its end, and one can argue that the developing impact of the book on the reader, rather than its alleged structure, is most important for the reader's experience in understanding the book. Second, Revelation is a difficult book to outline. Some structural elements are rather obvious—e.g., that chapters 2–3 contain the letters to the seven churches and chapters 4–22 consist of visions, or that there are seven seals, seven trumpets, and seven bowls—but others are not. For example, scholars frequently use the word "interlude" for chapter 7 or the section 10:1–11:14 because they seem to break up the seven seals and the seven trumpets, respectively.

With these qualifications in mind, and given that this commentary needs its own organizational structure, we make the following observations. Four times John describes an experience that he has "in the Spirit" (1:10; 4:1-2; 17:1-3; 21:9-10). The first such experience covers 1:9–3:22, the second 4:1–11:19, the third 17:1–20:15, and the fourth 21:1–22:6a. Between the second and third "in the Spirit" experiences are three signs in heaven (12:1, 3; 15:1). Given that the first two signs begin the section and the last introduces the seven bowls, which are followed immediately by the third "in the Spirit" experience, we may feel justified in treating the entire section (12:1–16:21) as a distinct unit. Hence, we will broadly organize the book as follows:

Prologue (1:1-8)
John's first "in the Spirit" experience (1:9–3:22)
John's second "in the Spirit" experience (4:1–11:19)
Three signs in heaven (12:1–16:21)
John's third "in the Spirit" experience (17:1–20:15)
John's fourth "in the Spirit" experience (21:1–22:6a)
Epilogue (22:6b-21).

We will even argue that this outline drives the story forward to its completion. But we have no intention of suggesting that these units are completely distinct from one another. Indeed, one thing that ties them together and propels the plot is that elements central to each unit are introduced in the previous one—e.g., the beast in 11:7, Babylon in 14:8, the Bride in 19:7. More generally, as we shall see, recurring images throughout the book tie the various sections together.

To mention "recurring images" is to raise a question, perhaps *the* question, that can be avoided only so long: how does one go about making sense of the strange imagery in this book? To some the answer seems obvious: take it literally (though one wonders how many really do so). But Revelation itself gives indication that the imagery is not to be understood in this manner. For example, is a promise to become a literal pillar in the temple of God *really* supposed to inspire the reader to become a conqueror (3:12)? Are we *really* to envision the rider on the white horse slaying his enemies with a literal sword that comes out of his mouth (19:21)? There is no virtue in taking literally something that is intended figuratively. Indeed, John essentially invites the reader to adopt a figurative approach to his book with the use in 1:1 of *esemanen* ("he made known"), a word that typically refers to making something known in "signs." The reader must recognize that figurative language abounds in Revelation.

To acknowledge the presence of figurative language in Revelation is not, however, to give free rein to readers to interpret it as they please. The reader's task is to focus on how John intended for his readers to understand the visual imagery he used. This requires taking into account two factors. First, painting pictures with words is never an exact science, especially when one is attempting to describe the indescribable—i.e., the things of God. Although it has inspired many an artist over the centuries, Revelation remains a literary document. Second, to paint his pictures verbally John uses imagery that is familiar to himself and, presumably, to his readers.

There are four main sources for John's imagery. First and most important is the Old Testament. Revelation breathes Old Testament imagery at virtually every turn, even though John never actually quotes an Old Testament passage outright. But two cautions must be expressed here. First, we must not assume, as is too often the case, that John simply assembles a list of Old Testament "prophecies" to which he adds his own, thereby creating a giant jigsaw puzzle of Daniel, Ezekiel, Revelation, and the like. An examination of the four living creatures in chapter 4, for example, demonstrates that John has combined images from both Isaiah and Ezekiel to create something fresh. Revelation is not part of a *larger* picture; rather it transforms Old Testament images into a *new* picture. Second, we must not assume that John creates this new picture by cavalierly lifting Old Testament images out of their contexts. Indeed, sensitivity to the original sense of the Old Testament passages to which John alludes will prove most beneficial to understanding his use of them, as we shall see.

A second source for John's imagery is Jewish books written between the Old Testament period and John's day, a period commonly known as the Second Temple period, especially those writings (or sections of writings) deemed by scholars as "apocalyptic." Apocalyptic literature (from the Greek *apokalupsis*, which means "unveiling" or "revelation") often includes, among other things, visionary journeys, end-times predictions, and bizarre imagery. Some of the more important Jewish writings of this sort (sometimes revised later by Christians) include *1 Enoch, 2 Enoch, 4 Ezra, 2 Baruch, 3 Baruch,* the *Apocalypse of Abraham*, and the *Apocalypse of Zephaniah*. Christians also wrote such books, including the *Shepherd of Hermas*, the *Apocalypse of Peter*, and the *Apocalypse of Paul*. (For a more exhaustive list, as well as a concise introduction to apocalyptic as a literary genre, see C. H. Talbert, *The*

Apocalypse: A Reading of the Revelation of John [Louisville: Westminster John Knox, 1994], 4-8.) While apocalyptic writings and generalizations drawn by scholars about them must not be given an overly privileged status in interpreting Revelation, readers who familiarize themselves with these writings will find the imagery in Revelation to be much less foreboding. Ancient authors really did write about weird-looking creatures with extra appendages, and they expected their readers to understand what they meant!

Third, John uses images from the Graeco-Roman world in which both he and his readers lived. Archaeological and literary knowledge of the seven cities of Asia and, more generally, the province of Asia itself can shed significant light on John's message (see, in addition to Friesen noted above, Ronald H. Worth Jr., *The Seven Cities of the Apocalypse and Greco-Asian Culture* [New York: Paulist Press, 1999], and *The Seven Cities of the Apocalypse and Roman Culture* [New York: Paulist Press, 1999]). The principle here is that certain images become part of a common culture and are readily understandable only as a part of that culture. The reader might consider, as a modern example, the way in which political cartoons use stock images of, say, elephants and donkeys to signify Republicans and Democrats, respectively.

Finally, as a first century Christian, John uses language that reflects the vocabulary of the early church. But a word of caution is in order here. While John's knowledge of the Old Testament is a given, the same cannot be said of his knowledge of other New Testament books. The New Testament as a collection did not yet exist. We cannot know which New Testament writings, if any, John (or his readers) knew. Therefore, we must not fall into the trap, as is often the case, of explaining a passage in Revelation by means of one from Paul or Mark. New Testament parallels perhaps *illustrate* what John is saying, but they do not *determine* it.

In this commentary we will pay careful attention to parallels of language and imagery from the Old Testament, from other Jewish (especially apocalyptic) writings, and from the larger Graeco-Roman culture, understanding that such parallels were readily available to John and his readers. These parallels we will treat as potentially *determinative* for John's meaning. On the other hand, we will use New Testament parallels as primarily *illustrative* of how John's ideas resonate with those of other early Christians. Three final words of caution are in order. First, at our distance, both chronologically and culturally, from the first century setting of Revelation, we cannot expect to be able to gain a clear grasp of all of John's images. We must allow that there will be things we do not fully understand. Second, the parallels noted in the commentary that follows are intended to be suggestive, not exhaustive; many more could be cited. Third, finding a parallel to an image in Revelation is not the same thing as explaining that image. The reader must always seek to distinguish meaningful parallels from those that are not. Furthermore, the most important concern must always be determining John's use of the image, not finding a parallel to it somewhere.

This last point all too often goes unrecognized. One of the distinctive features of Revelation is the consistency of imagery throughout the book, over against the episodic nature of the imagery that typically characterizes ancient apocalyptic writings (see Richard Bauckham, *The Theology of the Book of Revelation* [New Testament Theology; Cambridge: Cambridge University Press, 1993]). In literary terms, Revelation creates a "story world" into which everything in the book fits. It contains a series of interlocking pictures that form a seamless whole. John's images ultimately take their place as a part of this whole.

The reader must resist two common but unjustified temptations in attempting to understand John's "story world." First, because readers typically read, for example, chapter 20 *after* they read chapter 13, they often assume that the events recorded in chapter 20 take place *later in time* than those recorded in chapter 13. But this is not a necessary assumption. To be sure, John provides temporal indicators with respect to the order in which he receives the visions (e.g., "after this," "then"), but it does not follow that the visions (or parts of them) cannot overlap. Scholars often speak of "recapitulation" with respect to the visions in Revelation—i.e., that some parts of the book "recapitulate" (cover the same ground as) earlier parts. The point here is not to impose a particular scheme (either recapitulation or strict chronology) upon the book, but to raise the possibility that some parts of Revelation may treat the same period of time, but from different angles. With respect to issues of the temporal order of events, readers must take their cue *from the text*, not from assumptions based upon when they read things.

Second, in order to make sense of the puzzling imagery of Revelation, readers often try to read it allegorically, as if each detail "stands for" something in the real world. To be sure, John intends for his readers to adopt the perspective of his story world as the divinely-revealed key to understanding the real world, but one must first make sense of the story world as it stands. The lengthy description of the new Jerusalem, for example, may owe more to the way in which ancient cities functioned and were constructed than to some supposed connection between every detail and the real world. Again, the text must be primary.

"Blessed is he who reads . . .
and blessed are those who hear . . . and keep . . .":
An Invitation to Read Revelation

There is no doubt that Revelation is a strange book. But what obscures its meaning as much as anything is when readers bring to it all sorts of preconceived notions such as prophecy as prediction, Revelation as instantaneous transcription, a confused sense of what it means to take something "literally," the necessity of viewing Revelation within the larger context of Old Testament "prophecies," the priority of New Testament "parallels," order of reading as order of events, and Revelation as allegory, not to mention a vague (or sometimes very precise!) understanding of what Revelation is "supposed" to mean, at least according to self-styled "prophecy experts"! The reader who truly desires to "hear what the Spirit says to the churches" must lay aside all such preconceived notions and let the text speak for itself.

At the opening of the book John pronounces a blessing on the one "who reads aloud the words of the prophecy" and on "those who hear it, and who keep what is written therein" (1:3). John does not expect his readers to study his manuscript; rather, they will hear it read. As they hear it, they will make connections between one scene and another, sometimes being led to anticipate what will follow, at other times building upon images to which they have already been introduced. As they do so, they will reconstruct the story world underlying the revelation he has received. In other words, John invites his readers to use their imaginations.

As we embark on a reading of Revelation, I invite you to unharness your imagination, to enter into the story world of the book, to see it as a series of interlocking pictures that form a whole. And I would suggest that only by doing so will you truly begin to grasp its beauty and its power.

"The revelation of Jesus Christ"

Revelation 1:1-8

Revelation opens with a superscription in which the author briefly introduces the book and pronounces a blessing on those who read and hear it (1:1-3). There follows a typical letter introduction, complete with the identity of the addresser (John), the addressees (the seven churches in Asia), and a benediction (1:4-5a). The prologue is completed with a doxology to Jesus (1:5b-6), an oracle on the coming of Jesus (1:7), and a self-revelatory statement by God (1:8). The prologue is paralleled at the end of the book by an epilogue (22:6b-21).

In the superscription the author provides a twofold classification for his book: it is a "revelation" (1:1) and it is a "prophecy" (1:3). Any proper reading of the book must take into account these two terms of self-designation, which are closely related (see Introduction). A "revelation" involves the uncovering of something that is hidden; "prophecy" is the communication of a message from God. Hence, the author claims to have received a communication from God of something that has been hidden. His task is to pass along what has been revealed to him to those for whom it is intended. Specifically, the chain of revelation runs from God to Jesus to "his" (Jesus') angel to the author (identified simply as "John"; see Introduction) to the readers (1:1). The author will return, with slight variations, to the chain in 22:6b. The verbs used in the chain are instructive: God "gave" the revelation to "show" something to his servants; Jesus "made it known" by "sending" his angel; John "bore witness" to it (1:2). Only the angel's activity is left undefined. *same as in gospel of John*

John speaks in two ways of the manner in which he received the revelation. First, Jesus Christ "made it known" to him (1:1). The noun form of the verb *semaino* means "sign," and while the verb can simply mean "make known," it more typically has the connotation "make known by means of signs" (e.g., Dan 2:45 LXX). That the latter is intended here is confirmed by the author's second comment concerning his reception of the revelation: he bore witness to "all that he saw" (1:2)—i.e., the author received the revelation visually. The idea of receiving visions of divine matters (which, of course, includes hearing things, which will occur in John's case as well) is thoroughly rooted in the Old Testament (e.g., Isa 6:1-13; Jer 24:1-10; Ezek 1:1-28; Dan 7:1-28; Amos 7:1-9; Zech 1:7-17) and is characteristic of various Jewish writings in the Second Temple period (e.g., *1 Enoch, 2 Enoch, 4 Ezra, 2 Baruch, 3 Baruch, Apocalypse of Abraham, Testament of Abraham,* 4QShirShab). It is also found in the New Testament (e.g., Acts 10:9-16; 2 Cor 12:1-4) and continues into the post-apostolic period (e.g., *Shepherd of Hermas, Apocalypse of Peter, Apocalypse of Paul*). From the outset, then, the reader is alerted to the fact that understanding this book will be a challenge: it is indeed a revelation from God, but it is one communicated through signs (visions).

John, in turn, has passed along the revelation by writing it down after the fact. In 1:3 he speaks of "he who reads [it] aloud," presumably referring to the one in each church (cf. 1:11) who will read the book to the group of gathered believers. The public reading of the Old Testament was a staple of Jewish synagogue worship (e.g., Neh 8:2-8; Luke 4:17-20; Acts 13:15), and the public reading of Christian writings is attested elsewhere in the New Testament (Col 4:16; 1 Thess 5:27; cf. 1 Tim 4:13) and among other early Christian writers (e.g., Justin, *Apology* 67; Hermas, *Visions* 2.4.3). That John wrote the superscription *after* he received the visions is confirmed by the aorist tenses found in it ("he [God] gave . . . he [Jesus Christ] made known. . . he [John] saw"). In other words, the superscription informs the reader of the "literary" character of the book; John has had time to think about his experiences (see Introduction).

John describes the content of the revelation in two ways. First, it concerns "what must soon take place" (1:1). This expression will be repeated in 22:6b and, with variations, in 1:19 and in 4:1. The first part of the expression reflects the language of the LXX reading of Dan 2:28 (cf. Dan 2:29). Indeed, John has written the first verse against the backdrop of the LXX rendering of the story of God's revealing to Daniel Nebuchadnezzar's dream and its interpretation (Dan 2:14-47). "Revelation" recalls the use of the verb "reveal" (*apokalupto*) five times in this section of Daniel (Dan 2:28, 29, 30, 47 [twice]). In addition, the verb "make known" (*semaino*) occurs four times (Dan 2:15, 23, 30, 45). John's most significant alteration of Daniel is that he changes "what must take place *in the last days*" (Dan 2:28; cf. Dan 2:29, 45) to "what must *soon* take place." The implications of this alteration for understanding John's eschatological perspective will become clearer as the reader continues. At this point, it is at least evident that John believes that whatever

Daniel may have meant by "the last days," the revelation that he himself has received is not relegated to the distant future. John reaffirms this thought in 1:3 with the comment that "the time is near," an observation he will repeat at the end of the book (22:10). The notion of "the time" as a special time of great eschatological significance is based upon Daniel 7:22 (LXX; cf. Dan 8:17; 9:27; 11:35; 12:4, 7) and is also picked up in the Gospel tradition (Mark 1:14; Luke 21:8).

John further describes the content of the revelation as "the word of God" and "the testimony of Jesus Christ" (1:2), an expression that will be repeated (without "Christ") in 1:9 and in 20:4. In addition, "the word of God" will recur in 6:9 and 19:13 and, in the plural ("words"), in 17:17 and 19:9; John will mention "the testimony of Jesus" again in 12:17 and 19:10 (twice). In each case the genitive should be understood subjectively—*God's* word and *Jesus'* testimony, rather than the word *about* God and the testimony *about* Jesus. John uses the full expression "Jesus Christ" (Hebrew "Messiah," which means "Anointed One") only at the beginning (1:1, 2, 5) and the end of the book (22:21). "Jesus" will be found nine more times, most often in the expression "the testimony of Jesus" (1:9; 12:17; 19:10 [twice]; 20:4; cf. 1:9; 14:12; 22:16, 20); "Christ" will be found four more times, twice in the expression "his [i.e., God's] Christ" (11:15; 12:10) and twice in the passage on the 1,000 years (20:4, 6). Although the concept of an "Anointed One" took on a number of different connotations in both the Old Testament and Second Temple Judaism, many Jews, on the basis of 2 Sam 7:12-16, maintained a strong connection between the Messiah and the line of David (e.g., Ps 18:50; Isa 9:7; 11:1; Jer 23:5; 30:9; 33:15; Ezek 34:24; 37:24; Amos 9:11; 4QpIs^a[4Q161] 2.18; 4Q285 frag 5.3-4; 4QpGen^a[4Q252] 5.1-4; 4QFlor[4Q174] frags 1-3 1.10-13; *Psalms of Solomon* 17:21; *4 Ezra* 12:32; cf. Matt 1:1; Mark 10:47; Luke 1:32; John 7:42; Rom 1:3). Jesus' Davidic connection will be alluded to in 1:5a and explicitly affirmed in 3:7; 5:5; 22:10.

John also characterizes his readers in two ways. First, they are called "servants" (1:1: *douloi*), a designation John also uses for himself (1:1) and that will be repeated as the book unfolds (2:20; 7:3; 10:7; 11:18; 19:2, 5; 22:3, 6). There might be an allusion here to Amos 3:7 (LXX): "Surely the LORD God does nothing unless he reveals [*apokalupto*] his plan to his servants [*douloi*] the prophets" (cf. 10:7), though John does not identify God's "servants" as "prophets" here. Since there is no reason to believe John's intended readers are a specific subgroup of Christians (prophets or otherwise), an intentional allusion to Amos might serve to introduce the notion that *all* Christians are prophets (see further on 11:18).

Second, John speaks of his readers as those who "hear" and (he hopes!) "keep" the things written in this prophecy (1:3). In both the Old Testament and the New Testament "keeping" words or commandments typically carries the connotation of obedience (e.g., 1 Sam 15:11; Dan 9:4; Matt 19:17; John 14:15; 1 John 2:3; cf. Sir 6:26). The importance of both "hearing" and "keeping" will be underscored as the book progresses. "Hearing" what the Spirit says to the churches will become a repeated refrain throughout the letters to the seven churches (2:7, 11, 17, 29; 3:6, 13, 22; cf. 3:3, 20; 13:9); "keeping" Jesus' works (2:26) and word (3:8, 10), what they have received and heard (3:3), and the commandments of God (12:17; 14:10) will also be a theme (cf. 16:15). Indeed, at the close of the book John will return to the importance of both "hearing" and "keeping" the words of the prophecy of this book (22:7, 18; cf. 22:9, 17).

The superscription concludes with a beatitude (1:3), the first of seven in the book (cf. 14:13; 16:15; 19:9; 20:6; 22:7, 14). Beatitudes are a traditional form of Jewish blessing ("Blessed is . . .") found in the Old Testament (e.g., Deut 33:29; Job 5:17; Ps 1:1; Prov 3:13; Isa 56:2), in Jewish writings of the Second Temple period (e.g., 4Q525; Wis 3:13; Sir 14:1-2; *Psalms of Solomon* 6:1; *2 Enoch* 42:6-14), and in the New Testament (e.g., Matt 5:1-11; Luke 6:20-22; John 20:29; Rom 14:22; Jas 1:12). John's blessing is upon the reader and the hearers/keepers of his book.

1:4-5a constitutes the opening of a letter. The mention of the addresser, followed by the addressee(s), is standard in letters from this period; the benediction extending grace and peace, which comes next, is reminiscent of the letters of both Paul and Peter. The author has taken the revelation he received and put it into the form of a letter, which he now sends to those for whom the revelation is intended.

The author identifies himself as "John" (1:4; cf. 1:9; 22:8). He does not describe himself any further—as, e.g., an apostle, or one of the Twelve, or the son of Zebedee, or the brother of James (see Introduction). His readers are "the seven churches that are in Asia" (1:5; see Introduction). The seven churches will be named in 1:11. "Asia" is the designation for a Roman province that constitutes much of what is now western Turkey.

The rather lengthy benediction (contrast, e.g., Rom 1:7; 1 Cor 1:3; 2 Cor 2:2; 1 Pet 1:2; 2 Pet 1:2) extends grace and peace from three sources (1:4-5a). The first source is "the one who is and who was and who is to come" (1:4). The expression will be repeated in 1:8 and, with the first two relative clauses reversed, in 4:8; the first two clauses will be repeated in 11:17 and 16:5. Each of these later passages contains an explicit reference to God. The expression, which stretches the limits of the Greek language, is based upon the self-revealed name of God in Exod 3:14 ("I AM"). John's use of the present participle (lit., "is coming"), rather than a future tense ("will be"), might reflect the use of the present participle in the LXX rendering of Isa 41:4, which is an elaboration of Exod 3:14: "I, the LORD, the first, and to the coming things, I am He."

The second source of grace and peace is "the seven spirits who are before his [i.e., God's] throne" (1:4). In the Old Testament, to sit upon a throne meant to rule as king (e.g., 1 Kgs 1:13, 17, 20, 24). The throne was also a place from which judgment was dispensed (e.g., 1 Kgs 7:7; Ps 9:7-8; Dan 7:10, 26). God's throne is mentioned frequently in the Old Testament (e.g., Ps 9:4; Isa 6:1; Ezek 1:16; Dan 7:9) and will become a central element in John's visions (see on 4:2). "The seven spirits" will be found again in 3:1; 4:5; and 5:6. That they are said to be "before his throne" anticipates the vision beginning in 4:1 (cf. 4:5). It is likely that John is referring to the Holy Spirit here—the seven spirits do, after all, stand in the presence of God. Furthermore, although John never uses the expression "the Holy Spirit," he does use the singular "spirit" in such a way as to suggest that he is speaking of the Holy Spirit (2:7, 11, 17, 29; 3:6, 13, 22; 14:13; 22:17). In addition, the number seven has already become the number of completeness in Judaism (for numerous examples see 4QShirShab; cf. *1 Enoch* 77:5-6; *Jubilees* 5:24; Tob 12:15) and will apparently be used in such a manner throughout Revelation (seven churches, seven lampstands, seven stars, seven seals, seven angels, seven trumpets, seven thunders, seven thousand, seven heads, seven plagues, seven bowls, seven kings). John's source for the notion of "seven" spirits is probably Zech 4. In Zech 4:2 the prophet sees a gold lampstand with seven lamps, each with seven tips, upon it; the seven are interpreted in Zech 4:10 as "the eyes of the LORD, which range through the whole earth" (cf. Rev 5:6). In between, God speaks to Zechariah about "my Spirit" (Zech 4:6).

The third source mentioned in the benediction is Jesus Christ. Jesus is further identified in three specific ways (1:5a). First, he is "the faithful witness," an expression that will be repeated in a slightly expanded form in 3:14. Given the concern with bearing witness (RSV: "testimony") already expressed twice in 1:2, the expression here testifies to Jesus' faithful transmission of the revelation (1:1). Second, Jesus is "the first-born of the dead." While this particular expression is found in Revelation only here (cf. Col 1:18), the importance of Jesus' resurrection will be emphasized in other ways. Third, Jesus is identified as "the ruler of kings on earth" (lit., "the kings of the earth"). The significance of this "political" characterization is left unspecified for now, but John will have much to say about kings, including "the kings of the earth" (6:15; 17:2, 18; 18:3, 9; 19:19; 21:24). "Ruler" (*archon*), found only here in the book, may well be drawn from the LXX rendering of Isa 55:4: "Behold, I have given him as a witness among the nations, a ruler [*archon*] and commander of the nations."

John's fundamental designation of Jesus in 1:5a is drawn from the description of David in Ps 89. As David is appointed by God to be "first-born" (Ps 89:27), Jesus is the "first-born *of the dead*"; while David is the "*most exalted* of the kings of the earth" (Ps 89:27), Jesus is "*ruler* of the kings of the earth"; and as God's promise to sustain David's line is compared to the moon, "the faithful witness in the sky" (Ps 89:37), for John it is Jesus who is "the faithful witness." John's use of Ps 89 in 1:5a, therefore, serves to suggest to the reader from the outset that Jesus is to be understood in Davidic terms.

Following the epistolary introduction is a doxology that characterizes Jesus in a threefold manner that is distinctive in the New Testament (1:5b-6). First of all, Jesus "loves" [present tense] us" (1:5b). Although Jesus' present love for his people will be mentioned again in 3:19 (cf. 3:9), Jesus' love is uniformly viewed elsewhere in the New Testament in relation to his death and, hence, is expressed in the past (aorist) tense (e.g., Gal 2:20; Eph 5:2). Second, Jesus "freed" (lit., "loosed") us from our sins (1:5b). While elsewhere in the New Testament the more general notion of Jesus delivering people from their sins is common (e.g., Matt 1:21; John 1:29; Acts 13:38; 1 Cor 15:3; Gal 1:4; Heb 2:17; 1 Pet 2:24; 1 John 2:2), the expression "freed/loosed from sin" is found only here. Third, Jesus "made us a kingdom, priests to his God and Father" (1:6). Although John will repeat the thought with slight variations in 5:10 and with more variations in 20:6, and although 1 Peter picks up the notion of Christians as priests (1 Pet 2:5; cf. Isa 61:6), John's coupling of kingship with priesthood in describing Christians is unique in the New Testament.

The lack of close New Testament verbal parallels to John's characterization of Jesus in the doxology throws into sharp relief the presence of such parallels in the Old Testament. In Hos 3:1 God tells Hosea that "the LORD loves [present tense] the people of Israel" (cf. Job 42:9; Isa 43:4; Jer 12:7). Similarly, in Isa 40:2 (LXX) the prophet says of Israel that "her iniquity is loosed." Finally, and perhaps most significantly, in Exod 19:6 God tells Moses to inform Israel about the covenant he intends to institute with them. Included in this brief but defining passage is the promise that "you shall be to me a kingdom of priests and a holy nation" (cf. Isa 61:6; *Jubilees* 16:18).

John's use of Old Testament language in the doxology can hardly be accidental. Two themes emerge. First, John has applied to *Jesus* language that in the Old Testament depicts *God*. To be sure, John goes on to complete the third clause by speaking of "his [Jesus'] God and Father," maintaining a certain distinction at this point between God and Jesus. Yet it is clear that in some respects John invites the reader to consider Jesus in terms previously used for God. Second, John has applied to *Christians* language that in the Old Testament depicts *Israel.* Indeed, John gives the reader no reason to distinguish Israel from the Church.

The importance of recognizing how John uses Old Testament language in 1:5b-6 cannot be overstated. The doxology is determinative for a proper reading of the book: the reader is to understand Jesus in terms that had previously been reserved for God, and Christians in terms that had previously been reserved for Israel. John's further development of Jesus as God and the Church as Israel will be central themes in the book. *The failure to understand what John is doing in the doxology leads many interpreters into much confusion regarding what they mistakenly view to be the separate roles of Israel and the Church in the visions that unfold.*

The doxology also introduces the reader to the importance of Jesus' death. John specifies that Jesus' act of loosing people from sins is accomplished "by his blood" (1:5b). The blood of Jesus is a major New Testament theme (cf. Matt 26:28; Mark 14:14; Luke 22:20; John 6:55; Rom 3:25; 5:9; 1 Cor 10:16; 11:25, 27; Eph 1:7; 2:13; Col 1:20; Heb 9:12, 14; 10:19, 29; 13:12, 20; 1 Pet 1:2, 19; 1 John 1:7), and John will have more to say about it later (5:9; 7:14; 12:11). In addition, Jesus is said to have "made us a kingdom, priests to his God and Father" (1:6). Just how this was done is left unspecified at this point, but the fact that the verb is in the aorist tense indicates that the action is perceived as having already been completed. In 5:9-10 this action will be attributed directly to Jesus' blood—i.e., his death.

Finally, the doxology directs "glory" and "power" to Jesus forever (1:6). Although John will speak a number of times about giving glory to God (4:9, 11; 5:12; 7:12; 11:13; 14:7; 16:9; 19:1, 7), he will bring "glory" and "power" (along with other attributes) together only in the climactic passage 5:13, when the whole creation gives praise to the one who sits upon the throne and to the Lamb. "Amen," which underscores both the solemnity and the truth of the doxology, is used in a similar manner seven more times in Revelation (1:7; 5:14; 7:12 [twice]; 19:4; 22:20, 21).

The doxology is followed by an oracle (1:7), consisting of four clauses, concerning one who "is coming." The first clause is based upon Dan 7:13, which speaks of "one like a son of man" who comes "with the clouds" (cf. Matt 24:30; 26:64; Mark 13:26; 14:62; Luke 21:27) and approaches the Ancient of Days. John will return to Dan 7:13 later (1:13; 14:14 [twice], 15, 16). The last three clauses of the oracle are based upon Zech 12:10. Within the context of the restoration of Jerusalem (Zech 12:1-9), God promises to "pour out on the house of David and the inhabitants of Jerusalem a spirit of compassion and supplication, so that, when they look on him [MT: me] whom they have pierced, they shall mourn for him, as one mourns for an only child, and weep bitterly over him, as one weeps over a first-born" (Zech 12:10). As a result, there will be both redemption—God will cleanse the people from their sin and uncleanness—and judgment—God will rid the land of idols and false prophets (Zech 13:1-6). In Daniel the "coming" one is clearly distinguished from God ("the Ancient of Days"), while in Zechariah (MT), the one "whom they pierced" is God himself ("me"). John's juxtaposition of these two passages serves to identify the "coming" one with the "pierced" one. Given the immediately preceding verses, this figure must be Jesus, with the "piercing" alluding to the crucifixion (1:5b; cf. John 19:37, which quotes Zech 12:10). Once again John has applied to Jesus an Old Testament passage pertaining to God.

John has made two primary changes to Zech 12:10 in composing this oracle. He has specified the subjects of those who will see and those who will mourn as "every eye" and "all the tribes of the earth," respectively. While the first expression is not picked up elsewhere by John, he will speak further of "tribes," especially with reference to Israel (5:5; 7:4, 5 [three times], 6 [three times], 7 [three times], 8 [three times]; 21:12), but also in a broader sense (cf. 5:9; 7:9; 11:9; 13:7; 14:6), which is confirmed here by the addition of the phrase "of the earth." The oracle therefore stands as both a promise and a warning: *all* will see and mourn the coming of Jesus, which, as in Zechariah, will lead to both redemption and judgment, as the rest of the book will make clear. The oracle is underscored by the double addition of "even so" (cf. 14:13; 16:7; 22:20) and "Amen" (see on 1:6), both brought together again only for a similar promise/warning at the end of the book (22:20).

But what about Jesus' "coming"? An initial reading of this statement might lead the reader to infer that John is speaking of the second coming of Jesus, a widespread expectation in early Christianity (e.g., Matt 25:31-36; Acts 1:11; 1 Thess 4:15-17). But one might reasonably expect a reference to the second coming of Jesus to be in the future tense. John, however, uses the present tense, which reminds the reader of the present tense of the same verb (*erchomai*), used of God, in 1:4. The use of the future tense in the second and fourth clauses confirms this "coming" as in some sense future, but why is the future mixed with the present? Is there a sense in which Jesus is already—or even always—coming? The timing of the events mentioned in Revelation is one of the most puzzling aspects of the book. The reader will do well to follow John's terminology carefully. He certainly is not finished with the subject!

This section closes with a self-revelatory statement by God (1:8). "The Lord God" (cf. 4:8, 11; 11:17; 15:3; 16:7; 18:8; 19:6; 22:21; 22:5, 6) identifies himself in three ways. The first and last letters of the Greek alphabet (Alpha and Omega) characterize God's eternal nature. John will repeat this expression in 21:6 and 22:13. The repetition of the peculiar formula from 1:4 underscores God's neverending activity and serves as an inclusion to bracket 1:4-8 as a unit. "Almighty," a common Old Testament appellation stressing God's sovereignty (e.g., 2 Sam 7:8; 1 Chr 1:9; Job 11:7; Ezek 1:24; Amos 3:13; Mic 4:4; Hag 1:2; Zech 1:3; Mal 1:4), will be John's favorite title for God (cf. 4:8; 11:17; 15:3; 16:7, 14; 19:6, 15; and 21:22). God will speak again in Revelation only in 21:5-8.

As a literary unit that John composed after he received his visions (and, hence, had had some time to reflect on them), 1:1-8 deserves close attention from the reader. Among the themes John introduces in this unit, four will stand out in the overall scheme of the book: Jesus as God, the Church as Israel, the death of Jesus, and the coming of Jesus.

"Write what you see in a book and send it to the seven churches"

Revelation 1:9–3:22

The greater part of the book can be organized around four references John makes to being "in the Spirit" (1:10; 4:2; 17:3; 21:10). To be specific, John records four "in the Spirit" experiences (1:9–3:22; 4:1–11:19; 17:1–20:25; and 21:1–22:6a), the second and third of which are separated by a unit (12:1–16:21) in which John speaks of three "signs" (RSV "portent") in heaven (12:1; 12:3; 15:1). The first "in the Spirit" experience contains John's account of his call (1:9-20), along with seven letters Jesus dictates to him for the seven churches of Asia (2:1–3:22). In the second "in the Spirit" experience John is taken up to heaven (4:1-3), where he witnesses the dramatic transferal of the sealed scroll from the one sitting upon the throne to the Lamb (4:3–5:14), followed by the breaking of the seven seals (6:1–8:6) and the blowing of the seven trumpets (8:7–11:19). The unit on the three signs introduces the woman clothed with the sun who is about to give birth (12:1-2), the dragon (12:3), and the ensuing conflict between the dragon and his cohorts, the beast and the false prophet on the one side and the woman and her offspring on the other (12:4–14:5), followed by the announcement of judgment (14:6-20) that leads to the third sign (15:1), seven angels with seven last plagues (the seven bowls of the wrath of God) that are poured out on the earth (15:1–16:21). In John's third "in the Spirit" experience, he is taken to a wilderness (4:3), where he witnesses the judgment of the great harlot Babylon (17:1–19:4), followed by the announcement of the marriage of the Lamb (19:5-10) and the judgment of the beast, the false prophet, and their armies (19:11-21), the dragon (20:1-10), and those whose names are not written in the book of life, along with Death and Hades (20:11-15). John's final "in the Spirit" experience takes him to a great, high mountain (21:1-10) from which he sees the Bride, the wife of the Lamb, the holy city Jerusalem coming down out of heaven from God (21:9–22:6a).

"Write what you see, what is and what is to take place hereafter": John's Commission
Revelation 1:9-20

The author turns to the circumstances surrounding his call to pass along the revelation. This section contains four subsections: (1) the setting of John's revelatory experience (1:9), (2) the beginning of that experience when John heard a voice speaking to him (1:10-11), (3) what John saw when he turned to look at the speaker (1:12-16), and (4) John's response, along with the subsequent response of the speaker (1:17-20).

To set the stage for recounting how he received the revelation, John begins by identifying himself, first by name (cf. 1:1, 4) and then by his relationship with his readers (1:9). John speaks of himself as a "brother" (for "brother" in the sense of fellow Christian, see also 6:11; 12:10; 19:10; 22:9; Acts 21:7; Rom 1:13; Heb 3:1; Jas 1:2; 1 Pet 3:8; 1 John 3:13) and one "who shares" (only here in the book). He and his readers share three things, all combined by a singular definite article and qualifier ("in Jesus"): the tribulation, kingdom, and patient endurance. John will speak of tribulation again in 2:9, 10, 22; 7:14. "Tribulation" refers to a time of distress, though the actual cause for that distress (e.g., poverty, persecution) is not inherent in the word itself. Indeed, the prophets even viewed tribulation as something God can bring in judgment upon Israel (e.g., Isa 30:20; Jer 10:18; Ezek 12:18; Hos 5:15). Dan 12:1 speaks of a future tribulation "such as never has been since there was a nation till that time" (see further on 3:10). It is noteworthy that John perceives the tribulation to be *present*. Presumably his readers understand the character of this tribulation. "Kingdom" picks up John's previous ascription of this term to the Church (1:6). "Patient endurance," an appropriate trait for those undergoing tribulation, will be used again by John in 2:2, 3, 19; 3:10; 13:10; 14:12. John and his readers share the kingdom *now* as they patiently endure the tribulation.

John next identifies the place where he received the revelation: the island of Patmos (1:9; see Introduction). "Was" could indicate that John was no longer on the island when he wrote down the revelation, but such an inference is not necessary. That he is on Patmos "on account of the word of God and the testimony of Jesus" (1:9) is probably an indication that he is in exile, though the specific details of his exile are not known.

John describes his commission in terms drawn from the Old Testament. His mention of being "in the Spirit" (1:10) is probably an allusion to Ezekiel's various experiences where the Spirit entered him, lifted him up, and even took him places (Ezek 2:2; 3:12, 14, 24; 11:1; 43:5). The fact that in this state John sees visions may well be an indication of some sort of trance (e.g., Acts 10:10; 11:3; 22:17; cf. 2 Cor 12:2-4). The "loud voice like a trumpet" (cf. 4:1) is reminiscent of the loud trumpet blast that accompanied God's appearance to Moses at Mount Sinai (Exod 19:16, 19). Finally, the command to write in a book what he sees (1:11) reminds the reader of similar commands given to Isaiah (Isa 30:8) and Jeremiah (Jer 30:2). Throughout the book John will receive other commands to write (1:19; 2:1, 8, 12, 18; 3:1, 7, 14; 14:13; 19:9; 21:5). All of this serves to underscore for the reader the authority of John's book as truly a revelation from God.

John's reference to "the Lord's Day" (1:10) is the only such reference in the New Testament and the earliest in Christian literature. The phrase became more common in the second century (e.g., Ignatius, *Magnesians* 9:1; *Didache* 14:1; *Gospel of Peter* 35, 50). The presence of the possessive "Lord's" suggests that the day was probably understood to have been the day of Jesus' resurrection—i.e., Sunday (cf. Matt 28:1; Mark 16:2; Luke 24:1; John 20:1). Though the connection between Sunday and the resurrection of Jesus was not made explicit until the second century (e.g., *Gospel of Peter* 35, 50; *Epistle of Barnabas* 15:9; Justin, *Apology* 67), it is clear that as early as the 50s Christians were already attaching special significance to Sunday (1 Cor 16:1-3; Acts 20:6-7).

John is commanded to send his book to "the seven churches" (1:11; cf. 1:4), which are named and which will serve as the addressees of individual letters in chapters 2 and 3 (see Introduction).

When John turns to see "the voice" that was speaking to him, he first sees "seven golden" lampstands (1:12-13). Once again (cf. 1:4) John probably intends an allusion to Zech 4:2, where Zechariah has a vision of a single golden lampstand with seven lamps upon it. God had earlier commanded the Israelites to make a seven-branched, golden lampstand as part of the furniture for the Tabernacle (Exod 25:31-37). In 1:20 the one whom John sees identifies the seven lamps as the seven churches (cf. 1:4, 11).

Standing among the lampstands is the one who had been speaking to John (1:13-16). The modern reader needs to keep several things in mind when reading John's description of this individual. First, visions of bizarre figures are not uncommon in the Old Testament (e.g., Isa 6:2; Ezek 1:8-12; Dan 10:5-6) and continue into Second Temple Judaism (e.g., *Apocalypse of Abraham* 11:2-3; *Apocalypse of Zephaniah* 6:11-12; *2 Enoch* 1:5; *Joseph and Aseneth* 14:9). A first century reader would probably not find John's description to be particularly shocking. Second, John is not unaware of this tradition when he writes about what he saw; in fact, his description is rich in

Old Testament allusions, as we will see. Third, some of the details (e.g., a sword coming out of the mouth) are such that the reader cannot understand them literally without making a mockery of the whole scene. But to suggest therefore that the description is symbolic is not to say that it is necessarily allegorical—i.e., that each detail has one and only one "deeper" meaning. If John indeed had such a vision, and there is no reason to doubt that he did, then he is describing the indescribable, and no language will adequately capture what he actually saw. He naturally used language with which he was familiar—that of the Old Testament—to communicate his vision.

The expression "one like a son of man" (1:13) is taken from Dan 7:13, a passage John has already echoed in 1:7. In Daniel "one like a son of man" approaches the Ancient of Days and is given an eternal kingship (Dan 7:13-14). A "long robe" (1:13: *podere*) is a distinctive garment worn by the priest (LXX *podere*: Exod 25:7; 28:4, 27 [31]; 29:5; 35:9; Zech 3:5[4]; Wis 18:24; Sir 45:8; cf. Ezek 9:2, 3, 11). Although the priestly attire included gold decorations (Exod 28:30; cf. Josephus, *Antiquities* 3.7.4), the reference to a "golden belt" (RSV "girdle"; cf. *Apocalypse of Zephaniah* 6:12) probably reflects the influence of Dan 10:5, where Daniel sees a man, apparently the angel Gabriel (cf. Dan 9:20-23), clothed in linen with gold around his waist (cf. 1 Macc 10:89, where a "gold buckle" is associated with royalty). The description of the head and the hair as "white as white wool, white as snow" (1:14) recalls Dan 7:9, where the clothing of the Ancient of Days (God) is described as being "white as snow" (cf. *Apocalypse of Abraham* 11:2) and his hair "like pure wool." Given John's demonstrated concern to apply to Jesus Old Testament language used to describe God (1:5b, 7), that he does so again here should not be lost on the reader.

The eyes being like "a flame of fire" (1:14) combines Daniel's characterization of the throne of the Ancient of Days as "a flame of fire" (Dan 7:9 LXX) with his characterization of the man in Dan 10:5 as having eyes like "flaming torches" (Dan 10:6). The feet "like burnished bronze" (1:15; cf. *Apocalypse of Zephaniah* 6:12) recall Daniel's continued description of the man in Dan 10:5 as having arms and feet "like the gleam of burnished bronze" (Dan 10:6), as well as Ezekiel's description of the legs and the feet of the four living creatures as sparkling "like burnished bronze" (Ezek 1:7). The specific metal alloy John mentions here is unknown; John's word for it (*chalkolibanon*) is found only here and in 2:18 in all of Greek literature. That it is mentioned again in the letter to the church at Thyatira might be an indication that this compound was a distinctive product of one of the trade guilds of that city, specifically metalworking. That this alloy has been refined in the "furnace" (1:15; cf. Dan 3:6) indicates its purity (cf. 3:18).

Daniel continues by describing the sound of the man's words as being like "the noise of a multitude" (Dan 10:6). John also describes the voice next, but by comparing it with "the sound of many waters" (1:15)—a rushing river or even a waterfall—he continues to draw upon Ezekiel's opening vision, where the sound of the wings of the four living creatures is said to be "like the sound of many waters" (Ezek 1:24; cf. Ezek 43:2). John's description of the figure as having a "sharp, two-edged sword" issuing "from his mouth" (1:16; cf. Heb 4:12) is reminiscent of Isa 49:2, where the servant of God is said to have a mouth "like a sharp sword." The "right hand" of God is a common Old Testament expression denoting both God's power (e.g., Exod 15:6; Deut 33:2; Ps 20:6) and protection (Ps 16:8; 17:7; Isa 41:10). While the notion of holding stars in the right hand is not an Old Testament expression, that of God controlling the stars is (e.g., Job 38:31-32). There is no need to find an astrological explanation for the "seven" stars; the number simply matches that of the "seven" churches, whose "angels" they represent (1:20). Finally, the face like "the sun shining in full strength" (1:16; cf. *Apocalypse of Zephaniah* 6:11) recalls Judg 5:31, where the "friends" of God are compared to "the sun as he rises in his might."

Although it is important to take note of these allusions, the reader must take care not to let the specifics of the vision get in the way of its overall impact: the one whom John sees is clearly a figure of extraordinary power and authority. John will return to most of these details as the book progresses: walking amid the lampstands (2:1), one like a son of man (14:14), a golden belt around the waist (15:6), eyes like a flame of fire (2:18; 19:12), feet like burnished bronze (2:18), a voice like the sound of many waters (14:2; 19:6), holding seven stars in the right hand (2:1; 3:1), and a sharp, two-edged sword coming out of the mouth (2:12, 16; 19:15, 21).

John's response upon seeing this bizarre figure is to fall at his feet as though dead. Such an action is not surprising; Daniel's response to his vision in Dan 10 is quite similar (Dan 10:8-9, 15; cf. Dan 8:17-18; Josh 5:14; Ezek 1:28; Matt 17:6; Acts 9:4; *1 Enoch* 14:14; *Apocalypse of Zephaniah* 6:13; *Joseph and Aseneth* 14:10). In both instances the figure reaches out to touch the prophet and says, "Fear not" (1:17; Dan 10:9, 16-19; cf. *Joseph and Aseneth* 14:11). John specifies that the figure extends his "right hand," which is the same one in which he holds the seven stars (1:16). The speaker reveals several things about himself. "The first and the last" (1:17) is reminiscent of the self-designation of God in Isa 44:6 (cf. Isa 48:12). Here the expression immediately brings to mind "the Alpha and the Omega" of 1:8; John will use both expressions together in 22:13. "The living one" (1:18: *ho zon*) echoes Josh 3:10: "the living God" (*theos zon*; cf. Tob 13:1; Matt 16:16; Acts 14:15;

Rom 9:26); the exact expression (*ho zon*) is found in Sir 18:1. Here it is defined further by what follows: "I died, and behold I am alive for evermore" (both Tob 13:1 and Sir 18:1 add "for evermore"). This is a clear reference to the death and resurrection of Jesus, which John has already mentioned (1:5; cf. 1:7). Contrary to modern usage, Hades is not a synonym for Hell—i.e., the place of punishment. It is the Greek equivalent of the Hebrew "Sheol," the place of the dead (i.e., the grave). "Death" and "Hades" are frequently combined in the Old Testament (e.g., Job 33:22; Ps 6:5; Prov 2:18; Cant 8:6; Isa 28:15; Ezek 31:14-15; Hos 13:14; Hab 2:5; cf. Wis 16:13; Sir 14:12; 2 Macc 6:22-23), and are always combined in Revelation (cf. 6:8; 20:13, 14). That Jesus holds "the keys" of Death and Hades gives him the power to unlock death and its consequences. Jesus has already conquered Death for himself; he has the power to do so for others. John will develop this notion of "keys" further in 3:7.

The speaker's charge to John to "write" (1:19) recalls 1:1 and forms an inclusion with 1:11. The shift from "what must *soon* take place" (1:11: *en tachei*) to "what is (*mellei*; cf. Isa 48:6) to take place *hereafter*" (1:19: *meta tauta*) simply picks up more closely the allusion to Dan 2 (see on 1:1), where Dan 2:45 (Theod) has "what must take place *hereafter*" (*meta tauta*; cf. v. 29). Similarly, the variations in the tense of the verb "see" from 1:1 (aorist) to 1:11 (present) to 1:19 (aorist) are insignificant. To suggest here a threefold breakdown of the revelation—i.e., what John *saw*, what *is*, and what *will be*—is to miss the allusions back to 1:1 and 1:11. Jesus is repeating his previous injunction for John to write what he sees, and here he further specifies the content of what John sees in a twofold manner: "what is and what is to take place hereafter." To view even this twofold characterization as an outline of the book—i.e., what *is* will be described in chapters 2–3 and what *will be* in chapters 4–22—is not only artificial but ignores the presence of future elements in chapters 2–3 and present elements in 4–22. Indeed, in Dan 2 "hereafter" (2:29 Theod) refers to events past, present, and future (Dan 2:36-45).

Jesus calls the stars and the lampstands a "mystery" (1:20). The concept of "mystery," drawn from Daniel (2:18, 19, 27-30, 47, 47), is that of something God alone knows but that he might choose to make known to people (see further on 10:7). That Jesus explains this mystery to John encourages the reader to believe this book that calls itself a "revelation" will indeed "reveal" divine truths.

John has set the stage for the rest of his book. He has recounted the circumstances surrounding his commission to write to the seven churches of Asia. He has presented a powerful (and distinctive) portrait of the One who commissioned him: Jesus. While details of the portrait conjure up certain Old Testament associations (e.g, the priesthood), a fuller appreciation for them will come only as John continues to unfold the revelation. In addition, John has once again called attention to Jesus' death and applied to Jesus language traditionally associated with God. The reader is assured that Jesus stands amid the churches, with their "angels" in his powerful hand.

The Letters to the Seven Churches: An Overview

Each of the letters to the seven churches contains a specific message for one of the churches named in 1:11. In four of the letters (Ephesus, Pergamum, Thyatira, and Sardis) Jesus both praises and criticizes the church. In two of the letters (Smyrna and Philadelphia) there is no criticism; in one (Laodicea) there is no praise. The letters to the seven churches follow, with minor differences, the same basic form: (1) addressee, (2) command to John to write, (3) self-identification of speaker (Jesus) in terms from the previous chapter and introduced by the expression "The words of . . .," (4) acknowledgment of the situation in the church by the words "I know your works," (5) exhortation to the church, (6) warning or promise, (7) challenge to hear, (8) promise to "him who conquers." As an example, one might note the letter to Ephesus:

(1) "To the angel of the church in Ephesus" (2:1)
(2) "Write" (2:1)
(3) "The words of him who holds the seven stars in his right hand, who walks among the seven golden lampstands" (2:1; cf. 1:13, 16)
(4) "I know your works . . ." (2:2)
(5) "Remember then from what you have fallen, repent and do the works you did at first" (2:5)
(6) "If not, I will come to you and remove your lampstand from its place" (2:5)
(7) "He who has an ear, let him hear what the Spirit says to the churches" (2:7)
(8) "To him who conquers I will grant to eat of the tree of life, which is in the paradise of God" (2:7).

Minor differences include self-identification of Jesus in terms beyond those of chapter 1 in the letters to Thyatira, Philadelphia, and Laodicea; changes in the wording of (4) in the letters to Smyrna and Pergamum; the reversal of elements (5) and (6) in the letters to Thyatira and Philadelphia; and the reversal of elements (7) and (8) in the letters to Thyatira, Sardis, Philadelphia, and Laodicea.

Although each of the letters is addressed to an individual church, each of the churches was expected to read the other six letters. This is underscored not only by the fact that every manuscript of Revelation contains all seven letters, but also by the fact that each letter contains the refrain "what the Spirit says to the church*es*" (2:7, 11, 17, 29; 3:6, 13, 22). Yet all of the letters are different and reflect, in varying degrees, the local color of the city in which the particular church is found (see especially W. M. Ramsay, *The Letters to the Seven Churches of Asia and Their Place in the Plan of the Apocalypse* [London: Hodder and Stoughton, 1904; updated ed.; Peabody MA: Hendrickson, 1994]; and C. J. Hemer, *The Letters to the Seven Churches in Their Local Setting* [JSNTS Supplement Series 11; Sheffield: JSOT Press, 1986]). One must recognize, however, that a church cannot simply be identified with a city; literary allusions, as well as local references, must be used in understanding the letters.

One of the thorniest—and perhaps least significant—issues in Revelation is the identity of the "angels" of the seven churches. Not only is there an absence of clear parallels outside the book to the expression "the angel of the church in . . .," but the word *aggelos* need not imply a supernatural being at all; it can simply mean "messenger." Suggested identifications include a church's pastor, prophetic leadership, apostolic delegation, guardian angel, or even "prevailing spirit." That the letters are addressed to these "angels" and dominated by the second person *singular* pronoun, yet contain references to people *within* the churches and communicate the Spirit speaking to the *churches*, suggests that the angels in some sense serve as (spiritual?) counterparts to the churches, though the dynamic of this relationship is far from clear.

"You have abandoned the love you had at first": The letter to the church at Ephesus
Revelation 2:1-7

An important commercial center on the Aegean Sea at the mouth of the Cayster River, Ephesus had become the most prominent city in the province of Asia by John's day. It had long been the home for the cult of the goddess Artemis, whose temple was hailed as one of the seven wonders of the ancient world. Destroyed by arson in 356 BC, the temple had been rebuilt to a size of 425 feet by 220 feet by 60 feet. It contained 127 marble pillars, 36 of them overlaid with gold and jewels. Ephesus was the third city in Asia to become a provincial center for the emperor cult and boasted a magnificent temple erected to the Flavian emperors (Vespasian, Titus, and Domitian). Paul visited Ephesus briefly near the end of his second missionary journey (Acts 18:19-21) and made it his primary base of teaching on his third missionary journey (Acts 19:1–20:1; cf. Acts 20:17-38).

Jesus identifies himself as the one who holds the seven stars in his right hand and who walks among the seven golden lampstands (2:1; cf. 1:12, 16). This self-designation, the "mystery" of which he has just explained to John (1:20), constitutes an appropriate opening to the seven letters and serves to anticipate the threat of removing the lampstand in 1:5.

Jesus praises the church for its toil (2:2) and endurance (2:2, 3). He mentions the latter twice, elaborating the second time in terms of bearing up for his name's sake and not growing weary (2:3). This is probably to be understood within the context of those false teachers whom the Ephesians have successfully countered. That Jesus speaks of "those who call themselves apostles" (2:2) shows that these teachers claimed not only to be Christians but also to have positions of authority within the church (cf. Paul's warning to the Ephesian elders in Acts 20:29-30). How the Ephesians "tested" these self-proclaimed apostles is not clear, but the Ephesians correctly determined these individuals to be "false." Just why these people are deemed false is also not clear, nor is their connection, if any, with the Nicolaitans (2:6), a group also present at Pergamum (2:15). Their positive reception among at least some of the Christians there suggests that the Nicolaitans, if not claiming to be Christians themselves, at least did not come across as being overtly opposed to the church. Here Jesus speaks merely of their "works," which both he and the Ephesians "hate" (2:6; cf. Ps 139:21).

The problem with the church at Ephesus is that it has abandoned "the love you had at first" (2:4). The result is that the church has suffered a significant fall and no longer does "the works you did at first" (2:5). The thought is that of Jer 2:2, where the Lord tells Jeremiah to proclaim in Jerusalem: "I remember the devotion of your youth, your love as a bride, how you followed me in the wilderness in a land not sown." The "love you had at first," therefore, is the initial zeal and commitment that characterizes a relationship. For the church at Ephesus, as for Israel, that initial zeal for God has waned. That is why the situation at Ephesus is so serious. The ability to identify and oppose false teachers is meaningless if it is not matched by a fervent love for God. The only recourse is that the Ephesians "repent" (twice in 2:5) and do the works—unspecified here—they did at first, which demonstrate their love for God (2:5). The significance of repenting or not repenting will be an important theme in the book (cf. 2:16, 21, 22; 3:3, 19; 9:20, 21; 16:9,

11). The threat of the removal of their lampstand (2:5)—i.e., church—is both serious and readily understandable to the inhabitants of a city whose landscape was constantly changing. Ephesus faced the neverending problem of its harbor silting up, and today the coastline is six miles away from the ruins of first century Ephesus.

The promise to the conqueror is that he will eat of the tree of life, which is in the "paradise" of God (2:7). "Paradise" (*paradeisos*) can simply mean "garden" (e.g., Ecc 2:5), and the source of John's image is Gen 2:9 (cf. 13:10), which mentions the tree of life amid the "garden" (LXX *paradeisos*: thirteen times in Gen 2–3; cf. *Life of Adam and Eve* 1:1) of Eden. In the LXX "paradise of God" is found four times (Gen 13:10; Ezek 28:13; 31:8, 9). In Gen 3, God expels Adam and Eve from the "garden" lest they eat of the tree of life "and live for ever" (Gen 3:22); he then places cherubim and a flaming sword "to guard the way to the tree of life" (Gen 3:24). In Judaism there developed the notion of a future paradise in which will be planted the tree of life (e.g., *Testament of Levi* 18:10-11; *2 Enoch* 8:3-7; *4 Ezra* 8:52), though sometimes paradise was mentioned without a reference the tree of life (e.g., *1 Enoch* 32:3; *4 Ezra* 7:123; *2 Baruch* 4:3-6; Luke 23:43; 2 Cor 12:3), and vice versa (e.g., *Apocalypse of Moses* 18:4; *5 Ezra* 2:12; cf. *1 Enoch* 24:4–25:6). In a passage strikingly similar to this passage, *Testament of Levi* 18:10-11 reads, "And he shall open the gates of paradise; he shall remove the sword that has threatened since Adam, and he will grant to the saints to eat of the tree of life." Overall, it is clear that the tree of life had become an important symbol among some Jews regarding their hope for the future. This is certainly true for John, who will mention the tree of life—but not paradise—again (22:2, 14, 19).

Although this Jewish background is the most natural setting within which to understand the tree of life in paradise, one should also note that a sacred tree was associated with the temple of Artemis in Ephesus. The notion of *God's* (rather than Artemis's) special tree would perhaps have had particular relevance for the Ephesian Christians.

Once again, the use of the present tense to speak of Jesus as "coming" (2:5; RSV "will come") is striking (cf. 1:7). To be sure, it is followed by a future ("[I will] remove"), but the reader gets the impression that Jesus is in some sense *always* "coming."

"For ten days you will have tribulation":
The letter to the church at Smyrna
Revelation 2:8-11

Thirty-five miles to the north of Ephesus lay another harbor city, Smyrna. For exports from the province, it was second only to Ephesus. Smyrna was the second city in Asia to become a center for emperor worship: in AD 26 it had been selected, out of eleven applicants, to build a temple to the emperor Tiberius. Claiming to be the birthplace of Homer, Smyrna was well known for its civic pride. It was especially famous for its wealth, fine buildings, and devotion to science and medicine. Coins depict Smyrna as "first of Asia in beauty and size."

Jesus identifies himself as the first and the last, the one who died and came to life (2:8; cf. 1:17-18), comforting words indeed for a church facing the problems mentioned in this letter.

The church at Smyrna is one of two churches (the other being Philadelphia) that receive no criticism. Rather than speaking of knowing their "works," Jesus speaks of knowing their "tribulation" and "poverty," along with the "slander" (lit., "blasphemy") they have been experiencing (2:9). John will speak later of "blasphemy" in connection with the beast (13:1, 5, 6; 17:3) and with those who refuse to repent at the pouring out of the seven bowls (16:9, 11, 21). The slanderers are characterized in terms similar to those of the false apostles in Ephesus: they "say that they are Jews and are not" (2:9; cf. 2:2). But rather than being "false," like the self-proclaimed apostles, this group is called a "synagogue of Satan" (2:9). The reference to "synagogue" suggests that Jesus is speaking of actual Jews. In the middle of the second century, some local Jews in Smyrna participated in the persecution and martyrdom of a number of Christians, most notably the bishop Polycarp (*Martyrdom of Polycarp*). While we must not read the later situation back into the time of John, it is certainly possible that some Jews in Smyrna were causing trouble for the Christians in John's day. Jesus speaks of what the church is "about to suffer" and warns them of imprisonment, testing, tribulation "for ten days," and even death (2:10). The church both has (2:9) and will have (2:10) tribulation; John has already identified himself as one who shares in the tribulation of the churches (1:9).

The Devil, who is explicitly identified as Satan in 12:9 and 20:2, is the principal enemy of God and his people in this book. "(The) Devil" ([*ho*] *diabolos*; lit., "[the] slanderer") is the standard LXX rendering of the Hebrew word *hasatan*. *Satan* means simply "adversary" (e.g., Num 22:22; 1 Sam 29:4; 1 Kgs 11:25). Only with the definite article (*hasatan*) does the word take on the connotation of a specific adversary—i.e., "the Adversary," or "Satan." This figure is mentioned in three Old Testament books. In 1 Chronicles Satan, portrayed as standing "against" Israel, incites David to institute a census (1 Chr 21:1; cf. 2 Sam 24:1). Job presents a more complex picture of Satan. First, Satan is one of "the sons of God" who present themselves before the Lord periodically (Job 1:6; 2:1). Second, he goes "to and fro" on the earth (Job 1:7; 2:2). Third, he accuses Job of fearing God only because he lives a happy life; bereft of it, Satan argues, Job will curse God (Job 1:8-11; 2:3-5). Finally, Satan has the power to inflict severe misfortunes on Job (1:12-19; 2:6-8). In Zechariah Satan is depicted as the accuser of the high priest Joshua before God; in response God replaces Joshua's filthy garments with clean ones (Zech 3:1-2). Satan is also found in the *Testaments of the Twelve Patriarchs* as a deceiver (*Testament of Dan* 3:6; 5:6; cf. *1 Enoch* 54:6) who leads people into committing evil acts (*Testament of Dan* 3:6; 5:6; 6:1; *Testament of Gad* 4:7; cf. *Testament of Asher* 6:4). The LXX translates *hasatan* ("Satan") with (*ho*) *diabolos*—i.e., "(the) slanderer" or "(the) Devil." Elsewhere "the Devil" will be found again in 12:9, 12; 20:2, 10, while "Satan" will be found in 2:13, 13, 24; 3:9; 12:9; and 20:2, 7. Outside of Revelation "Satan" is found twenty-six times in the New Testament (e.g., Matt 4:10; Mark 8:33; Luke 10:18; John 13:27; 1 Cor 5:5) and "devil" thirty-two times (e.g., Matt 25:41; Luke 8:12; John 8:44; Eph 6:4; Heb 2:14; Jas 4:7; 1 Pet 5:8; 1 John 3:8; Jude 9).

The reference to being "tested" (*peirazo*) for "ten days" (2:10) is drawn from Dan 1. Chosen along with fellow Jews Hananiah, Mishael, and Azariah to live and be educated in King Nebuchadnezzar's palace (Dan 1:3-6), Daniel resolves not to "defile himself with the king's rich food, or with the wine which he drank" (Dan 1:8). He therefore proposes to the steward that he and his compatriots be tested (LXX *peirazo*) for "ten days": they will be given only vegetables and water, and at the end of the period their health will be compared to that of the other young men eating the rich food and drinking the wine (Dan 1:12-13). The steward agrees to the test, and at the end of ten days Daniel and his fellow Jews are found to be in better health than the others (Dan 1:14-15). What is significant about this "testing for ten days" is that the issue is not one of *persecution* but of *accommodation*. This may well be the situation at Smyrna. It is not so much that Christians are being persecuted for their faith; rather, they are being pressured to accommodate themselves to pagan practices. Imprisonment, which is not a typical form of Roman punishment as such, could then be used to coerce Christians to adopt such practices, with the threat of death if they refused. There is no way of knowing exactly what the Christians in Smyrna faced, but it is probably safe to say that, given the allusion to Daniel 1, there is no reason to take the "ten days" literally. The close association between "testing" and "tribulation" will recur in 3:10.

To call the opposing Jews in Smyrna a synagogue "of Satan" is striking indeed, and Jesus will use the expression again in 3:9. The rhetoric here reminds the reader that John has already begun to portray the Church in terms used to describe Israel in the Old Testament (cf. 1:5b-7). Thus, the rhetoric is not intended as an ethnic statement—i.e., that all ethnic Jews are necessarily on the side of Satan—but as a theological one—i.e., that the church has taken ethnic Israel's place as the true Israel (cf. Rom 2:28-29). To deny these individuals the name "Jew," therefore, is to affirm that their opposition to the church shows that they are on the side not of Jesus, but of Satan.

Though the city might appear wealthy and the Smyrnean Christians poor, Jesus, in an ironic twist, assures them that they are indeed the ones who are truly "rich" (2:9). His exhortations to them are two: "do not fear" and "be faithful unto death" (2:10). If they are indeed faithful, he promises to give them "the crown of life," which is not mentioned elsewhere in the book (but cf. 3:11). While "crown of life" is found only in Jas 1:12, the notion of a "crown" as a future reward for the righteous is found in both Judaism (e.g., Wis 5:16; *Testament of Benjamin* 4:1; 1QS 4.7; 1QH 17(9).25; *2 Baruch* 15:8) and early Christianity (e.g., 1 Cor 9:25; 2 Tim 4:8; 1 Pet 5:4; *2 Clement* 7:3; *Martyrdom of Polycarp* 17:1; *Ascension of Isaiah* 9:10, 25). The motif of a "crown" was also strong at Smyrna, especially as a mark of civic honor, and perhaps as a metaphor for the beauty of the city as well. As the one who died and came back to life (2:8), Jesus has the power to grant life to his followers. The promise to the conqueror is that he will not be harmed by "the second death" (2:11), a concept John will develop later (20:6, 14; 21:8).

"Where Satan's throne is":
The letter to the church at Pergamum
Revelation 2:12-17

Once the royal capital of the Attalid Empire (241–133 BC), Pergamum was the original capital of the Roman province of Asia, though by John's day it had been eclipsed in importance by Ephesus (and had perhaps seen the transfer of its provincial supremacy to that city; the evidence is not clear). Lying forty miles north of Smyrna and fifteen miles inland from the Aegean Sea, and with its citadel situated on a hill towering over the surrounding valley, Pergamum still remained an impressive and prosperous city. In 29 BC Pergamum became the first city in Asia to build a temple to the emperor, and it continued to be a center for the emperor cult. It boasted impressive temples to Zeus and to Asclepius, the god of healing, the latter temple giving the city widespread acclaim as an important medical center. Pergamum was also famous for its library and its book production.

Jesus identifies himself as the one who has the sharp, two-edged sword (2:12; cf. 1:16). The prospect of Jesus as the bringer of judgment contrasts sharply with Pergamum's longtime status as wielder of Roman authority and provides a sobering beginning to this letter.

This is the only letter in which Jesus begins "I know *where* you live" (2:13). It is the setting of the church, therefore, that creates its immediate problem. Pergamum is the place "where Satan's throne is"—i.e., "where Satan dwells" (2:13). Although an allusion to the temples of Zeus or Asclepius is possible here, it is much more likely that "Satan's throne" is a reference to the emperor cult (if not to Pergamum's status as the capital of the province, if that were still the case), given Pergamum's preeminence in that regard. What is important is that the environment in Pergamum is particularly hostile to Christianity. The result is pressure upon the Christians not to "hold fast to my name" but rather to "deny my faith" (i.e., faith in Jesus), which has already resulted in the martyrdom of a Christian named Antipas (2:13). "Faithful" is precisely the quality urged upon the church at Smyrna (2:10). Why Antipas was martyred is not known, but he is honored with the same title ("[my] faithful witness") that was used previously of Jesus (1:5). That Jesus speaks of "the days of" Antipas suggests that the incident that led to Antipas's martyrdom lay in the past; that he singles out by name one martyr suggests that widespread martyrdom is not yet an experience of the church at Pergamum, despite the fact that the church has not succumbed to the pressure to deny Jesus (2:13).

The church's problem lies rather in its toleration of false teachers. Some of the Christians at Pergamum hold to the teaching of "Balaam" (2:14). Balaam was a Moabite prophet at the time of the exodus. Although he is probably best known for owning a talking donkey (Num 22:1–24:25), Balaam also played a major role in leading the Israelites into apostasy at Peor, where they participated at the invitation of Moabite women in sacrifices to the Moabite gods (Num 31:16; cf. Num 25:1-2). The tradition that Balaam "taught Balak" (2:14), the king of Moab (Num 22:4), to entice the Israelites in this manner, though absent in the Old Testament, is found in first century AD Jewish writings (*Pseudo-Philo* 18:13-14; Philo, *On the Life of Moses* 1.294-99; Josephus, *Antiquities* 4:126-40). There is no reason to believe there was actually anyone named "Baalam" in Pergamum; Jesus' point is that as Balaam led astray "the sons of Israel" (2:14), so also the teaching at Pergamum is leading astray some Christians. One should note again the correspondence between Old Testament Israel and the Church.

The selection of Balaam as the Old Testament example of false teaching here, instead of other possibilities, may well be due to a certain similarity between the problems at Peor and Pergamum. Jesus' characterization of "Balaam's" false teaching in terms of eating food offered to idols and immorality recalls Israel's "playing the harlot" with the daughters of Moab (Num 25:1) and sitting down to eat their sacrifices to their gods (Num 25:2). Offering animal sacrifices to the gods was a common practice in John's day. Only part of the animal was used in the sacrifice, however; some of it was given to the priests and the rest often ended up being sold in the meat market or used in banquets held, more often than not, in the god's (or goddess's) temple. The issue of whether or not a Christian could eat food offered to idols troubled the church at Corinth (1 Cor 8:1-13; 10:14-33) and was addressed by the Jerusalem Council (Acts 15:20, 29). In Revelation it will be found again only in the letter to Thyatira (2:20).

"Immorality" in Judaism can have a broad range of meanings in the sense of sexual practices contrary to the Mosaic Law (e.g., incest, adultery), but it was also used metaphorically in the sense of being unfaithful to God by following pagan practices (e.g., Jer 2:1–3:9; Ezek 23; Hos 4:10-15). The metaphorical sense dominates Revelation (14:8; 17:2, 4; 18:3, 9; 19:2; cf. 9:21; 21:8; 22:15) and is to be preferred here. That does not exclude the possibility, or course, that involvement in pagan rituals may sometimes have included sexual debauchery, as may have been the case at Peor. Certainly cult prostitutes were a staple in the Graeco-Roman world. But the problem here is more the assimilation of the Christians to the pagan culture around them, perhaps in the context of trade guilds (see on 2:18-29). The point is that *any* participation in pagan practices represents a "stumbling block" for Christians and is therefore to be avoided. In 2:15 Jesus compares the teaching of Balaam to that of the Nicolaitans. Given the similarity of language, it is best to see the Nicolaitans as the group about whom Jesus is speaking in 2:14; hence, there is one group of teachers, not two. The church at Pergamum has not been as successful in warding off the influence of the Nicolaitans as the church at Ephesus has been (cf. 2:6).

Jesus' exhortation to the church is simple: repent (2:16; cf. 2:5). If the church does not repent, "I will come [present indicative—cf. 2:5] to you soon" (cf. 3:11; 22:7, 12, 20) and "war [cf. 12:7; 13:4; 17:14; 19:11] against them with the sword of my mouth" (cf. 2:12; 1:16). As in 2:5, this "coming" seems to be one of judgment within history upon an unrepentant church. The graphic "war against [*polemeo*] them with the sword of my mouth" (2:16) can hardly be taken literally. The metaphorical use of God "making war" against his people can be seen, for example, in Jer 21:5, where God warns Zedekiah, king of Judah, that "I myself will fight [LXX *polemeo*] against you with outstretched hand and strong arm, in anger, and fury, and in great wrath." Similarly, the Messiah smiting his enemies with the word of his mouth is found in *Psalms of Solomon* 17:24, 35, 36. The connection of the sword—a common image for judgment (e.g., Rom 13:4)—with the mouth suggests that Jesus will speak words of judgment against the church (cf. *4 Ezra* 13:37-38). Proper attention to the imagery here will prevent the reader from misunderstanding similar imagery later in the book, including the climactic scene of 19:11-21.

Jesus' promise to the conqueror has several parts (2:17). First, he is promised "the hidden manna." Manna was the food God miraculously provided the Israelites in the desert following the exodus (Exod 16:4-36). God commanded them to save an omer of manna in a jar and keep it in the sanctuary (Exod 16:32-34). According to Jewish legend Jeremiah hid the manna just before the Babylonians conquered Jerusalem (2 Macc 2:4-7; *Lives of the Prophets* 2:11-19; *4 Baruch* 3:9-18; cf. *2 Baruch* 6:7-10). Second, the conqueror is promised a white stone. What significance this would have had to the original readers escapes us. The more likely suggestions include (1) a vote of acquittal, (2) a token of admission, (3) an amulet inscribed with the name of the deity, and (4) a token given by a deity and inscribed with a new name given to the deity's disciple. (3) and (4) represent diametrically opposed interpretations of another problem: upon the white stone will be written a new name that no one knows except the one who receives it (2:17). But whose "new name" is it? the deity's? the disciple's? In Isa 62:2 God promises a "new name" to Jerusalem (cf. Isa 1:26; 60:14, 18; 62:4, 12; 65:15; Jer 3:7; 33:16; Ezek 48:35; Zech 8:3). Since the only other reference to a "new" name in Revelation is 3:12, where Jesus speaks of writing upon the conqueror "the name of my God, and the name of the city of my God, the new Jerusalem . . . and my own new name," the "new name" probably belongs to Jesus. What the conqueror receives is not a new name but a white stone, and only those who are given the white stone will know Jesus' new name. Perhaps multiple senses of the white stone are intended: it is a token of admission to the new Jerusalem inscribed with the name of the Lamb whose death has brought acquittal to his followers (cf. 12:10-11). All that can be said with certainty is that the color of the stone is the same as that of the clothes promised to the conqueror elsewhere (3:5; cf. 3:4, 18) and is consistent with other positive uses of "white" in Revelation (1:14; 4:4; 7:9, 13; 14:14; 19:11, 14 [twice]; 20:11).

"You tolerate the woman Jezebel, who calls herself a prophet": The letter to the church at Thyatira
Revelation 2:18-29

Forty miles to the southeast of Pergamum lay Thyatira, the least important of the seven cities to which John is instructed to write. Built as a military garrison city at the beginning of the third century BC, Thyatira eventually became a center of trade. It was most noteworthy for its large number of trade guilds, many of which were associated with a significant textile industry. Paul's first convert in Philippi was Lydia, a dealer in purple cloth from Thyatira (Acts 16:14). According to local legend, Thyatira had been founded as a shrine to the sun god Apollo Tyrimnaeus.

Jesus identifies himself as "the Son of God, who has eyes like a flame of fire, and whose feet are like burnished bronze" (2:18). "Son of God," a common title for Jesus in the New Testament (e.g., Matt 14:33; Mark 1:1; Luke 1:35; John 1:49; Rom 1:4; Heb 4:14; 1 John 5:5), is found neither in chapter 1 nor anywhere else in Revelation. The title might be an allusion to Ps 2:7 ("He said to me, 'You are my son, today I have begotten you'") in anticipation of the references to Ps 2:8-9 (2:26-27) and "my Father" (2:28; cf. 3:5, 21; 1:6 ["his Father"]) at the end of the letter. In addition, it probably functions polemically against the mingling together, evidenced by Thyatiran coins, of Apollo Tyrimnaeus and the emperor as sons of the god Zeus. The polemic is pushed even further if *chalkolibanon* ("burnished bronze") was an alloy distinctive to this city (see on 1:15): though the city's patron god was Apollo Tyrimnaeus, it is Jesus whose feet are like *chalkolibanon*. Having eyes "like a flame of fire" anticipates Jesus' comment in 2:23 that he searches the mind and heart and judges according to one's works. This self-identification draws upon a common Old Testament characterization of God, especially Jer 17:10: "I the LORD search the mind and try the heart, to give to every man according to his ways, according to the fruit of his doings." That God knows people's minds and hearts is a common theme in both the Old Testament (1 Sam 16:7; 1 Kgs 8:39; 1 Chr 28:9; Ps 7:9; Prov 24:12; cf. Sir 42:18; *2 Baruch* 83:3) and the New Testament (Acts 1:24; 1 Cor 4:5; Heb 4:12-13), as is the notion that God judges people according to their works (Ps 62:12; Prov 24:12; Isa 59:18; Jer 17:10; Rom 2:6; 2 Tim 4:14; cf. Sir 16:12; *Psalms of Solomon* 2:16). The latter will be found again in Revelation (18:6; 20:12-13). Once again Old Testament language for God is used to describe Jesus.

Jesus praises the church for its love, faith, service, and patient endurance (2:19). "Love" is found in Revelation only in 2:4; "faith" in 2:13; 13:10; 14:12; "service" nowhere else; and "patient endurance" in 1:9; 2:2, 3; 3:10; 13:10; 14:12. "Faith" and "patient endurance" are linked together in 13:10 and 14:12. Jesus also acknowledges that the church's "latter works exceed the first."

That the letter to Thyatira is the longest of the seven letters is an indication that the problem at Thyatira is especially acute. At its center is a woman who has set herself up as a leader in the church. Jesus calls this woman "Jezebel" (2:20), an allusion to the wicked wife of the Old Testament king Ahab. The Old Testament Jezebel's devotion to the Canaanite god Baal had a profound influence on her husband and the northern kingdom of Israel, which he ruled (1 Kgs 16:31-33). She attempted to exterminate the prophets of God (1 Kgs 18:4), set herself firmly against Elijah the prophet (1 Kgs 19:2), and was remembered for her "harlotries and sorceries" (2 Kgs 9:22). The "Jezebel" in the church at Thyatira calls herself a "prophet" (2:20). (The reader should not be confused by the RSV translation "prophetess," as if there were some material distinction between male and female prophets. The difference between the Greek *prophetis* [feminine] and *prophetes* [masculine] is a matter of the structure of the Greek language, not of meaning.) As a "prophet" Jezebel "is teaching and beguiling" the Christians, whom Jesus calls "my servants" (cf. 1:1). Her teaching is identical to that of the false teachers in Pergamum: immorality and eating food offered to idols (2:20; cf. 2:14). The immorality, however, dominates the portrait of her here. Jesus has given her time to repent, but she refuses to repent of her "immorality" (2:21); hence, Jesus will "throw her on a sickbed (lit., "bed")" along with "those who commit adultery with her" (2:22).

Once again "immorality" should be taken metaphorically to suggest accommodation to pagan practices (cf. 2:14). Although we cannot be certain, the point at issue is probably participation in the various trade guilds in Thyatira. Since members of a guild sometimes gathered for cultic meals in pagan temples (note the reference to eating food sacrificed to idols in 2:20; cf. 1 Cor 8:10; 10:19-21), the question of Christian involvement in these guilds, important for one's economic well-being, would have been a relevant one. Jezebel may have been justifying Christian participation in such pagan rituals. Her teaching also involved "what some call the deep things of Satan" (2:24). Whether this is an ironic comment, as in 2:9 (cf. 3:9), where the Jews are said to be a "synagogue of Satan," or reflects the idea that Christians are somehow able to, and indeed should, probe Satan's mysteries is unclear. In the first instance, the attraction might be to learn "the deep things of God" (cf. 1 Cor 2:10); in the second, the sense might be that Christians can participate in idolatrous festivities unharmed (cf. Irenaeus, *Against Heresies* 1.24.5; cf. 1.6.5; Justin, *Dialogue with Trypho* 35).

That Jesus has given Jezebel "time to repent" suggests that she has already been warned. Being thrown onto a bed can indicate illness (cf. 1 Macc 1:5; Jdt 8:3), though it need not be taken literally. It is a deliciously ironic punishment for an "adulteress." Those who commit adultery with her will experience "great tribulation" (2:22: no definite article; cf. 7:14). The additional threat to "strike her children dead [lit., "kill . . . with death]" (2:23) need not cause confusion: they are the same as her paramours, both images being appropriate for those adversely affected by an adulteress. To kill "with death" is a Hebrew idiom (cf. 6:8; Ezek 33:27). The judgment of Jezebel and those whom she has led astray will demonstrate Jesus' authority to "all the churches" (2:23; cf. Ezek 33:29). There is still time, however, for repentance (2:22).

Not all of the Thyatiran Christians have followed Jezebel. Some do not hold to the teaching and have not "learned" the deep things of Satan (2:24). Upon these Jesus lays no "other" burden (cf. Acts 15:28), which is presumably to be explained (though rather vaguely) in light of the following: they are asked only to "hold fast what you have [cf. 3:11], until I come" (2:25). Again the question arises as to what "coming" Jesus is referring to (cf. 2:5, 16). That the conqueror is described as one who keeps Jesus' works (cf. 1:3) "until the end [*telos*]" (2:26) only compounds the problem, since what is meant by "the end" (e.g., of the conqueror's life? the return of Jesus?) is not made clear. The only other use of *telos* in the book is in the expression "I am the beginning and the end" (1:17; 2:23), which is of little value here.

The conqueror is given a twofold promise. First, Jesus will give to the conqueror "power over the nations" (2:26). This is a loose paraphrase of Ps 2:8a, which reads "the nations [as] your heritage." The change highlights the word "power," which will be a key theme in this book (e.g., 11:6; 12:19; 13:2; 17:12). Similarly, there will be frequent mention of the "nations," particularly in the sense of those outside of the church (e.g., 14:8; 16:19; 19:15; 20:3, 8). It is noteworthy that the first time these two words are used in the book, they are brought together in a promise to the conqueror. Jesus continues with a more literal citation of Ps 2:9 (2:27), which is alluded to again in 12:5 and 19:15. The image is one of a shepherd tending his flock (e.g., 7:17), but the mention of a staff (RSV "rod") made of iron (both in Ps 2 and in Revelation) is striking. The picture seems to be one of absolute power, even to the point of destroying those being ruled. In 12:15 and 19:15 it will be Jesus who has this power (cf. *Psalms of Solomon* 17:24). Here Jesus comments that he "received power from my Father" (2:28; cf. Matt 11:27; John 5:27). Not clear at this point is *when* Jesus actually received this power.

Second, Jesus will give to the conqueror "the morning star" (2:28). That the planet Venus appeared just before dawn, signaling the start of a new day, was well known as far back as ancient Babylon; hence, it was called the morning star, or the day star. Indeed, in Isa 14:12 "morning star" is used as an epithet for the king of Babylon himself. In Roman times the planet Venus was a symbol of sovereignty, and the Roman emperors claimed to be descendants of the goddess Venus. Among certain Jews, Num 24:17, which speaks of a "star" rising out of Jacob who will crush the enemies of Israel, was interpreted messianically (e.g., CD 7.18-21; 4QTest[4Q175] 9-13). In 22:16 Jesus will identify himself as the morning star. Perhaps the use of this expression in Revelation is intended as a polemic against the Roman Empire: true kingship resides in Jesus (and, by extension, with his followers).

Given the length of this particular letter, especially since Thyatira was the least significant of the seven cities, it is legitimate to ask how closely the controversy raised by "Jezebel" lies to the center of the concerns of the book. First, parallels with the letter to the church at Pergamum have already been noted. Second, that the punishment of Jezebel and her followers will reveal Jesus' role as divine judge to "all of the churches" (2:23) suggests that her activities were known beyond Thyatira itself. Third, there are clear parallels between the picture drawn of Jezebel here and that of Babylon later in the book (e.g., committing adultery with a harlot [2:21-22; 17:1-2; 18:3, 9] who "beguiles/deceives" people [2:20; 18:23]; the command not to participate in her sins [2:22; 18:4]; judgment according to one's deeds [2:23; 18:8]). Is it plausible to see the emphasis on "prophets" and "prophecy" in the book (1:3; 10:7; 11:6, 10, 18; 16:6; 18:20, 24; 19:10; 22:6, 7, 9, 10, 18, 19) as a response to the self-styled "prophet" of Thyatira? One might be tempted to ask the question, Is John's conflict with the rival prophet "Jezebel" the defining issue in the book (see P. B. Duff, *Who Rides the Beast? Prophetic Rivalry and the Rhetoric of Crisis in the Churches of the Apocalypse* [Oxford: Oxford University Press, 2001])? At this point the reader can do little more than ponder these questions. Clearly, however, the threat posed by "Jezebel" is a serious one.

"You have the name of being alive, and you are dead": The letter to the church at Sardis
Revelation 3:1-6

Sardis lay about thirty miles southeast of Thyatira, and its acropolis, rising grandly above the valley with almost perpendicular sides, provided a natural and virtually impregnable citadel. Once the center of the Lydian Empire (in the sixth century BC) and one of the most powerful cities in the ancient world, Sardis had waned somewhat in significance by the first century AD, though it remained an important commercial center. In AD 17 a devastating earthquake in the region hit Sardis especially hard; the emperor Tiberius granted Sardis an enormous amount of aid and exempted the city from paying taxes for five years. By AD 26 Sardis had recovered sufficiently to compete, albeit unsuccessfully, for the right to build a temple to Tiberius.

Jesus identifies himself as "him who has the seven spirits of God and the seven stars" (3:1). The first part of the expression comes from 1:4, though Jesus is not said to possess the seven spirits there. If the seven spirits represent the Holy Spirit (see on 1:4), then the close association between Jesus and the Holy Spirit here is striking. The seven stars, which Jesus is said to hold in his right hand in 1:16, have been previously identified as the seven angels of the seven churches (1:20). Perhaps the emphasis on the "sevens" here is intended as a warning that no church—even one that seems "alive"—escapes the notice of Jesus.

This is the first letter that contains no praise for the church at the beginning (the other is Laodicea). Jesus' charge that "you have the name of being alive, and you are dead" (3:1) contrasts starkly with his self-description as the one who died and came to life (1:18; 2:8). The church at Sardis apparently had an excellent reputation; Jesus sees through the reputation to the reality within. Jesus goes on to speak of "what remains and is on the point of death"; he has not "found your works perfect in the sight of my God" (3:2; cf. 2:5). Specifics about the church's problems are not given, but clearly its situation is grave. Indeed, that the Christians in Sardis have "soiled" (*moluno*) their robes (3:4) suggests accommodation to the pagan culture around them. The other use of *moluno* in the book (14:4) can be understood in this manner, and the only other occurrence of *moluno* in the New Testament is in the context of eating food sacrificed to idols (1 Cor 8:7).

Jesus' charge to the church is fivefold. First, the church is to "awake" (3:2, 3). The only other use of the verb in the book is in 16:15, a passage that recalls this one, where a blessing is given to the one who is awake and a warning to the one who is not. Elsewhere in the New Testament the idea is to watch, to be alert (Matt 26:38, 40-41; Acts 20:31; 1 Cor 16:13; Col 4:2; 1 Pet 5:8), especially with respect to the coming of Jesus/the Day of the Lord (Matt 24:42-43; 25:13; Mark 13:34, 37-38; Luke 12:37; 1 Thess 5:6, 10). This second element is in view in Jesus' warning that if the church does not "awake," he "will come like a thief [cf. 16:15], and you will not know at what hour I will come upon you" (3:3). The question, as we have seen several times, is *when* Jesus will come. Although the idea of Jesus/the Day of the Lord coming like a thief is strongly rooted in early Christian tradition (e.g., Matt 24:43-44; Luke 12:39-40; 1 Thess 5:2, 4; 2 Pet 3:10), the image would have provided a sobering reminder to the citizens of Sardis of the city's past history. According to Herodotus (*History* 1.84), during the siege of Sardis by Cyrus in 549 BC, a Persian soldier watched while one of the Lydian guards climbed down from the acropolis to retrieve a dropped helmet. During the night the soldier led a group of soldiers up the cliff by the same path and found the acropolis unguarded and everyone asleep. Polybius (*Histories* 7.15-18) records a similar incident during the siege of Sardis by Antiochus the Great in 214 BC. Not once, but twice the city of Sardis had fallen to its enemies because it had been so confident of its impregnability that it had failed to remain "awake." The second charge Jesus gives to the church is to "strengthen what remains and is on the point of death" (3:2; cf. Ezek 34:4). "Strengthen" is used only here in the book. Third, the church is to "remember" what it received and heard (cf. 2:5). Fourth, it is to "keep" what it received and heard (cf. 1:3; 2:26). Fifth, it is to "repent" (cf. 2:5 [twice], 16, 21 [twice], 22; 3:19).

Despite the grave state of the church overall, Jesus does observe that there are "a few names [cf. 3:5] in Sardis, people who have not soiled their garments" (3:4). This is the first mention of "garments" in the book, but not the last. These people are further declared to be "worthy," a word normally that will be reserved for God (4:11) and the Lamb (5:2, 4, 9, 12), but that will be used of "the saints and the prophets" in 16:6. To these believers Jesus promises that "they shall walk with me in white" (3:4). Unsoiled robes are not necessarily white. White, a color used in victory celebrations by the Romans, is already associated with Jesus (1:14) and with a promise to a conqueror (2:17). Here it also anticipates the reference to "white garments" in the promise to the conqueror in the next verse. "Walking" will be found again in 16:15.

"Thus" in 3:5 shows that the conqueror is understood in terms of the previous verse. The conqueror is given three promises. First, he will be clothed in "white garments" (cf. *1 Enoch* 108:12-15). "White garments" will be mentioned again in 3:18 and 4:4 (cf. 7:9, 13; 19:14). Second, his name will not be blotted out of "the book of life." The "book of life" will play an important role in this book. The concept of "the book of life [or the living]" was common in Judaism at this time (e.g., Ps 69:28; *Jubilees* 30:22; *1 Enoch* 47:3; 108:3; 4Q504 6.14-15; cf. Dan 12:1; Mal 3:16; 1QM 12.2-3; Luke 10:20; Phil 4:3; cf. Mal 3:16-18). The threat of being blotted out of God's "book" can be traced all the way back to Exod 32:32-33 (cf. Ps 69:28; *Jubilees* 30:22; *1 Enoch* 108:3). Over against this notion is the emphatic "will not" in 3:5. The conquerors' names are indelibly written in the book of life (cf. 21:27; *Joseph and Aseneth* 15:4); the names of others are simply not to be found there (13:8; 17:8; 20:15). Third, Jesus "will confess his name before my Father and before his angels" (cf. Matt 10:32; Luke 12:8).

"I will keep you from the hour of trial which is coming on the whole world":
The letter to the church at Philadelphia
Revelation 3:7-13

Located thirty miles southeast of Sardis at the intersection of several trade routes, including the main road leading into Phrygia to the east, Philadelphia was important both commercially and strategically. In addition, the fertile volcanic plain to the north was especially suitable for vineyards. But the land was also unstable; following the devastating earthquake of AD 17, tremors continued to be so frequent that most of the city's residents lived outside the city itself in the surrounding countryside.

Jesus identifies himself as "the holy one, the true one" (3:7), an expression not found in chapter 1 and elsewhere used only for God (6:10; cf. Isa 65:16). Indeed, the use of "holy" here anticipates the threefold declaration of God as "holy" in 4:8. Jesus will identify himself to the church as Laodicea as "the faithful and true witness" (3:14). He continues with an allusion to the "key" of 1:18, but rather than speaking of the "key of Death and Hades," as there, he speaks of "the key of David" in an allusion to Isa 22:22. The passage in Isaiah is part of a larger oracle against Shebna, the king's steward who controls access to the king (Isa 22:15-25). God tells Shebna that he will replace the steward with Eliakim, the son of Hilkiah. Eliakim is described in glowing terms, including those cited here about possessing the key to the house of David and having authority to open and shut. John has already described Jesus in Davidic terms (1:5) and will mention David two more times, both in connection with Jesus (5:5 and 22:16). The promise about no one being able to shut what he opens anticipates the next verse.

The church at Philadelphia is the second church (the other being Smyrna) to receive no criticism from Jesus. Jesus acknowledges that the church at Philadelphia has little power, yet it has kept (cf. 1:3) his word (3:10: word of endurance; cf. 2:2, 3) and has not denied his name (3:8; cf. 2:13). As a result, he has set before the church an "open door" (3:8). It is unlikely that the expression refers to a missionary opportunity (cf. 2 Cor 2:12); Revelation shows little interest in such matters. More likely is that the expression has to do with access to God. The same expression is used in 4:1, where John, seeing an open door in heaven, is caught up (presumably through that door) into heaven. The other use of "door" in Revelation is in 3:20, where Jesus refers to a door through which he will enter to eat with "any one" who opens it. The church at Philadelphia has little power; hence, Jesus himself has opened the door that enables its members to fellowship with God. Since he has the key of David, no one is able to shut the door (3:7-8).

Jesus' self-identification as the keyholder may well be relevant to the first promise he makes to the church. Once again Jesus speaks of a group of Jews. By characterizing them as "the synagogue of Satan who say that they are Jews" and affirming that they "are not, but lie" (3:9), Jesus combines his previous descriptions of the self-proclaimed Jews (2:9) and the self-proclaimed apostles (2:2). Further, he gives a strong indication that the Jews in Philadelphia are creating problems for the Christians. It is possible that (1) some of the Philadelphian Christians were Jews and were experiencing excommunication from the synagogue (e.g., John 16:2; cf. John 9:22; 12:42) or that (2) the Gentile Christians were encountering the argument that true salvation was to be found in Judaism (cf. Ignatius, *Philadelphians* 6:1; 8:2). But perhaps there is a more likely scenario. Judaism was a protected religion in the Roman Empire. As long as Christianity could claim an association with Judaism, it was exempt from emperor worship. But the Jews in Philadelphia were now officially repudiating the church, setting the Christians adrift to face Roman persecution. Against such a "shutting out," Jesus opens a door. Jesus' promise is that he will make the Jews "come and bow down before your feet" (3:9), a clear allusion to Old Testament promises given to Israel about Gentiles coming and bowing down before them (e.g., Ps 86:9; Isa 45:14; 49:23; 60:14). The irony is clear. Gentiles will not come and bow down before the Jews; rather, the Jews will come and bow down before the true Israel—i.e., the Church. Once again the reader encounters the theme that the Church is the true Israel (see on 2:9). Jesus adds that the reason for this reversal lies in himself: they will "learn that I have loved you" (3:9; cf. 1:5; Isa 43:3-4).

The second promise involves "the hour of trial which is coming on the whole world" (3:10). Several questions arise here. What is this "hour of trial"? Who is to experience it? What is the specific nature of the promise to the church at Philadelphia?

To begin with the second question, two expressions characterize those who will experience the hour of trial: "the whole world" and "those who dwell upon the earth." The first expression will be used twice more in the book, both in a negative sense—as those who are deceived by Satan (12:9) and as those whose kings are gathered for the battle on the great day of God Almighty (16:14). The same is true for "those who dwell upon the earth": they are guilty of the blood of the faithful (6:10); they are the recipients of the three "woes" (8:13); they gloat over the deaths of the two witnesses (11:10) who tormented them (11:10); they are astonished by the first beast (17:8) and worship it (13:8, 12); they are deceived by the second beast (13:14 [twice]); and they are intoxicated by the wine of the adulteries of the great harlot (17:2). It is clear that neither "the whole world" nor "those who dwell upon the earth" are merely neutral expressions intended to encompass the entire mass of humanity. Rather, both signify humanity in opposition to God. Indeed, "those who dwell upon the earth" will be twice identified explicitly as those whose names have not been written in the book of life (13:8; 17:8). Hence, the recipients of the "hour of testing" are not humans in general (godly and ungodly alike), but rather the ungodly.

What is this "hour of trial"? Although the noun "trial" (or "testing") (*peirasmos*) is used only here in Revelation, the verb "to try, to test" (*peirazo*) is found also in 2:2, where Jesus mentions a previous "trial" or "testing" of the false apostles by the church in Ephesus, and in 2:10, where he speaks of a ten-day "tribulation" the church in Smyrna will have to endure in order to be "tested." In both cases the "testing" is designed to verify genuineness (or lack thereof). Are the apostles in Ephesus *truly* apostles? Will the Smyrneans continue to be faithful in the face of pressure to accommodate to the surrounding culture? The "hour of trial" is therefore that which will verify once and for all that the ungodly are truly such. Although just what that "hour" will entail is not stated at this point, as the book progresses it will become clear that final judgment is in view (e.g., 6:15-17; 9:20-21; 16:9, 11, 21; 20:12-13).

The promise to the church is that it will be "kept from" the hour of trial. The only other use of "keep from" (*tereo ek*) in Greek literature is John 17:15, where Jesus prays concerning his disciples: "I do not pray that thou shouldst take them out of the world, but that thou shouldst keep them from [*tereo ek*] the evil one." It is clear that Jesus is asking for protection for his disciples *from* the evil one (cf. *1 Enoch* 100:5) *without* his disciples being physically removed from the world. Hence, any notion that the same expression in 3:10 depicts a physical removal (e.g., a pre-tribulational "rapture" of the church) is surely misguided. Rather, it again indicates protection *from*—in this case, from the final judgment. Such protection has been secured by Jesus' death, the significance of which has already been introduced (1:5) and will be developed throughout the book (e.g., 5:9-10; 7:14; 12:10-11). A similar thought is expressed in Dan 12:1, a passage reflected in Revelation at a number of points: "At that time shall arise Michael, the great prince who has charge of your people. And there shall be a time of trouble, such as never has been since there was a nation till that time; but at that time your people shall be delivered, every one whose name shall be found written in the book."

Jesus informs the church that he is "coming soon" (3:11; cf. 2:16; 22:7, 12, 20). Once again, the question arises as to what "coming" Jesus is talking about, although this time the "coming" is a promise, not a threat. He exhorts the Philadelphian Christians to "hold fast what you have [cf. 2:25], so that no one may seize your crown" (3:11). The "crown" is presumably the crown of life mentioned earlier by Jesus (2:10).

The conqueror is given two promises. First, Jesus will make him "a pillar in the temple of my God; never shall he go out of it" (3:12). Once again there seems to be an allusion to Isa 22, where God says that he will fasten Eliakim "like a peg in a sure place, and he will become a throne of honor to his father's house" (Isa 22:23). The "temple" of God will be mentioned throughout the book (7:15; 11:1, 2, 19 [twice]; 14:15, 17; 15:5, 6, 8 [twice]; 16:1, 17), though the promise to make someone a "pillar" can hardly be intended literally. The assurance of stability would be great comfort for residents of an earthquake-prone city, who often preferred being "outside" for safety reasons. Second, Jesus will write upon the conqueror three names: "of my God" (cf. Isa 18:7; 30:27; 56:6), "of the city of my God, the new Jerusalem that is coming down out of heaven from my God," and "my new name" (3:12; cf. 2:17). The emphasis on names would have a special meaning for residents of a city that had taken on, during the reigns of Claudius and Vespasian, the names "Neocaesarea" and "Flavia," respectively. On the name of God, see 11:18; 13:6; 14:1; 15:4; 16:9; 22:4. On the name of the new Jerusalem and the "new name" of Jesus, see on 2:17. The present tense used to describe the new Jerusalem as "coming down" is striking (cf. 21:2, 10). Is the point not that the new Jerusalem *will* come down—i.e., at the End—but that it is *already* descending from heaven? Certainly the reader is given something to ponder here.

"You are neither cold nor hot":
The letter to the church at Laodicea
Revelation 3:14-22

Situated in the valley of the Lycus river forty miles southeast of Philadelphia, Laodicea was closely associated with two other cities in the valley, Hierapolis to the north and Colossae to the east (cf. Col 4:13). Lying at the crossroads of two main trade routes, Laodicea was a major commercial center that flourished in the first century AD. The city became wealthy enough that following a catastrophic earthquake in AD 60, its inhabitants refused imperial assistance and rebuilt the city on their own. Given the Lycus Valley's excellent conditions for grazing sheep, the region became widely known for the production of black wool. Laodicea was also a banking center and the home of a famous medical school.

Jesus identifies himself as "the Amen, the faithful and true witness, the beginning of God's creation" (3:14). "Amen," from the Hebrew *ʾmn*, which means "truth, firmness, stability," is the standard word used by Jews to acknowledge agreement to the truth of what someone *else* says. For Jesus, the faithful (cf. 1:5) and true (cf. 3:7) witness, to be also "the Amen" is to acknowledge the truth of what he *himself* says. An allusion to Isa 65:16, which twice speaks of the God of truth (*ʾmn*), seems likely here. Once again, Old Testament language for God is applied to Jesus. This is the only instance in the New Testament of the use of "the Amen" as a title for someone. The final appellation is reminiscent of Jesus' identification of himself as "the first and the last" (1:17). Indeed, Jesus will later speak of himself as "the beginning and the end" (21:6) and ultimately as "the first and the last, the beginning and the end" (22:13). The "beginning" of creation presents Jesus in Wisdom terms: in Prov 8:22 wisdom is described as the "beginning" of God's works (cf. Sir 24:9).

Once again, as in the case of the church at Sardis, Jesus offers no praise to the church. Rather, he launches right into criticism: the church is lukewarm (3:16). The threefold repetition in 3:15-16 of the notion of the church being neither hot nor cold serves to underscore the seriousness of the church's condition. Hot water has its value (e.g., medicinal), as does cold (e.g., to quench thirst); hence, Jesus wishes they were one or the other (3:15). Lukewarm water, on the other hand, has no value; it is merely spit out of the mouth. The imagery of water temperature used here would have been clearly understood by the residents of Laodicea. Hierapolis, six miles to the north, was noted for its natural hot springs. The source of the drinking supply for Colossae, ten miles to the east, was the Lycus River, whose cold waters flowed in a narrow gorge past the city. "Lukewarm" water was known from two sources. First, Laodicea's water supply was brought in by aqueduct from the south; by the time it reached Laodicea, the water was lukewarm. Second, waters from the hot springs at Hierapolis, cooling as they crossed the plateau upon which the city was built, cascaded spectacularly to the bottom.

Furthermore, the church has an arrogant spirit: it claims to be rich, filled, and in need of nothing (3:17; cf. Hos 12:8; Zech 11:5). Jesus characterizes it rather as "wretched, pitiable, poor, blind, and naked" (3:17). Each element in the triple counsel Jesus gives to the church (3:18) stands as an ironic counterpart to something upon which the city of Laodicea boasted. First, in contrast to Laodicea's status as a banking center, the church needs to become truly rich by buying from Jesus (cf. Isa 55:1) gold refined by fire. Second, though the city prided itself on producing textiles made from black wool, the church needs from Jesus white garments to the cover the shame of its nakedness (cf. 3:4-5). Finally, in a region known for the manufacture of Phrygian eye powder for the healing of eyes (Pseudo-Aristotle, *On Marvelous Things Heard* 834b), the church at Laodicea needs from Jesus salve to anoint its eyes so that it might see.

Despite its bleak situation the church can take heart in knowing that Jesus reproves and chastens those whom he "loves" (3:19; cf. Prov 3:12). The remedy is direct: "be zealous [only here in the New Testament] and repent [cf. 2:5 (twice), 16, 21, 22; 3:3]" (3:19). Jesus continues with an offer (3:20), which must not be allegorized evangelistically—if one opens the "door" of one's heart, Jesus will "come in" to one's life. Jesus is speaking to those who are already Christians. The offer reflects first-century hospitality practices: when a visitor knocks on the door of your house, you invite him in and share meal fellowship with him. By their lukewarmness and arrogance, the Laodicean Christians have, in a sense, pushed Jesus outside. As they need gold, white clothes, and eye salve from Jesus, they also need fellowship with Jesus. What is significant about the offer is that it tempers the threat in 3:16. Though Jesus is about to spit them out of his mouth, he has not yet done so; they still have the opportunity to hear his knocking and invite him inside. This particular image serves as a contrast to the practice of corrupt Roman officials, who forced "hospitality" from Asian Christians. Jesus does not force himself upon anyone; he awaits the invitation to enter. Hence, fellowship with Jesus is genuine.

The promise to the conqueror that he will sit with Jesus on his throne, just as Jesus sat down with his Father upon his Father's throne (2:21; cf. *Ezekiel the Tragedian* 68-82), is truly breathtaking. Dan 7, which speaks of the transferal of the kingdom to the saints (Dan 7:22, 27; cf. 4Q521 frag. 2, 2.7), still distinguishes the throne of the Ancient of Days from other thrones (Dan 7:9). Similarly, Jesus speaks of his disciples sitting on twelve thrones and judging the twelve tribes of Israel (Matt 19:28; Luke 22:20). The promise is directly parallel to the promise of authority over the nations given to the conqueror in 2:26-27. The conqueror's role here is in some way analogous to that of Jesus and the Father. Further, Jesus notes that he took his place upon the throne of his Father as a result of his own "conquering." Both Jesus and the faithful Christian "conquer"; both Jesus and the faithful Christian take their seats upon the throne. How this applies to Jesus (5:5; 21:3) and to the conqueror (20:4) will be explained in due course. This is the third time a "throne" is mentioned in Revelation (cf. 1:4; 2:13); it will hardly be the last.

From the letters to the seven churches it is possible to construct a composite portrait of the conditions the churches in the province of Asia faced at the time of the writing of the book. Externally, the churches faced pressure from the culture—accommodation to pagan practices, opposition by local Jews, and the pervading specter of emperor worship. From within there were false apostles, false teachers, and a false prophet. In addition, various churches could be characterized as having lost their first love, being dead, and being lukewarm. Not every church faced all of these conditions, of course. But the composite portrait does indeed underscore the notion that, as a group, these churches were in need of a "prophecy."

John's Second "In the Spirit" Experience

"What must take place after this"

Revelation 4:1–11:19

John recounts his second "in the Spirit" experience in 4:1–11:19. Coming to be in the Spirit (4:2), he experiences a heavenly vision in which he is introduced to the one who will join God in dispensing judgment and to the group that will be able to stand before them (4:1–8:6), following which he learns of the precursors to that judgment and of mankind's response (8:7–11:19). Along the way John introduces his readers to a key motif (a sealed scroll that needs to be opened [5:1-4]); key themes (the coming judgment [6:12-14; 8:1–9:21], the failure to repent [9:20-21]); a key plea ("How long before thou wilt judge and avenge our blood on those who dwell upon the earth?" [6:10]); two key questions ("Who is worthy to open the scroll and break its seals?" [5:2], "For the great day of their wrath has come, and who can stand before it?" [6:17]); key characters (the one who is seated on the throne and his heavenly court [4:2-11], the Lamb [5:5-14], the 144,000/the Great Multitude [7:1-17], the two witnesses [11:3-12], the beast [11:7]); and a key result ("The kingdom of the world has become the kingdom of our Lord and of his Christ" [11:15]). Amid all of this, John himself receives something like a second commission (10:1–11:2).

The literary flow of this section is noteworthy. There is a sense in which chapters 4–5 form a complete unit introducing the Lamb (and what he has done), but not really: the seals still need to be opened, which leads into chapter 6. Similarly, chapters 6–7 seem to form a complete unit introducing the Great Multitude, but not really: the seventh seal still needs to be opened, which leads into chapter 8. In the same way, the section 8:6–11:14 more or less forms a complete unit introducing the failure to repent, but not really: the seventh trumpet still needs to be blown, which leads to 11:15-19. Finally, the abrupt introduction of the "beast" in 11:7 points beyond John's second "in the Spirit" experience altogether and prepares the reader for the next major section on the three signs in heaven (12:1–16:21).

"I saw in the right hand of him who was seated on the throne a scroll": Introducing the Lamb and the Great Multitude

Revelation 4:1–8:6

The primary—though not exclusive—focus in 4:1–8:6 is on action that takes place in heaven. Certainly heaven is the setting for the transferal of the sealed scroll from the one sitting upon the throne to the Lamb (4:1–5:14), as well as the vision of the Great Multitude (7:9-17) and the openings of the fifth (6:9-11) and seventh (8:1-6) seals. Even the openings of the first four and the sixth seals occur in heaven, though the effects are upon the earth. Similarly, as will be seen below, the sealing of the 144,000 (7:4-8), which to be sure has an earthly component to it (7:1-3), is ultimately tied to the identity of the Great Multitude. Through the asking and answering of two important questions, this section serves to introduce one major character and one major group into the story. Who is worthy to open the scroll and break its seals (5:2)? The Lamb (5:5-14). Who can stand before the great day of the wrath of him who is seated on the throne and of the Lamb (6:16-17)? The Great Multitude (7:1-17).

"Who is worthy to open the scroll and break its seals?": Meet the Lamb
Revelation 4:1–5:14

At the beginning of his second, third, and fourth "in the Spirit" experiences John is told that he will be "shown" something. Unlike the specificity of the third and fourth "in the Spirit" experiences, where an angel tells him he will be shown "the judgment of the great harlot" (17:2) and "the Bride, the wife of the Lamb" (21:9), the voice here tells him, rather ambiguously, that he will be shown "what must take place after this" (4:1). Alternate forms of this expression, which is taken from Dan 2:45 (Theod), are found in 1:1 and 1:19. Although the content of this expression awaits further definition through John's visionary experience that is to follow, the certainty of that content ("must") is indisputable.

The opening words of chapter 4 depict a new vision: "After these things I saw, and behold" (4:1; cf. Dan 7:6). Seeing an open door in heaven and hearing an invitation to ascend (4:1), John once again is "in the Spirit" (4:2). The first scene in this new experience consists of a description of the heavenly throne and the activity of those (the twenty-four elders and the four living creatures) surrounding it (4:2-11); the call for one to open the sealed scroll in the right hand of God, the failure of anyone to do so, and the ensuing interchange between John and one of the twenty-four elders (5:1-5); the coming of the Lamb to take the scroll (5:6-7); the initial response of the four living creatures and the twenty-four elders (5:8-10); the response of the multitudes of angels (5:11-12) and of all of creation (5:13); and the final response of the four living creatures and the twenty-four elders (5:14).

The primary purpose of this scene is to introduce the key character in the book: the Lamb. The scene does so by focusing on three elements: the asking of the question "Who is worthy to open the scroll and to break its seals?" (5:2), the coming of the Lamb to take the scroll in 5:7, and the response to that action that builds to a climax in 5:8-14.

As we shall see, much in this first scene serves to highlight the coming of the Lamb to take the scroll in 5:7 and the significance of this event. Certainly this is true with respect to the dramatic movement within the scene. In John's initial description of what he sees (4:2-11), there is no dramatic movement in the story. When he introduces the song of the four living creatures, for example, he observes that they "never cease to sing" (4:8). Thus, even though the reader encounters the song for the first time in 4:8, she assumes that it has been going on endlessly. The same is true for the song of the twenty-four elders (4:11), who fall down and worship the one who is seated on the throne (4:10) "whenever" the four living creatures sing their song (4:9), which, as the reader has already learned, never ceases. John (and hence the reader) finds himself in the middle of the ongoing heavenly worship of God by the heavenly court. But all of this changes when John mentions the scroll in 5:1. Now dramatic movement begins. The call goes out: "Who is worthy to open the scroll and break its seal?" (5:2). But just as abruptly as the movement begins, it ends. No such individual is found anywhere. Indeed, no one can be found worthy enough even to look into the scroll, much less open it (5:3). John's tears (5:4) seem justified: the scroll will remain unopened. But now the dramatic movement begins again. This time it will not be aborted, and it will take up the remainder of the scene. The worthy one is introduced in 5:5-6, and the heavenly court (and beyond) will respond with—and redirect—their praise in terms of that worthiness in 5:8-14 (5:9: "Worthy art thou . . ."; 5:12: "Worthy is the Lamb . . ."). What causes their response is the climax of the dramatic movement. A new element is introduced into the heretofore unchanging heavenly worship: the Lamb comes and takes the scroll (5:7).

Second, the number of heavenly singers increases throughout the section. After the four living creatures and the twenty-four elders sing simultaneously but independently (4:8 and 4:10-11), they come together to sing a "new song" (5:8-10). What prompts the change? The Lamb comes and takes the scroll (5:7). Equally striking is that only after the Lamb's action is the size of the chorus increased beyond the four living creatures and the twenty-four elders—to "myriads of myriads and thousands of thousands" of angels (5:11) and, finally, to "every creature in heaven and on earth and under the earth and in the sea, and all therein" (5:13).

Third, there is a change in the recipient(s) of the heavenly songs. The first two songs are directed toward the one seated on the throne (4:8-11). The third and fourth are directed toward the Lamb (5:9-12). Finally, the fifth and final song is directed to the one who sits upon the throne and to the Lamb (5:13). Again, what prompts the shift is the Lamb coming and taking the scroll (5:7).

Fourth, there is a certain chiastic structure to the scene. Early in the scene the reader is introduced first to the twenty-four elders (4:4) and then to the four living creatures (4:6). The end of the scene reverses the references—the four living creatures (5:14a) and the twenty-four elders (5:14b). In the middle of the scene the four living creatures and the twenty-four elders are brought together in 5:6 and 5:8. Thus we have this chiasm:

A. The twenty-four elders (4:4)
   B. The four living creatures (4:6)
      C. The four living creatures and the (twenty-four) elders (5:6)
      C'. The four living creatures and the twenty-four elders (5:8)
   B'. The four living creatures (5:14a)
A'. The twenty-four elders (5:14b)

Between C and C' is the center of the action: the Lamb comes and takes the scroll (5:7).

Fifth, the central action of the Lamb coming and taking the scroll is explained twice, setting up a simple chiastic structure:

A. before the action: "has conquered" (5:5)
   B. the action: the Lamb comes and takes the scroll (5:7)
A'. after the action: "thou wast slain and by thy blood didst ransom men for God" (5:9)

After again (cf. 1:10) characterizing himself as coming to be "in the Spirit" (4:2), John describes what he sees in heaven. That the first thing he mentions is a "throne" picks up immediately the promise concerning the "throne" at the end of the letter to the Laodiceans (3:21). John provides no description of the throne, but its centrality is assured by the characterization of everything else in the vision in terms of its spatial relationship with the throne: "on the throne" (4:2; 5:1, 7, 13 [RSV "upon"]), "round the throne"

(4:3, 4), "from the throne" (4:5), "before the throne" (4:5, 6), and "round the throne, on each side of the throne" (4:7). To describe what he sees John will draw especially upon the language and imagery of the four great "throne" visions of the Old Testament—Isa 6:1-11; Ezek 1:1-28; 10:1-22; and Dan 7:1-28.

John observes that there is "one seated on the throne" (4:2), a figure who will be mentioned repeatedly in the book (4:9, 10; 5:1, 7, 13; 6:16; 7:10, 15; 19:4; 20:11; 21:5; cf. 1:4; 4:3) and who will be explicitly identified as God in 7:10 (cf. 1 Kgs 22:19; Pss 11:4; 47:8; 103:19; Isa 6:1; 22:19; Ezek 1:26-27; Dan 7:9; Sir 1:8; cf. Ezek 10:1). As noted previously (see on 1:4), "sitting" upon a throne meant possessing royal and judicial authority. Although both functions will be exercised here, the emphasis, as the reader will see, will be on the latter. First Kings 7:7 speaks of Solomon's "Hall of the Throne where he was to pronounce judgment" (cf. 1 Kgs 2:19; Dan 7:9-10, 13-14). In Daniel 7, a passage to which John has already alluded (1:7, 13, 14) and upon which he will draw over and over throughout the book, Daniel has a magnificent vision of the Throne Hall of God that ends in the heavenly court sitting in judgment (Dan 7:26-27). Similarly, in the *Book of Watchers* "Enoch" has a vision of God sitting upon the throne specifically in his role as judge (*1 Enoch* 14:19-20; cf. *1 Enoch* 13:4-6; 15:1–16:3). John's vision is of the Throne Hall of God (cf. *1 Enoch* 14:8-25; 69:27-29), where judgment will be dispensed (cf. 20:11-15).

John gives no detailed description of God; he merely says he had the appearance of "jasper and carnelian" (4:3), two precious stones. In Ezekiel's opening vision God's throne is said to have the appearance of sapphire (Ezek 1:27; cf. Ezek 10:1). Jasper will be mentioned again in John's description of the new Jerusalem (21:11, 18, 19), as will carnelian (21:20).

Round the throne is, first, "a rainbow that looked like an emerald" (4:3). Ezekiel compares the brightness surrounding the one sitting upon the throne to a rainbow (Ezek 1:28). This is the only mention of an "emerald" in the book.

Also round the throne are twenty-four thrones, upon which sit twenty-four "elders" (4:4). Daniel also speaks of thrones in association with the throne belonging to the Ancient of Days (Dan 7:9). One should note that there is one group of twenty-four elders, not two groups of twelve—e.g., the twelve patriarchs and the twelve disciples. Twenty-four is the number of priestly families appointed to serve in the Temple (1 Chr 24:1-19), a practice that persisted in Judaism until the Temple was destroyed in AD 70 (cf. 4QMishmarot[4Q320-330]; 4QOtot[4Q329]; 1 Macc 2:1; Luke 1:8-9). The priestly character of the number brings to the reader's mind the identification of the church as priests in 1:6. That the twenty-four are "clothed in white robes" recalls the similar promise to the conqueror in 3:5 (cf. 3:4, 18). That they are wearing "crowns" calls to mind the identification of the church as a kingdom in 1:6, as well as the promise of a crown (though not specifically a golden one) to the conqueror (2:10; 3:11). "Golden" crowns will later be associated with marauding locusts (9:7) and with "one like a son of man" (14:14).

Given that John's description of the twenty-four elders draws so much upon his earlier characterizations of Christians, does it follow then that the twenty-four elders *are* Christians? The answer is No, and the clearest indication of this is 7:13-14, where one of the elders explains to John the identity of the Great Multitude as the Church, thereby indicating that the elder himself does not belong to that group. Rather, the twenty-four elders are angels. John is picking up the terminology of Isaiah 24:23, where God's heavenly court is characterized as "elders": "on Mount Zion and in Jerusalem and before his elders he will manifest his glory." Throughout the book John will draw an extensive picture of the heavenly Temple. The twenty-four elders represent the twenty-four angelic priestly families that serve in the heavenly Temple. That they wear crowns is not inconsistent with their role as priests. Indeed, God commanded Zechariah to take "silver and gold and make a crown, and set it on the head of Joshua, the son of Jehozadak, the high priest" (Zech 6:11). The similarities between the descriptions of the twenty-four elders and Christians in Revelation is due to the fact that Christians are portrayed precisely in priestly and royal terms. The twenty-four elders form a heavenly counterpart, as it were, to the church on earth.

Not to be missed is that John has combined two pictures here: that of a Throne Hall and that of a Temple. Such a composite picture is also found in Isa 6, which speaks both of God's throne (Isa 6:1) and the "altar" (Isa 6:6), and in Ezek 10 (cf. *Testament of Levi* 5:1), which mentions a throne (Ezek 10:1) and "burning coals" (Ezek 10:2) and "fire" (Ezek 10:6-7), both of which presumably come from an altar (cf. 2 Macc 1:19-22). In 5:8 John will speak of the twenty-four elders holding golden bowls full of incense, which brings to mind the incense altar in the Temple (Exod 30:6; see on 6:9).

From the throne come "flashes of lightning, and voices and peals of thunder" (4:5). Thunder and lightning were associated with the presence of God at Mount Sinai (Exod 19:16). These three terms, along with "earthquake" (cf. Exod 19:18), will recur at key manifestations of God's presence in the book (8:5; 11:19; 16:18).

Before the throne John sees first of all seven lamps burning (4:5). John identifies these as the seven spirits of God, which he has already mentioned as being before the throne (see on 1:4; cf. 3:1). Second, John sees "a sea of glass, like crystal" (4:6). Once again John draws upon Old Testament imagery. In Exod 24:9-10 Moses and his entourage see God: "and there was under his feet as it were a pavement of sapphire stone, like the very heaven for clearness." Similarly, Ezekiel speaks of "the likeness of a firmament, shining like crystal" under God's throne (Ezek 1:22, 26). The sea of glass will be mentioned again (twice) in 15:2. An analogy with crystal will also be used for the new Jerusalem (22:11) and the river of the water of life (22:1).

Around the throne and on each side (lit., "in the midst") of it are four living creatures (4:6). In appearance they have several features in common: each is full of eyes in front and in back (4:7, 8), each has a face (though their faces differ from one another: 4:7), and each has six wings (4:8). The description of the four living creatures is based primarily upon the four living creatures in Ezek 1:5-11, which are identified in Ezek 10:3-14 as cherubim. The four faces are the same, but in Revelation each creature has a different face, while in Ezekiel each has all four faces, one on each side of the head (Ezek 1:10; 10:14). Also, the order of the faces is different. In Revelation the order is lion, ox, man, eagle; in Ezekiel it is man, lion, ox, eagle (Ezek 1:10) and cherub, man, lion, eagle (Ezek 10:14). In addition, the creatures in Ezekiel have four, not six, wings (Ezek 1:6, 11). Ezekiel says nothing about the creatures being full of eyes, though he does speak of a wheel associated with each of them (Ezek 1:15-21; 10:9-13) and observes that the wheels were full of eyes all around (Ezek 1:18; 10:12). Ezekiel also describes other characteristics of the living creatures John omits (e.g., their feet). In Isa 6 Isaiah sees the Lord sitting upon a throne attended by the seraphim who have six wings (Isa 6:2). No mention is made, however, of the seraphim's faces, of their being full of eyes, or of their being four in number. Neither the specific details nor the differences between Revelation and Ezekiel/Isaiah should be pressed. John has combined the visions of the two prophets into a single vision in his own unique way so as to depict the heavenly court and to align himself with those two great prophets: what they saw, he saw.

John continues by recording the song of praise the four living creatures do not cease to sing day or night (4:8). Like the song of the seraphim in Isa 6, this one begins with a triple appellation of the Lord as "holy" (4:8; Isa 6:3). Isaiah's "the LORD of hosts" has now become "the Lord God Almighty" (cf. 11:17; 15:3; 16:7; 19:6; 21:22), returning to the characterization of God in 1:8. "Who was and is and is to come" picks up 1:4 and 1:8, though in those passages the first two elements are reversed. The four living creatures thus praise God for his holiness, his power, and his timelessness. John goes on to characterize the song as one of "glory and honor and thanks" (4:9).

"Glory" and "honor" will be found together again in 4:11; 5:12, 13; 7:12 (along with "thanks" [RSV "thanksgiving]); 21:26 (cf. Pss 29:1; 96:7; 1 Chr 29:11).

John observes that "whenever" the four living creatures sing their song, the twenty-four elders sing one of their own (4:9-10). In each case, they sing to "him who is seated on the throne" and "who lives for ever and ever" (4:9, 10; cf. Dan 4:34; 6:26; 12:7). Specifically, John says, the elders "fall down before" and "worship" God (4:10). To "fall down and worship" is typically understood as a single act in Jewish literature (e.g., Dan 3:5, 6, 10, 11, 15; *Joseph and Aseneth* 28:9; Matt 2:11; Acts 10:25; 1 Cor 14:25); the terms will be so paired in 5:14; 7:11; 11:16; 19:10; 22:8. What is rare here is that the heavenly court, rather than humans, does so (cf. Ps 29:1-2; *Apocalypse of Moses* 27:5). Furthermore, they "cast their crowns before the throne" (4:10). Defeated kings were sometimes stripped of their crowns by their conquerors in a symbolic act of newly imposed subordination (cf. 2 Sam 12:30). By contrast, this act of subordination by the twenty-four elders is voluntary. The song of the elders is a bit more elaborate than that of the four living creatures. This song and the next two begin, "Worthy art/is . . ." (4:11; 5:9, 12). Just who is or is not worthy will provide the dynamic for the movement of the scene through all three songs (cf. 5:2, 4). Here the one designated as worthy is "our Lord and God." He is viewed as worthy "to receive glory and honor and power," thus reaffirming the song of the four living creatures. But the elders go further by expressing *why* God is worthy: he is the creator of "all things" by his "will" (cf. Wis 1:14; Sir 18:1, 3; 3 Macc 2:3; Acts 4:24). This is the only use of "will" in the book.

Movement now enters the story. John observes ("And I saw . . .") "in the right hand of the one sitting upon the throne [cf. 4:2, 3, 9, 10] a scroll written within and on the back, sealed with seven seals" (5:1). Since scrolls are ordinarily written on only one side, John seems to be alluding to Ezek 2:9-10, where Ezekiel sees a hand holding a scroll that has writing on both sides. Unlike the scroll in John's vision, the one Ezekiel sees is not sealed. When it is spread out for him he observes that it contains "words of lamentation and mourning and woe" (Ezek 2:10). Is this the content of the scroll in Revelation? The reader will have to read on to find out. But given the Throne Hall setting of John's vision, there is little doubt that the scroll has something to do with judgment. "Sealing" important documents with wax, typically with a signet ring to verify the sender or owner, was a common practice in the ancient world, though a single seal was all that would be necessary to prevent unauthorized people from reading it. That this scroll is sealed with seven seals (cf. 4QProtoEsther[a][4Q550] 4-5) suggests the completeness of the sealing. The "right hand" of God is an expression used frequently in the Old Testament to refer to God's power (e.g., Exod 15:6; Ps 18:35; Isa 41:10). A scroll sealed with seven seals in the right hand of God . . . no one will be able to open this scroll without God's permission!

There is more movement. John sees ("And I saw . . .") "a strong angel proclaiming with a loud voice, 'Who is worthy to open the scroll and to break its seals?'" (5:2). A "strong angel" will appear again in 10:1 and 18:21 (cf. Dan 4:13, 14, 23). The reader remembers that God has just been designated as "worthy" (4:11); surely God is able to open his own scroll! Apparently another "worthy" individual must be found. But none are, whether they be "in heaven or on earth or under the earth" (5:3). (A similar threefold cosmology of sky or heaven [both the Hebrew *shamayim* and the Greek *ouranos* have a dual meaning] and earth and under the earth is found in Phil 2:10 [cf. 9:1; Exod 20:4; Deut 5:8; Ignatius, *Trallians* 9:1].) No one can even look into the scroll (5:3). The reader identifies with John's reaction: weeping (5:4). The repetition in 5:4 of the phrase "no one was found worthy to open the scroll or to look into it" underscores the seriousness of the situation: God has a scroll, but no one has access to it (cf. Isa 29:11-12, which speaks of a sealed scroll that cannot be read).

But the situation is not hopeless. One of the elders tells John not to weep. There is one who "can open the scroll and its seven seals" (5:5). That one is identified as "the Lion of the tribe of Judah, the Root of David" (5:5). The two expressions derive from two Old Testament passages that were viewed as Messianic by Jews. The first is taken from Judah's blessings of his twelve sons in Gen 49. He speaks of Judah as "a lion's whelp" (Gen 49:9) and goes on to promise kingship to Judah's descendants (Gen 49:10), a promise that was picked up in later Jewish Messianic expectation (e.g., 4Q252 5.1-4; *Jubilees* 31:18-20; *Testament of Simeon* 7:1; *Testament of Judah* 24:1-6; cf. *Testament of Naphtali* 8:2-3; *Testament of Joseph* 19:11). *Fourth Ezra* 12:31-32 depicts the Messiah as a lion. John will speak no further in Revelation of the Lion of the tribe of Judah, but the image of a lion fits well what the figure has accomplished (he "has conquered") and serves as a striking contrast with the continued development of Jesus as a lamb in what follows (5:6). The second expression is taken from Isa 11, which speaks of a shoot from the stump of Jesse (Isa 11:1, 10; cf. Isa 4:2; 16:5), who was the father of David (1 Sam 16:1-13). The concept of the righteous "Branch" of David, which comes from this passage, is picked up by Jeremiah (Jer 23:5; 33:15; cf. Zech 3:8; 6:12; 4Q485 frag. 5.3-4; 4Q174 1.10-13; 4Q161 2.18). For the place of David in Jewish Messianic expectation, see on 1:2. Jesus, having already been characterized in Davidic terms in 1:5a and having already mentioned that he holds the key of David (3:7), will identify himself as "the root and offspring of David" in 22:16. The angel, then, uses expressions from two classical Jewish messianic texts to identify the one who will open the scroll.

The angel does not say that the Lion is "worthy"; rather, he says he has "conquered" (5:5). Apparently conquering makes him worthy, as John will see (5:9). The word reminds the reader not only of the promises to the conqueror in each of the letters to the seven churches, but also of Jesus' comment that he himself "conquered" (3:21). Surely an elaboration of when and how Jesus "conquered" is about to take place here.

John looks again ("And I saw . . .") and sees that something has been added to the scene he originally described. "In the midst of [cf. 4:6; RSV "Between"] the throne and of the four living creatures and in the midst of [RSV "among"] the elders" stands a . . . Lamb (5:6). The reader is expecting a Lion. Why is a Lamb present? Where is the Lion?

The Greek word John uses here (*arnion*) can mean a male sheep of any age, from immature ("lamb") to mature ("ram"). One might argue, given the reference to the "horns" in this verse, that "ram" is the best translation. This would certainly fit the notion of "conquering" (5:5) better. But given John's emphasis in the verses that follow on the *arnion* as having been slain, it seems clear that he has in mind the Old Testament sacrificial system, where both rams and lambs were slaughtered (e.g., Isa 1:11). Since there is a special emphasis on killing lambs at, e.g., Passover (Exod 12:5; cf. Isa 53:7), we shall, along with the RSV, use "Lamb." But the age issue should not be pressed.

The Lamb has several unusual characteristics. First, he has seven horns (5:6). Horns are the primary weapon possessed by certain animals, such as bulls and oxen (cf. Ps 22:21). The idea of such an animal "goring" another led to the metaphorical use of "horn" as representing power, especially in defeating one's enemies (e.g., Deut 33:17; 1 Sam 2:10; 2 Sam 22:3; 1 Kgs 22:11; Dan 7:8; Mic 4:13; Zech 1:18-21; Sir 47:5-11; *1 Enoch* 90:6-12, 37; Luke 1:69). The reference to the Lamb's horns is therefore appropriate for one who has "conquered." One would expect a male sheep—a ram—to have *two* horns (cf. 13:11). That the Lamb has seven signifies the totality of power he possesses. Other characters in the book who will be said to have horns will be the dragon (12:3: ten horns), the first beast (13:1: ten horns), and the second beast (13:11: two horns).

The Lamb also has seven eyes (5:6). The reference to seven eyes is based upon Zech 4, a passage John has used previously in connection with the seven spirits (1:4). In Zech 4:10 the seven lamps with seven tips that the prophet has seen in Zech 4:2 are interpreted as "the eyes of the LORD that range over the whole earth." Here they are further identified with "the seven spirits of God sent out into all the earth" (5:6), the latter phrase being a clear allusion to Zech 4:10 (cf. 2 Chr 16:9). John has just identified the seven spirits with seven lamps burning before the throne (4:5). Now he identifies them as the seven eyes of the Lamb. Such an identification is consistent with the suggestion that the seven spirits represent the Holy Spirit. After all, while Jesus addressed each of the seven churches in chapters 2 and 3, the Spirit was said, in the refrain at the end of each letter ("He who has an ear . . ."), to speak to the churches.

Finally, the Lamb stands "as though it had been slain" (5:6). The image is drawn from the Old Testament (e.g., Isa 53:7; Jer 11:19). A more unexpected picture would be difficult to find. John has heard about a conquering Lion, but all he sees is a slain Lamb. Yet it is precisely this slain Lamb who will take the scroll and open it (5:7-8; 6:1-17; 8:1-2). The remarkable fact is that the slain Lamb is one and the same as the conquering Lion. The implications of this fact are enormous. First, the reader is given an important key for understanding the book: what John *hears* and what John *sees* may appear to be different, but that is not necessarily the case. In 1:10 John *hears* a voice; in 1:13 he *sees* one like a son of man. In 5:5 John *hears* conquering Lion; in 5:6 he *sees* slain Lamb. Second, the principle of *non-literal* revelation is confirmed once and for all: this is *not* a literal lion. Third, the astonishing juxtaposition of a conquering Lion with a slain Lamb can only be intended to indicate how Jesus, in fact, conquered: by being slain (cf. 1:6, 7). And the fact that the slain lamb is "standing"—i.e., alive—reminds the reader of Jesus' self-identification as the one who died but is now alive (1:18). "Slain" will be used to describe the Lamb two more times in this section (5:9, 12) and once later on (13:8).

The slain Lamb who is alive again now acts: he comes and receives (RSV "took") the scroll from the right hand of the one seated upon the throne (5:7). The perfect tense of the verb for "receive" reminds the reader of Jesus' observation that he "has received" power from his Father (2:28). The transfer of the scroll from the one sitting upon the throne to the Lamb results in a new action in heaven: the four living creatures and the twenty-four elders fall down before the Lamb (5:8). Previously the twenty-four elders had fallen down before and worshiped the one sitting upon the throne (4:10). Here the four living creatures join them in falling down before—but not yet worshiping—the Lamb. The Lamb is clearly someone special, but how special? The twenty-four elders are given two further characteristics here: they each hold a harp and golden bowls full of incense (5:8). In the Old Testament the Temple musicians used harps (1 Chr 25:1, 6; cf. Ps 33:2), and the priests offered incense (e.g., 1 Chr 6:49). The twenty-four elders have thus added musical duties to their priestly ones. Once again John identifies one aspect of the imagery: the golden bowls full of incense are the prayers of the saints (5:8). Ps 141:2 compares prayer to incense that goes up before God. Tob 12:15 depicts the angel Raphael as the one who presents the prayers of the saints before God (cf. Tob 12:12). John makes the explicit identification between those prayers and the incense. To what prayers of the saints is John referring? He does not say yet. Whereas the four living creatures and the twenty-four elders were previously singing separate songs of praise, they now join together in a "new song" (5:9; cf. Pss 33:3; 40:3; 96:1; 98:1; 143:9; 144:9; 149:1; Isa 42:1; Jdt 16:13). John will mention a "new song" again in 14:3.

The new song begins "Worthy art thou . . ." (5:9). In 5:2 the angel had asked, "Who is worthy . . .?" and in 5:4 John had lamented that "no one was found worthy." At last, a "worthy" one has appeared: the Lion who "conquered" (5:5) has been deemed "worthy." The first line of the song acknowledges what has already taken place: in light of the event recorded in 5:7, the Lamb is acknowledged to be worthy "to take the scroll" (5:9). The second line draws the obvious inference. The angel had not asked who is worthy to *take* the scroll but who is worthy to *open* it and break its seals (5:3). Since the Lamb has been judged worthy to take the scroll from God's hand, then it follows that he must also be worthy to open its seals (5:9).

That the Lamb is worthy to take the scroll is evident from God's giving it to him. But on what *basis* is the Lamb "worthy"? The song continues, using three verbs to indicate what the Lamb has accomplished to demonstrate (5:9: "for") his worthiness. First, he was "slain" (5:9; cf. 5:6). Second, he "didst ransom [i.e., purchase] men for God" (5:9; cf. 14:3, 4; Hos 3:1-2; 1 Cor 6:20; 7:23; 2 Pet 2:1). Those ransomed are "from every tribe and tongue and people and nation" (5:9; cf. Dan 3:4; 7:14). Fine distinctions among these four groups should not be pressed; they simply but clearly indicate the universal nature (note "every") of the Lamb's purchase—no group is omitted. These four groups will be brought together again (though always in a different order) in 7:9; 11:9; 13:7; and 14:6; the last three in 10:11 (along with "kings") and in 17:15 (along with "multitudes"). The fact that the Lamb purchased these people for God by his "blood" (5:9) shows that this second activity is really a subpoint under the first. Third, the Lamb "made" them a kingdom and priests to God (5:10). The language here is almost identical with that in 1:6. In addition, in both cases the statement is in close proximity to a reference to Jesus' death (1:5; 5:9). Clearly, the Lamb "making" people into a kingdom and priests is in some sense a result of his death. Somewhat surprisingly the heavenly choir adds one more element to the song: a comment about the role of those who have been made a kingdom and priests. The choir promises that "they shall reign on earth" (5:10; reading the future with Codex Sinaiticus and other early witnesses; cf. 20:6; 22:5). This additional comment serves to underscore for the reader the practical implications of this otherwise theological statement concerning the death of the Lamb.

Does the connection between the Lamb's right to take the scroll and his death give a clue as to the content of the scroll? Since the Lamb is deemed worthy to take the scroll and open its seals *because* he purchased people for God, does it not follow that the scroll must have something to do with those very people? What scroll used in judgment would be associated with those who will not be harmed by it? Certainly not a scroll containing their sins (cf. 20:12). But what about a scroll containing their names—i.e. the book of life, which has already been mentioned in 3:5? It will certainly be used in the climactic judgment scene in 20:11-15. The reader must not be led astray by English translations here—i.e., "scroll" vs. "book." The Greek word used throughout chapter 5 is *biblion* (5:1, 2, 3, 4, 5, 8, 9), which is the word John will use most frequently in the phrase "the book of life" (13:8; 17:8; 20:12; cf. *biblos* in 3:5; 20:15 [= *biblios* in 20:12]). It follows, then, that the scroll the Lamb receives from the one seated on the throne is none other than the book of life. Indeed, it is precisely by virtue of his having purchased them through his death that their names are *in* the book of life!

As impressive as the new song is, the scene is not yet over. Something new is added as John sees and hears ("Then I looked, and I heard") the voice of "many angels" around the throne and the living creatures and the elders (5:11). How many angels? Drawing upon the language of Dan 7:10, John says "their number was myriads of myriads and thousands of thousands" (5:11; cf. *1 Enoch* 14:22; 40:1; 60:1; 71:8, 13). A myriad equals ten thousand. The number of participants in the heavenly choir has increased indeed! This is the first time in the book that John is interested in the "number" of something; it will not be the last (7:4; 9:16; 13:17-18; 15:2; 20:8). This new choir sings with "a loud voice" (5:12). Once again the song begins with "Worthy . . ." (5:11; cf. 5:9), but this time it is in the third person ("Worthy is the Lamb"), not the second ("Worthy art thou"). Unlike the "new song," therefore, this song is not directed toward the Lamb himself. Once again the focus is on the death of the Lamb ("who was slain"; cf. 5:6, 9), so much so that the death of the Lamb becomes its distinguishing attribute: it is no longer "Worthy art thou . . . *for* thou wast slain" (5:9), but "Worthy is the Lamb *who* was slain" (5:11). In addition, the Lamb is no longer viewed simply as worthy "to take the scroll" (5:9), but now as worthy "to receive power and wealth and wisdom and might and honor and glory and blessing" (5:12). The slain Lamb is worthy of heavenly praise.

But the scene is still not over. Now John hears "every creature" (5:13). John specifies them as those "in heaven and on earth and under the earth and in the sea and all therein" (5:13). The first three expressions were used in 5:3 as John recounted the failure of anyone to open the scroll or even to look inside. The last is found only here in the book (cf. Exod 20:11; Neh 9:6; Ps 146:6; Jer 51:48). The point is that the choir John hears sing this last song in this scene is made up of all of creation—no one is omitted. Indeed, they comprise all who were unable to open the scroll themselves. To put it another way, the size of the chorus singing praise moves from four (4:8) to twenty-four (4:11) to twenty-eight (5:8-10: four + twenty-four) to myriads of angels (5:11) to all of creation!

The song is directed to "him who sits upon the throne" (5:13). This is certainly reasonable in that the one who sits upon the throne created those who sing (4:11). But the song is also directed to "the Lamb" (5:13). This juxtaposition of the one who sits upon the throne and the Lamb is astonishing. There is to be no distinction between them as recipients of praise. They are to be praised together, equally. To the one who sits upon the throne *and* to the Lamb are given "blessing and honor and glory and might for ever and ever" (5:13). The first three of these terms were used in the previous song about the Lamb. The third and fourth were used in John's own doxology directed toward Jesus in 1:6.

How will those in heaven respond to the audacity of every creature in praising God and Jesus on equal terms? The heavenly response to the song is recorded briefly, yet powerfully. The four living creatures say "Amen" (5:14), indicating their complete agreement with the song. As for the twenty-four elders, John says that "they fell down and worshiped" (5:14). That they now worship both the one sitting upon the throne *and* the Lamb completes their response to the Lamb, before whom they had previously fallen down (5:8). The response of the four living creatures and the twenty-four elders leaves the reader with no doubt—the Lamb is worthy to be worshiped as God himself. There is no distinction between the two.

Reminiscent of other New Testament passages that identify Jesus as God (e.g., John 1:1-4; Phil 2:5-11; Col 1:15-20), this unit presents a breathtakingly exalted picture of Jesus. As the Lamb who was slain, he now holds the sealed scroll of God and receives equal worship with him. Such a picture serves as a stark response to all who would promote the worship of the Roman emperor. He cannot even look inside the scroll, much less take and open it; Jesus is in control, not the emperor. The reader should note carefully that it is this scene, not the opening of the seven seals or the blowing of the seven trumpets or the pouring out of the seven bowls or 666 or Armageddon, that is the first to follow the letters to the seven churches. To put it differently, what the reader learns here about Jesus will provide the lens through which the rest of the book must be read.

"Who can stand before the great day of their wrath?": Meet the Great Multitude
Revelation 6:1–7:17

Since 5:1 the tension has been building concerning the scroll belonging to the one seated on the throne. In 5:2 the angel asks, "Who is worthy to open the scroll and break its seals?" The absence of anyone worthy "to open the scroll or to look into it" causes John to despair (5:3-4). But then John is told of a Lion who "has conquered, so that he can open the scroll and its seven seals" (5:5). The Lamb appears (5:6), receives the scroll from the one sitting upon the throne (5:7), and is hailed by the four living creatures and the twenty-four elders as "worthy . . . to take the scroll and to open its seals" (5:9). The intervening songs of praise, though enormously significant for presenting a distinctive portrait of Jesus, nonetheless interrupt the storyline concerning the opening of the scroll, thus building suspense. Now, with the Lamb appropriately exalted, the sealed scroll returns to the center of John's vision.

There are two questions asked during the opening of the first six seals. The first is asked by "those who had been slain . . ." at the fifth seal: "How long before thou wilt judge and avenge our blood . . .?" (6:10). It is answered in two ways. Initially, the plaintiffs are told "to rest a little longer, until the number of their fellow servants and their brethren should be complete, who were to be killed as they themselves had been" (6:11). But then with the opening of the very next (the sixth) seal, as the heavens and the earth are shaken to their core, those who are terrified lament that "the great day of . . . wrath has come" (6:17). "How long" it has taken to get from the fifth seal to the sixth the reader is not told. She can only surmise that enough time has elapsed for the number of slain fellow servants and brethren now to be complete. The time for judgment and vengeance is here . . . almost. John does not yet describe the actual judgment itself. The reader—not to mention "those who had been slain"—must wait "a little longer."

The second question is asked by the terrified ones at the close of the sixth seal: at the great day of wrath "who can stand?" (6:17). Those haunting final words—"who can stand?" ("before it" in the RSV is an explanatory addition)—continue to echo in the reader's mind as the scene now shifts. But the reader does not have to wait long for an answer: in 7:9 John sees a Great Multitude "standing before the throne and before the Lamb." Who can stand? The Great Multitude can stand. And given the first question and its first answer, it follows that the Great Multitude must comprise all of the fellow servants and brethren who were to be killed (6:11).

The Lamb is about to open the seals, one at a time. Seven times there will be a recurring refrain: "When he [seal #1: "the Lamb"] opened the [first, second, and so forth] seal . . . ." The first four seals follow a pattern (6:1-8). The opening of the seal is announced; one of the four living creatures (numbered in accordance with the number of the seal) says, "Come!"; and John sees a horse of a particular color and its rider. Then the fifth (6:9-11) and sixth (6:12-17) seals are opened. But instead of coming to the seventh seal next, John has two more visions instead (7:1-8, 9-17). Only after those visions is the seventh seal opened (8:1).

The imagery of the four horses is drawn from Zechariah. In Zech 1:8-11 the prophet has a vision of a man riding a red horse; behind him are red, brown, and white horses. Zechariah learns that these have been sent by the Lord to go throughout the earth. In Zech 6:2-9 the prophet sees four chariots drawn by red, black, white, and dappled horses, respectively. They are characterized as "going forth to the four winds of heaven, after presenting themselves before the LORD of all the earth" (Zech 6:5). They travel throughout the earth in the direction of the four points of compass. In Revelation the colors are in a different order (white, red, black, and pale), and all of the horses have riders, as in Zech 1:8-11. There is no mention of them going in different directions.

The first horse is white; its rider has a bow and "was given" a crown (6:2). The expression "was given [*edothe*] to him" reflects the common Jewish idiom called the divine passive—that is, God is understood to be the unexpressed subject of the verb. This is the first of many such divine passives in the book that have to do with something being "given" (6:4, 4, 8, 11; 7:2; 8:2, 3; 9:1, 3, 5; 11:1, 2; 12:14; 13:5, 5, 7, 7, 14, 15; 16:8; 19:8; cf. 20:4). God is ultimately in control. The rider goes out "conquering and to conquer" (6:2).

The second horse is bright red; its rider "was permitted [*edothe*] to take peace from the earth, so that men should slay one another and was given [*edothe*] a great sword" (6:4). Two of the details in the description of the rider will be picked up again in the section on the dragon and the beast: the "bright red" color of the dragon (12:3) and death by the "sword" (13:10; cf.

13:14). John will speak more about some who have been "slain" at the sixth seal (6:9; cf. 18:24).

The third horse is black; his rider holds a balance scale in his hand (6:5). John's narration is broken at this point as he hears a voice—undoubtedly the Lamb's—"in the midst of the four living creatures" (6:6). The voice sets prices on two commodities and gives a command regarding two more. A quart of wheat was considered a day's ration for a person, and three quarts of barley for a horse; a quart of wheat and three quarts of barley thus constituted a day's ration for a cavalryman. In 2 Kgs 7:1 the cost of a quart of wheat is figured at a shekel (= one eighth of a denarius) and that of a quart of barley at half a shekel. In the New Testament period a denarius was considered to be a day's wage for an average worker (Matt 20:1-16; cf. Tob 5:14). Even taking into account natural inflation from the ninth century BC to the first century AD, the prices here—"a quart of wheat for a denarius, and three quarts of barley for a denarius"—are enormously high. An average worker would have to use his entire wage just to feed himself, never mind his family. Such staggering prices would probably be brought on by drought or famine. If so, then the command "Do not harm oil and wine," which is directed toward the rider, would represent a lessening of the impact of whatever caused the famine. The effect of serious drought on olive trees and vineyards would be long-lasting. The Lamb is ultimately in control.

The fourth horse is pale; his rider's name is Death, and Hades follows him (6:8). This is the second pairing of Death and Hades in the book: the reader has already learned that Jesus holds the keys of Death and Hades (cf. 1:18; cf. 20:13, 14). The personification of Death and Hades is not unusual in Jewish and early Christian literature (e.g., Hos 13:14; 1 Cor 15:55; and, in a particularly vivid description, *Testament of Abraham* 17:16-20). There is "given" to them power over a fourth of the earth to kill (6:8). This is the first use of a fraction in the book. One fourth is a significant, but limited, amount. Later the reader will encounter a larger fraction: one third (8:7-12). The use of a fraction to describe the impact of judgment may well be derived from Ezek 5:12 (see on 8:7). The combination of sword, famine, pestilence, and wild beasts is derived from Ezek 14:12-21 (cf. Ezek 5:12, 17; 33:27; Jer 14:12; 15:3; 21:7).

What is the reader to make of the first four seals? Are they to be understood as chronological events in human history? They are certainly not portrayed as such; they are simply four seals on a scroll. Any "chronology" that exists has to do with when they are opened, not when they "happen." In addition, as we will see, the fifth seal does not at all fit the category of a historical event and makes no sense in terms of "chronology." Any suggestion, then, that the seven seals represent seven successive events in human history simply has no basis in the text. Are they four distinct "plagues"? Again, they are not portrayed as such. The second and fourth seals overlap to the extent that they both involve death, and the third and fourth seals both involve famine. The first seal is not necessarily "bad" at all, as we shall see. To suggest that it must be "bad" because the other three are bad amounts to circular reasoning and imposes an interpretation onto the text rather than allowing it to speak for itself.

What, then, does the first seal represent? The identity of the rider on the white horse has engendered considerable controversy among interpreters. One common suggestion is that the rider would have conjured up in the minds of John's readers the Parthians, the archenemies of the Romans and the only mounted archers in the first century. Understood in this way, the seal is "bad"—i.e., it represents invasion by a hostile power.

But one can make a rather different case from a purely literary perspective. What should strike any sensitive reader of the book are the positive traits associated with this figure. First, the horse is white. To this point in the book, "white" has always had positive associations—with Jesus (1:14; 3:18), with the conqueror (2:17; 3:4-5), or with the twenty-four elders (4:4). Indeed, white will continue to have positive connotations at every point throughout the rest of the book: those slain on account of the word of God and the witness of Jesus will be given white robes (6:11); the Great Multitude will be dressed in white robes (7:9, 13); one like a son of man will be seated upon a white cloud (14:14); Jesus will come riding upon a white horse (19:11) along with the armies of heaven, who will also be riding white horses and will be dressed in pure white linen (19:14); and God will preside as judge while sitting upon a great white throne (20:11). Second, that someone is wearing a crown is familiar to the reader. So far, the crown of life has been promised to the conqueror (2:10; cf. 3:11), and the twenty-four elders are wearing gold crowns (4:4, 10). The woman clothed with the sun will be said to have a crown of stars upon her head (12:1), and one like a son of man, who is seated upon a white cloud, will wear a gold crown (14:14). Unlike the theme of whiteness, there will be, however, one negative use of "crown": the locusts from the abyss will have crowns "like gold" upon their heads (9:7). Third, the rider's task—"conquering and to conquer"—has always had positive connotations up until now in the book. Each of the letters to the seven churches ends with a promise to "the conqueror," and Jesus is also said to have conquered (3:21; 5:5). As the book progresses, some will be said to have conquered their accuser (12:11) or the beast, its image, and the number of its name (15:2); the Lamb will conquer ten kings

(17:14); and once again a promise will be given to "the conqueror" (21:7). But as in the case of "crown," "conquer" can take on negative connotations as well. The beast will conquer the two witnesses (11:7) and the saints (13:7).

What is one to make of the fact that symbols containing positive associations—exclusively with "white," primarily with "crown" and "conquer"—dominate the description of the rider on the white horse? Is it not reasonable, even probable, that John intends the reader's first impressions about this figure to be positive?

The obvious answer is that the rider is Jesus. After all, Jesus has already been identified in terms of his having "conquered" (5:5). Indeed, Jesus will come riding on a white horse in 19:11, a passage that will be introduced by the same nine Greek words: *kai idou hippos leukos kai ho kathemenos ep' auton* (lit., "and behold a white horse and one sitting upon it"). Such extensive verbal agreement between the two passages can hardly be accidental; surely John intends at 19:11 for the reader to remember 6:2. In addition, in 14:14 "one like a son of man" (Jesus) will be wearing a golden crown.

But what about the bow? God using his bow in his role as judge is a common Old Testament symbol. Ps 7:11-13, for example, reads as follows (cf. Isa 41:2-4; Lam 2:4; 3:12-23; Hab 3:8-15; Zech 9:13-14; 10:4):

11 God is a righteous judge,
    a God who expresses his wrath every day.
12 If he does not relent,
    he will sharpen his sword;
    he will bend and string his bow.
13 He has prepared his deadly weapons;
    he makes ready his flaming arrows.

Jesus has already been presented in his role as ransomer (5:9-10); now he rides out as judge, a notion that has already been introduced (1:16; 2:4, 16, 22-23, 27; 3:3, 16) and that anticipates not only 19:11-21, but also the sixth seal itself, which will speak of "the wrath of the Lamb" (6:16).

The opening of the first seal sets in motion the judgment: Jesus rides out as judge, people kill one another, prices are exorbitantly high, people (one fourth of the earth) die by various means. But the reference to Death and Hades reminds the reader that Jesus has the keys to Death and Hades (1:18). In whatever manner his followers might die, they have the assurance that Jesus has conquered Death. The judgment, then, will be upon all who have *not* been ransomed by Jesus (cf. 5:9): Jesus the judge is also Jesus the Lamb who was slain. For the attentive reader, then, the section containing the first four seals begins and ends with Jesus.

With the opening of the fifth seal comes the breaking of the pattern repeated in the first four. Gone are the four living creatures saying, "Come!"; gone are the different colored horses and their riders; gone is the focus upon the earth. Rather, the scene is once again heaven. For the first time in the book John speaks explicitly of an "altar," though one was implied in 5:8. The mention of an altar confirms that John understands his vision as one of a heavenly Throne Hall/Temple (see on 4:4; cf. Isa 6:1-6; Ezek 10:1-7). The Jewish Temple, modeled after the Tabernacle in the time of Moses, had two altars: the altar for burnt offerings, located outside the entrance of the Tabernacle/Temple proper (Lev 4:18; cf. Exod 27:1), and the incense altar, located within the Tabernacle/Temple itself, just outside the curtain that set off the holy of holies (Exod 30:6; cf. Lev 4:18; Luke 1:11). Both altars had four "horns" (Exod 27:2; 30:2). The altar for burnt offerings was overlaid with bronze (Exod 27:2), and the altar of incense was overlaid with gold (Exod 30:3). The Greek word used here by John (*thusiasterion*) is used in the LXX for both altars. Which does John have in mind here? Either is possible, but in 8:3, 5 he will mention the altar again, explicitly identifying it as the incense altar (cf. 5:8). Given that he will speak there of the incense mingling and rising "with the prayers of the saints," and given that the only prayers of the saints recorded in the book prior to that point are those mentioned in 6:10 (cf. 5:8), it seems likely that the incense altar is intended here. Because "those who had been slain" are *under* the incense altar, their prayers mingle and rise with the incense to God (cf. 5:8).

Under the altar John sees "the souls of those who had been slain" (6:9). The reason these individuals have been slain recalls John's reason for being on the island of Patmos: "for the word of God and for the witness they held" (6:9: RSV "had borne"; cf. 1:9). The slain seek a specific kind of judgment— vengeance for their blood (6:10). The cry to God to avenge the blood of the righteous, typically prefaced by "How long?", is proverbial in Jewish litera-ture (e.g., Deut 32:43; 2 Kgs 9:7; Ps 79:5; Zech 1:12; *1 Enoch* 22:6-7; 47:1-4; 104:3; *Psalms of Solomon* 3:3; Luke 18:6; *4 Ezra* 4:33-37). Further concern for the shedding of the blood of God's people will be found later in the book (16:6 [twice]; 17:6 [twice]; 18:24; 19:2). The vengeance is to be taken upon "those who dwell upon the earth." The reader has already learned of a time of testing that is to come upon those who dwell upon the earth (3:10). The expression will appear again, always in a negative sense (8:13; 11:10, 10; 13:8, 12, 14, 14; 17:2, 8). This is the only use of "Master" (*despotes*; RSV "Lord") in the book (cf. Luke 2:29; Acts 4:24; 2 Pet 2:1; Jude

4). Since Jesus is the one who previously identified himself as "the holy one, the true one" (3:7), he is presumably the one being petitioned here. Given that such petitions are typically directed to God, this is another indication that Jesus is being portrayed in terms usually reserved for God.

The response to the question of the slain is twofold. First, each is given a white robe (6:11). Earlier, the conquerors were promised white robes to wear (3:5; cf. 3:18; 4:4). The word used there is *himation*, a general term used to refer to any kind of robe or outer garment. Here John uses *stole*, which is a long, flowing robe indicating high social status. Second, the slain are told that they must "rest a little longer, until the number of their fellow servants and their brethren should be complete, who were to be killed as they themselves had been" (6:11; cf. *1 Enoch* 47:4; *4 Ezra* 4:36). Other references in the book to God's people being "killed" are 2:13 (Antipas); 11:7 (the two witnesses); 13:15 (those who do not worship the image of the beast); cf. 20:4 (those who were "beheaded"). "A little longer" will also be found in 20:3 (RSV "a little while").

Who is John talking about here? When does the fifth seal "take place"? That John is not speaking of disembodied "souls" that have left their bodies at death and "gone to heaven" is made clear by his use of *psuche* throughout the book (cf. 8:9; 12:11; 16:3; 18:13, 14; 20:4). This popular misconception is, regrettably, reinforced by most modern translations, which, like the RSV, do not translate *psuche* consistently as "soul." Hence, the reader will undoubtedly be surprised to learn that John speaks twice of sea creatures as having (8:9) or being (16:3) souls (*psuche*). Nor is John speaking to the issue of where people—or martyrs—go after they die. He is describing his vision, all of the details of which cannot be pressed literally, as we have seen. It is also unlikely that he is speaking of literal martyrs here. Indeed, since a *stole* is a kind of *himation*, there is no reason to view "those who had been slain" as anyone other than the conquerors. The further specification of the robe received not only illuminates the special status given to "those who had been slain"/conquerors, but also serves to anticipate the description of the Great Multitude, who will be wearing white robes (7:9, 13-14 [cf. 22:14]: *stole*) and who will not be characterized as martyrs. As we will see, John portrays the entire Church as a martyr church (e.g., 11:7; 13:7, 10, 14; 20:4). That is his picture of the Church, but it does not necessarily mean every Christian will be martyred, and it certainly does not mean that those who do become martyrs receive some kind of special reward. Finally, 5:8 speaks of the prayers of the saints—not the martyrs—without specification. 6:10 records the first such prayers in the book. The connection of *both* prayers with the incense altar is surely intended to lead the reader to connect them. The prayers of the saints are none other than the prayers that God will avenge their blood. This will be the theme throughout the book. The sixth seal, then, is timeless: the prayers mentioned in it are always going up to God from a Church continually battered by its enemies.

John does not at this point answer the question of how much longer it will be until God avenges the blood of his servants, but the reader is assured that God will, in fact, do so. How and when it will take place remains to be seen.

With the opening of the sixth seal, the focus shifts back to the earth. The aftermath of the opening of the seal consists of two parts: a series of natural upheavals (6:12-14) and the response of the mass of humanity (6:15-17). The natural upheavals number six: there is a great earthquake, the sun becomes black as sackcloth, the full moon becomes like blood, the stars fall from the sky to the earth, the sky vanishes like a rolled-up scroll, and every mountain and island is removed from its place. John's language draws upon vivid Old Testament imagery for judgment (e.g., Isa 13:10; 34:4; 50:3; Ezek 26:18; 32:7-8; 38:19-20; Joel 2:10, 31; 3:15; Amos 8:9; cf. *Sibylline Oracles* 3.382). Of these upheavals, only the sky vanishing will have no counterpart in the rest of the book. Earthquakes will be found (8:5; 11:13, 13, 19; 16:18, 18), as well as plagues affecting the sun (8:12; 9:2; 16:8), the moon (8:12), the stars (8:12), and the mountains and islands (16:20). Can this be anything other than the hour of trial that is coming on the whole world, to try those who dwell upon the earth (3:10)?

The upheavals spark a response from the following groups of people: "the kings of the earth and the great men and the generals and the rich and the strong, and every one, slave and free" (6:15; cf. Isa 24:2). The last two groups clearly indicate that all people are included. The first five groups designate various people of privileged status, who would otherwise seem to be secure in their positions. That the natural upheavals affect them in the manner John describes demonstrates how serious the crisis is. Five of these groups (kings, generals, the strong, slaves, and the free) will be brought together again in 19:18, and three of them (the rich, slaves, and the free) in 13:16; the great ones will be found again only in 18:23. A chiliarch (RSV "general")—literally, the leader of 1,000 men—was a high-ranking military officer. In John's day the term could be used specifically to designate a Roman military tribune, who commanded a cohort (about 600 men).

The response of these seven groups is to act and to speak. First, they hide themselves "in the caves and among the rocks of the mountains" (6:15). Then they speak to the mountains and the rocks: "Fall on us and hide us" (6:16; cf. *1 Enoch* 104:5; *Sibylline Oracles* 3.607). The language is drawn from Old Testament passages where people hide before the terrible majesty of God (e.g., Isa 2:10, 19, 21; cf. Jer 8:3; Hos 10:8). From what or whom are they so desperate to hide? "From the face of him who is seated on the throne and from the wrath of the Lamb" (6:16). What is the occasion for such terror? "The great day of their wrath has come" (6:17). Their awareness of the consequences of that day is apparent not only in their attempts to hide but also in their question: "Who can stand?" (6:17). This cry echoes Malachi 3:2: "But who can endure the day of his coming, and who can stand when he appears?" A similar question is found in Joel 2:11: "For the day of the LORD is great and very terrible; who can endure it?" Though the question is rhetorical, the answer that is presumed is undoubtedly the same as the answer to the question in 5:2 ("Who is worthy to open the scroll and break the seals?"): no one.

The Day of the Lord as a great day of terrible judgment is a common theme in the Old Testament (e.g., Isa 13:9-13; Ezek 30:1-9; Joel 2:1-11; Amos 5:18-20; Obad 15; Zeph 1:14-18; Zech 14:12-15; Mal 4:5; cf. Jdt 16:17; *1 Enoch* 100:4; *Jubilees* 24:30; *Testament of Levi* 3:3; *Psalms of Solomon* 15:12; 1QpHab 12.14; *4 Ezra* 7:38) and is also found in the New Testament (e.g., 1 Thess 5:2-3; 2 Thess 1:9-10; 2 Pet 3:10). The wrath of God will also be mentioned in 11:18; 14:10; 16:19; 19:15. "The great day" will return again in 16:14. What is especially striking here is the expression "the wrath of the Lamb." Any attempt to soften the force of this expression by suggesting that these fearful ones only *think* (mistakenly, to be sure) that the loving Lamb can be wrathful is not only a romantic theologizing of the text but also misses the clear inclusion with 5:13. As praise is given "to him who sits upon the throne and to the Lamb," so also wrath is shared by them. They are equal in status.

The first six seals set in motion the coming judgment. They do not constitute a series of successive events in history but serve to picture the Lamb as coming in his role as judge, particularly as avenger of the blood of his servants, who cry out to him. The Lamb is in control. The sixth seal brings the reader right up to the time of the judgment—to the Day of the Lord itself. It is a day from which none will escape and of which all should be terrified. No one will be able to stand before the one seated on the throne and the Lamb on that day. The reader is braced for the seventh seal, which surely must describe that day. Instead, the reader gets a surprise: an unexpected answer to the question, "Who can stand?"

Before the opening of the seventh seal John has two visions, each introduced in a similar manner: "After this I saw . . ." (7:1) and "After these [RSV "this"] I saw [RSV "looked"]. . ." (7:9). In the first, John witnesses an exchange between four angels standing at the four corners of the earth and an angel ascending from the rising of the sun (7:1-3), following which he hears the number of the servants of God who receive a seal upon their foreheads (7:4-8). In the second, John sees and hears a great multitude standing before the throne (7:9-10), witnesses the response of the angels, the elders, and the four living creatures (7:11-12), and engages in a brief conversation with one of the elders, who explains to him the identity of the Great Multitude (7:13-17).

7:1-17 is sometimes called an "interlude" because it seems to interrupt the opening of the seven seals: the sixth seal was opened in 6:12-17, and the seventh will not be opened until 8:1. To be sure, this section heightens the suspense surrounding the opening of the seventh seal. The first six seals are opened in rapid fashion, but the opening of the seventh is delayed. But to view this chapter as little more than a delaying tactic is to miss its clear connection with what precedes it. In 6:17 the question is asked: "Who can stand [before the one seated on the throne and the Lamb]?" 7:1-17 answers that question. 7:9 identifies those who can stand as "a great multitude which no man could number, from every nation, from all tribes and peoples and tongues." The entire unit serves to elaborate on the identity of these people. Hence, the opening of the seventh seal is delayed until the question of 6:17 is answered—i.e., until the identity of those "who can stand" is revealed.

The parallels between 7:1-17 and 4:1–5:14 are strong. Both center on a single action: the Lamb comes and takes the scroll (5:7) and the Great Multitude cries out in praise to God and to the Lamb (7:10). In both cases the throne is the place of action: "between the throne and the four living creatures" (5:6) and "before the throne and before the Lamb" (7:9). Both describe the key actor (the Lamb/the Great Multitude) as "standing" (5:6; 7:9). Both use the hear/see pattern (5:5 and 5:6; 7:4 and 7:9). In both there is a chiastic structure centering on and informing the central action:

A. before the action: "has conquered" (5:5); were "sealed" (7:4)
   B. the action: the Lamb comes and takes the scroll (5:7); the Great
      Multitude cries out in praise (7:10)
A'. after the action: "by thy blood didst ransom . . . and hast made" (5:9-10);
   "they have washed their robes and made them white in the blood of the
   Lamb" (7:14)

The difference is that while the Lamb is always the actor (conquered, purchased, made), the Great Multitude is described initially as the recipient of an action (were sealed). Even their action of washing their robes and making them white is dependent upon a prior action by another: the Lamb shedding his blood. Hence, when the Great Multitude stand before the throne, they also stand before the Lamb (7:9): it is only because of the Lamb that they can stand at all.

Other connections with 4:1–5:14 include the (twenty-four) elders (4:4, 10; 5:8, 11, 14; 7:11), the four living creatures (4:6-8; 5:8; 7:11), angels (5:2, 11; 7:11), songs of praise (4:8, 11; 5:9-10, 12, 13; 7:10, 12), worship (4:10; 5:14; 7:11), white garments (4:4; 7:9, 13-14), an elder speaking to John (5:5; 7:13-14), and the blood of the Lamb (5:9; 7:14). Indeed, 7:9 picks up where 5:14 left off—with the Lamb at the throne. Finally, the key characters (the Lamb and the Great Multitude) are introduced in response to questions: "Who is worthy?" (5:2) and "Who can stand?" (6:17; cf. 7:13).

In the first vision John sees "four angels standing at the four corners of the earth, holding back the four winds of the earth, that no wind might blow on earth or sea or against any tree" (7:1). The "four corners" of the earth (e.g., Isa 11:12; *Testament of Asher* 7:2; Job 37:3; Isa 41:9; Ezek 7:2; Irenaeus, *Against Heresies* 3.11.8) and the "four winds" (e.g., Ezek 37:9; Dan 7:2; 8:8; 11:4; Zech 2:6; 6:5; *1 Enoch* 18:2; *4 Ezra* 13:5; Mark 13:27; Irenaeus, *Against Heresies* 3.11.8) are traditional Jewish concepts. In Jer 49:36 the four winds are viewed as destructive: "I will bring upon Elam the four winds from the four quarters of heaven" (cf. 1QapGen[1Q20] 13.13-19; *1 Enoch* 76:4). In Ezek 20:47 the burning of trees is seen as a picture of God's judgment (cf. 8:7; 9:4; 1QapGen[1Q20] 13.13-19). The four angels are described further as those "who had been given power to harm earth and sea" (7:2). The four angels, then, are apparently getting ready to unleash the four winds to wreak havoc upon the earth.

Before they do so, however, "another angel" (7:2) intervenes. John sees him "ascend from the rising of the sun" (7:2)—i.e., the east. "The rising of the sun" will be mentioned again in 16:12. The angel is carrying "the seal of the living God" (7:2). "The living God" is a common characterization of God in Jewish literature (e.g., Deut 5:26; Josh 3:10; 1 Sam 7:26; 2 Kgs 19:4; Ps 42:2; Isa 37:4; Jer 10:10; Dan 6:20; Hos 1:10 *1 Enoch* 5:1; *Testament of Abraham* 17:11; *Testament of Job* 37:2; *Joseph and Aseneth* 8:5) and early Christian literature (e.g., Matt 16:16; Acts 14:15; Rom 9:26; 2 Cor 3:3; 1 Thess 1:9; 1 Tim 3:15; Heb 3:12; *2 Clement* 20:2; Hermas, *Visions* 2.3.2; cf. 15:7). Crying out "with a loud voice," the angel commands the four angels not to do their injurious work "till we have sealed the servants of our God upon their foreheads" (7:3). The first person plural "we" is odd; perhaps it is intended to include the other four angels (7:1).

The practice of marking the servants of God upon their foreheads recalls Ezek 9. In Ezek 9 six executioners come to Jerusalem to implement God's judgment upon sinners in the city (Ezek 9:1-2). But before they do, the Lord orders "a man clothed in linen" to go through Jerusalem and mark on their foreheads all who are chagrined over the sins committed in the city; those so marked will be spared execution (Ezek 9:2-6). The judgment is carried out, and those marked are left untouched (Ezek 9:6-11). A similar thought is expressed in PssSol 15:6-7, where the righteous are marked for salvation, preserving them from famine, sword, and death. The sealing on the forehead here in chapter 7 has two consequences. First, it marks out those sealed as servants of God. It does not make them such—they already are. Second, it keeps them from being harmed by the four winds. Having (or not having) God's "seal" or "name" on one's forehead will be an important theme in the book ("seal": 9:4; "name": 14:1; 22:4), as well as having (or not having) the "mark" of the beast upon one's forehead (13:16; 14:9; 20:4; cf. 13:17; 14:11; 16:2; 19:20).

John does not witness the actual sealing of the servants of God, but he does learn "the number of the sealed": 144,000 (7:4). John speaks of the "number" of something nine times elsewhere in the book: five times with reference to the number of the beast (13:17, 18 [three times]; 15:2), twice with reference to the number of the troops of calvary at the sixth trumpet (9:16 [twice]), once with reference to the angels praising the Lamb (5:11), and once with reference to the nations gathering for battle against "the camp of the saints" (20:8). John further specifies that the 144,000 are sealed "out of every tribe of the sons of Israel" (7:4; cf. 21:12) and goes on to list each of the twelve tribes, along with the number 12,000 as those who are from that tribe (7:5-8).

The listing of the twelve tribes in 7:5-8 is marked by several oddities. First, the order of the list is unique in Jewish literature. Second, both the tribe of Joseph and one of the half tribes descended from him are listed. Third, the tribe of Dan is missing.

With respect to order, it should be pointed out that earlier Jewish lists typically differed from one another as well. The traditional order of birth of the twelve sons of Jacob is narrated in Gen 29–30 (cf. *Jubilees* 28:17-24; 32:3): four sons of Leah (Reuben, Simeon, Levi, Judah), two sons of Bilhah (Dan, Naphtali), two sons of Zilpah (Gad, Asher), two more sons of Leah (Issachar, Zebulun), and two sons of Rachel (Joseph, Benjamin). In Gen 35:22-26 the sons are grouped by mother: six sons of Leah, two sons of Rachel, two sons of Bilhah, and two sons of Zilpah (also *Jubilees* 33:22; *Pseudo-Philo* 8:6; *Testaments of the Twelve Patriarchs*). Sometimes the order of the mothers is altered: Leah, Bilhah, Zilpah, and Rachel (*Pseudo-Philo* 26:10-11; cf. *Pseudo-Philo* 8:11-14). Other lists of the twelve tribes headed by Reuben (the oldest) include Gen 49:2-27; 1 Chr 21:2; Ezek 48:30-34; and *Pseudo-Philo* 10:3, and, omitting Simeon, Deut 33:6-25 and *Pseudo-Philo* 25:9-13—all with differing orders. The list in Revelation is one of only a few that begin with Judah (cf. 11QTemple[11Q19-20] 24.39-41, 44-45; *Pseudo-Philo* 25:4), though the orders of these lists differ. The precedence of Judah in Rev 7 may well be explained by the identification of Jesus as "the Lion of the tribe of Judah" in 5:5. Whether or not there is any significance to the unique order of names following Judah is not clear.

With respect to Joseph and the half tribes, sometimes the lists include one or both of the half tribes Manasseh and Ephraim, the sons of Joseph (cf. Gen 48:1-6). Manasseh replaces Joseph in *Pseudo-Philo* 25:4, and Ephraim replaces Joseph in Num 13:4-14. Both replace Joseph in Num 1:5-15 and Ezek 48:1-7, 23-28 (where Levi is also omitted but the orders otherwise differ) and in *Pseudo-Philo* 25:4 (where Dan is also omitted). But only in Rev 7 does the list include both Joseph and one of the half tribes (Manasseh). Whether or not there is any significance to this fact—or to the mention of Manasseh rather than Ephraim—is not clear, though the corruption of Ephraim (Israel) is detailed at length in Hosea 5:3–14:9.

Finally, only Rev 7 (and perhaps *Pseudo-Philo* 25:4, though there has probably been a corruption of the text here) omits Dan from the list of tribes. Whether this omission is deliberate or accidental is not clear, though it should be pointed out that in the time before the exile the tribe of Dan was the site of an altar in the north that competed with the legitimate altar of God in the south (1 Kgs 12:28-30; 2 Kgs 10:29; Amos 8:14; cf. Jdg 18:11-31). Indeed, in *Testament of Dan* 5:6 "Jacob" states bluntly to "Dan," on the basis of an otherwise unknown tradition "in the book of Enoch," that "your prince is Satan." Whether John was influenced by any of this tradition is unknown; he certainly makes no attempt later to connect either Satan or the beast(s) to the tribe of Dan. Irenaeus's later observation that the Antichrist would come from the tribe of Dan (Irenaeus, *Against Heresies* 5.30.2; cf. Hippolytus, *Treatise on Christ and Antichrist* 14:5-6) is a comment on Rev 7, not a source for it.

The sealing of the 144,000 is a logical, if unexpected, sequel to the opening of the sixth seal, which has brought the reader to the great day of wrath, before which none can stand. Now the reader learns that there is a group of people who will not be harmed by the coming destruction, which is depicted here by the four winds. 144,000 "Jews" will be exempt. There is no need to press the literalness of the number 144,000, which is the product of

12, 12, and 1,000. Both 12 and 1,000 are stock numbers in Judaism. Twelve was, of course, the number of the sons of Jacob and hence the number of tribes of Israel. A thousand was a standard designation given to the largest grouping of Israelite soldiers. Num 31:48, for example, reads, "Then the officers who were over the thousands of the army, the captains of the thousands and the captains of the hundreds, came near to Moses." Indeed, the Qumran community was organized into thousands, hundreds, fifties, and tens (e.g., 1QS 2.21-22; 1QSa 1.14-15; 1QM 4.1-2). Given that a "thousand" is the largest such group, the number 12,000 (from each tribe) would be a reasonable way to combine the largest military group (1,000) with the number of completeness in Israel (12). 144,000, therefore, would represent the totality of Israel.

But are the 144,000 ethnic Jews? The reader has no reason to believe so. John has already taken great care to characterize the Church using language that in the Old Testament was applied to Israel (e.g., 1:6; 5:10; cf. 2:9; 3:9). A reasonable inference on the part of the reader, then, is that the 144,000 is yet another way of speaking about the Church. But what might that way be? Censuses in the Old Testament were typically designed to determine how many men from each tribe were available to fight in an army (e.g., Num 1:2-3; 26:1-2; 2 Sam 24:1-9; 2 Chr 21:1-5). To characterize the Church in this way, then, is to characterize the Church in military terms. In some way the Church is an army (cf. the promise in each of the seven letters to him who "conquers"). John will develop this theme as the book progresses (e.g., 14:1-5; 19:14; cf. 11:7; 13:7; 20:9).

Finally, the sealing of the 144,000 reminds the reader of the promise to those "who have kept my [Jesus'] word of patient endurance" that they will be kept from the hour of trial that is coming on the whole world (3:10). God's people will be sealed—i.e., protected—from the coming "harm."

The reader's suspicions that the 144,000 represent the Church are confirmed in the next vision. John sees "a great multitude which no man could count, from every nation, from all tribes and peoples and tongues" (7:9). The reader, remembering 5:5-6, where John *heard* about a Lion but *saw* a Lamb, observes that John *heard* 144,000 from Israel and *saw* a "great multitude" from all ethnic backgrounds. The reader realizes that just as the Lion and the Lamb are one and the same, so also must be the 144,000 and the Great Multitude. Furthermore, the reader remembers that what John saw *explained* was what John heard: Jesus can be portrayed as a conquering Lion *because* he is, in fact, a slain Lamb. It follows, therefore, that the group in view in this chapter can be portrayed as an army of 144,000 from Israel *because* they are, in fact, a Great Multitude from all ethnic backgrounds who, as the reader will discover, "washed their robes and made them white in the blood of the Lamb" (7:14).

There is a two-part structure to 7:9-17: the scene with the Great Multitude (7:9-12) and the explanation of the scene (7:13-17). In the scene itself John sees the Great Multitude and describes their appearance (7:9). Next, he records what they say (7:9), followed by the response of the angels (7:11-12). The explanation itself has its own two-part structure: the identification of the Great Multitude through a question and answer exchange between one of the elders and John (7:13-14) and a commentary upon the identification (7:15-17: "Therefore . . ."). The commentary has a chiastic structure:

A. God (7:15a)
    B. he who sits upon the throne (7:15b)
    B'. the Lamb in the midst of the throne (7:17a)
A'. God (7:17b)

This chiastic structure further strengthens the link between the one sitting on the throne (God) and the Lamb (cf. 5:13).

John sees a "great multitude" (7:9). John will hear the voice of a "great multitude" again in 19:1, 6. As in 5:9, "every nation . . . all tribes and peoples and tongues" (7:9) indicates the universal nature of the Great Multitude; no group is omitted. The reader remembers that these same groups were brought together in 5:9 as those out of which the Lamb had purchased people with his blood. John sees the Great Multitude "standing *before* the throne and *before* the Lamb" (7:9). The juxtaposition of the throne (and, presumably, the one seated on it) and the Lamb recalls both the praise directed to God and to the Lamb in 5:13 and those who sought to hide themselves from the one seated on the throne and from the Lamb in 6:17. Indeed, in 5:6 John saw the Lamb standing *between* the throne and the four living creatures and *among* the elders: God and the Lamb now share the throne.

The Great Multitude has nothing to hide. John observes further that those in the Great Multitude are "clothed in white robes" (7:9). Again the reader recalls the promises to the conqueror (3:4-5, 18) and, most recently, the fact that "those who had been slain" were given white robes to wear (6:9-11). Since this is the first mention after 6:9-11 of someone wearing white robes, it is reasonable to identify the Great Multitude in 7:9 with the slain in 6:9-11, especially since both passages use the same word: *stole*. 6:9-11 speaks of them *before* receiving the white robes; 7:9 *after*. Finally, John notes that the members of the Great Multitude have "palm branches in their hands" (7:9). While palm branches were used in the celebration of the Feast of Tabernacles (e.g., Lev 23:39-43; Neh 8:14-15; 2 Macc 10:7; *Jubilees* 16:31), they more commonly represented victory (e.g., 1 Macc 13:51; 2 Macc 14:4), the most likely connection here, given that the 144,000 have just been characterized in military terms. This is a victory celebration for the one who sits upon the throne and for the Lamb (5:5) and his army (7:4-8). Although palm branches will not be mentioned in the rest of the book, John will make numerous allusions throughout the book to Zech 14, a chapter that concludes with a section on the importance of the Feast of Tabernacles (Zech 14:16-19: RSV "booths").

The connection with 5:13 is sustained and enhanced by a chorus of praise as the members of the Great Multitude cry out with a loud voice, "Salvation belongs to our God who sits upon the throne, and to the Lamb" (7:10; cf. Isa 12:2-3; 25:9). This is the first use of "salvation" in the book; it will recur in 12:10 and 19:1. The Greek word *soteria* can also mean "deliverance." Many other expressions of praise were directed toward God by the heavenly choruses in 4:1–5:13 (4:8, 11; 5:13) and will be so again in this very passage (7:12), but "salvation" is reserved for the Great Multitude only to sing. This is the first explicit identification of the one sitting upon the throne—which includes the Lamb—as God (cf. 19:4).

The cry of praise by the Great Multitude brings about a response in heaven. "All" the angels (presumably the "myriads of myriads and thousands of thousands" mentioned in 5:11), along with the elders (4:4, 10; 5:5, 6, 8, 11, 14) and the four living creatures (4:6-9; 5:6, 8, 11, 14; 6:1, 3, 5-6, 7), take their stand "round the throne" (7:11). They fall (cf. 4:10; 5:8, 14) upon their faces and worship (cf. 5:14) God (7:11). John will record similar scenes in 11:16 and 19:4. That their doxology begins with "Amen" (7:12) shows that they are in agreement with the song of the Great Multitude (cf. 5:14). In 19:4 there will be a similar formulation. This doxology consists of a string of seven expressions of praise directed to "our God for ever and ever" (7:12). All except "thanksgiving" were found in the doxology to the Lamb in 5:12. "Power" was also found in the doxology to God (4:11), "blessing" in the doxology to God and to the Lamb (5:13), and "glory" and "honor" in all three. Although the word "thanksgiving" does not occur in the doxology to God in 4:8, John characterizes that doxology as one of "glory and honor and thanks" (4:9). That there is no mention of this doxology being directed to the Lamb is an indication of how closely the one seated upon the throne and the Lamb can now be identified (cf. 5:13).

As in 4:1–5:14, John, after witnessing praise before the throne, is personally addressed by "one of the elders" (7:13; cf. 5:5). In 5:5 the elder provided John with an answer. Here he asks John a question: "Who are these, clothed with white robes, and whence have they come?" (7:13). Both questions are important. The Great Multitude has not been present in John's visionary experience of the heavenly throne up to this point: both their identity and their origin are unknown. Having previously been the recipient of information from one of the elders, John turns the tables: the elder knows the answer (7:14). The elder identifies the Great Multitude according to two characteristics. First, they are those "coming out [RSV "have come"] of the great tribulation" (7:14). The present tense is striking. It is not that the Great Multitude "came" (aorist) or "has come" (perfect) out of (*ek*) the great tribulation; they "are coming." "Tribulation" has already been portrayed as the present experience of John and the churches (1:9; 2:9; cf. Dan 12:1). It is also something the church of Smyrna is "about" to experience for "ten days" (2:10). "Great" has been associated with "tribulation" (without the definite article) as something into which Jesus intends to cast those who commit adultery with the prophetess Jezebel, if they do not repent (2:22). The reader also recalls that Jesus promises to keep the faithful in the church at Philadelphia "out of [*ek*, as in 7:14] the hour of trial which is coming on the whole world, to try those who dwell upon the earth" (3:10). For that matter, could anything be "greater" than the tribulation/terror experienced by those attempting to hide themselves as described after the opening of the sixth seal (6:15-17)? The Great Multitude will not experience the terror of the Judgment on the great day of wrath. On salvation from "tribulation," see Isa 33:2; 63:8-9 (LXX).

Second, those who make up the Great Multitude "washed their robes and made them white in the blood of the Lamb" (7:14). Those who "wash their robes" will receive a blessing at the end of the book (22:14). Why do the robes need to be washed? Are they dirty? The second verb clarifies the first: to wash one's robe is not simply to make it "clean," so that a dirty blue robe will become nice and blue again, but to make it "white." It is a symbol of consecrating oneself to God (e.g., Exod 19:10, 14). That they have done so "in the blood of the Lamb" recalls two passages. Given the strong associations between chapters 7 and 5, the reader can only conclude that making one's robe white in the blood of the Lamb must have something to do with the Lamb "ransoming" people by his blood (5:9). This in turn reminds the reader of 1:5, where John says Jesus "freed us from our sins by his blood." The need to have dirty robes washed and made white, the need to be ransomed, the need to be freed from one's sins—all of these needs, if they are not different ways of saying the same thing, are met by the blood of Jesus. One difference is that in 1:5 and 5:9 Jesus is the active party, while in 7:14 the members of the Great Multitude take action. Similarly, in 6:11 the slain are "given" white robes, while in 7:14 those who make up the Great Multitude wash their robes in order to make them white. One of the themes that pervades the book is that Christians are not *merely* passive recipients of actions performed by the Lamb. To be sure, the Lamb is the supreme actor, and he is in control. But Christians are still called, for example, to repent and conquer, as the letters to the seven churches make clear, and they will be described, for example, as those who bear witness (6:9; 12:11), prophesy (11:3), follow the Lamb (14:4), keep the commandments of God and the faith of Jesus (14:12), and do righteous deeds (19:8).

The elder next points out the effect of the Great Multitude's coming out of the great tribulation and having washed their robes and made them white in the blood of the Lamb: "Therefore they are before the throne of God" (7:15), which is where John sees them (7:9). It is on this basis ("Therefore") that the Great Multitude is able to stand before the throne (6:17). The elder continues by explaining what the Great Multitude is doing before the throne: "they serve him day and night within his temple" (7:15). Once again the reader observes that John's vision is of a heavenly Temple/Throne Hall. Since service in the Temple is a function carried out by priests (cf. Lev 1–9; 1 Chr 6:49; 24:1-19), that the Great Multitude is characterized in this manner picks up the earlier theme that Jesus has made his people priests (1:6; 5:10; cf. 20:6) and also reminds the reader of Jesus' promise to make the conqueror "a pillar in the temple of my God" (3:12). The idea of God's people "serving" him will be picked up again in the vision of the new Jerusalem at the end of the book (22:3). The elder continues with a promise that "he who sits upon the throne will shelter (*skenoo*) them" (7:15). The language is similar to Ezek 37:27: "My dwelling place [*kataskenosis*] will be with them" and picks up the image of the Tabernacle (Hebrew *mishkan*, Greek *skene*) that represented God's dwelling with the Israelites during their time in the wilderness (e.g., Exod 25:9; 26:30; cf. Acts 7:44; Heb 8:2; *1 Clement* 43:2-3). The verb form will be used again in 12:12; 13:6; 21:3. The noun form will be used in 13:6; 15:5; 21:3.

There follows a series of three promises recalling the language of Isa 49:10 that are based upon the continued activity of the Lamb, who, in a bit of remarkable irony, "will be their shepherd" (7:17). In the Old Testament God is sometimes portrayed as a shepherd (e.g., Ps 23:1-2; Ezek 34:11-16). In Ezekiel the task is also assigned to the coming son of David (e.g., Ezek 34:23). The other uses of the verb "to shepherd" in Revelation have to do with Jesus "shepherding" (or "breaking") his opponents "with a rod of iron" (2:27; 12:5; 19:15). The location here of the Lamb "in the midst of the throne" underscores the exalted position he now holds. First, the elder says "they shall hunger no more, neither thirst any more" (17:16). Though the notion of being hungry will not recur in the book, Jesus will give both a promise (21:6) and an invitation (22:17) to the thirsty at the end of the book. Second, "the sun shall not strike them, nor any scorching heat" (17:16). The fourth bowl will produce a plague in which the sun gives off scorching heat (16:8-9). Third, "he will guide them to springs of living water" (7:17). The elder has added the word "living" here (cf. Jer 2:13). Plagues will strike the "springs of water" in 8:10 and 16:4. The promise to the thirsty noted above includes the promise to give "from the fountain of the water of life without payment" (21:6). "The water of life" will be mentioned in 22:1, 17. Finally, in language reminiscent of Isa 25:8, the elder says "God will wipe away every tear from their eyes" (7:17), an expression that will be repeated in 21:4.

The question raised in 6:17 has now been answered. There are, after all, some who are able to stand on the great day of wrath, who will be kept from the judgment (3:10). By virtue of having come out of the great tribulation and having washed their robes and made them white in the blood of the Lamb, the Great Multitude from every nation, from all tribes and peoples and tongues, can stand before the throne of God. It is the Great Multitude, so many in number that it cannot be counted, that in fact completes the "number" of the fellow servants and brethren of those who cry out for vengeance (6:10-11). And it is precisely because the Great Multitude, which has no ethnic boundaries, is given its identity by its association with the blood of the Lamb that it can be understood to be the fullness of Israel (7:4-8), protected from the judgment of God that awaits the rest of humankind (7:1-3).

"The angel took the censer . . . and threw it on the earth": The judgment draws near
Revelation 8:1-6

The little unit 8:1-6 serves as a transition between 4:1–7:17 and 8:7–9:21. To be sure, the opening of the seventh seal in 8:1 completes the task begun in 6:1-17 (cf. 5:1-7). On the other hand, the mention of the seven angels with seven trumpets in 8:2 and 8:6 anticipates the blowing of the seven trumpets in 8:7–9:21 and 11:15-19. Hard and fast divisions in Revelation simply do not exist; that is part of the book's literary power. But the whole unit is best seen as one that moves the narrative from the question "Who can stand?"—the answer to which has occupied 7:1-19—to the question "How long before thou wilt judge and avenge our blood?" (6:10), which began to be answered in 6:12-17 but was not finished. The opening of the seventh seal in 8:1 sets the stage for what is to follow, and the reference to the seven angels with the seven trumpets in 8:6 forms an inclusion with 8:2.

After the delay in 7:1-19, it is at last time for the Lamb to open the seventh seal. The result is unexpected: "there was silence in heaven for about a half hour" (8:1). The sixth seal brought natural upheavals and terror in anticipation of the Day of the Lord. The reader expects some sort of judgment scene. But the silence is not just unexpected; it also stands in stark contrast to the picture of heaven sketched so far by John, in which songs and doxologies dominate (4:8, 11; 5:9-10, 12, 13; 7:10, 12). Yet silence in heaven is not at all inappropriate. Habakkuk observed, "The LORD is in his holy temple; let all the earth keep silence before him" (Hab 2:20; cf. Zeph 1:7). That there is silence in heaven is an indication that God is in his Temple, a concept to which John will return in 11:19 after the blowing of the seventh trumpet. That the silence lasts "about half an hour" builds suspense. With the breaking of the seventh seal the reader expects the scroll to be opened at last. Instead, John sees seven angels who are given seven trumpets (8:2). After a brief description of another angel taking incense from the heavenly altar and casting it to earth (8:3-5), the seven angels prepare to blow their trumpets (8:6). There is an air of anticipation: something is about to happen.

John sees "the seven angels who stand before God" (8:2). They are given seven trumpets (8:2). In Josh 6, with the children of Israel poised to enter the promised land, God instructs Joshua that to be included in the entourage marching around the city of Jericho seven times are seven priests carrying seven trumpets before the ark of the covenant, blowing them continually (6:2-4). On the seventh day the priests are to give one long blast on the trumpets, which the people are to follow with a great shout, at which the walls of the city will fall down (Josh 6:5; cf. Josh 6:6-21). Although the details in Joshua and Revelation are not identical (e.g., priests vs. angels, blowing the trumpets at the same time vs. one at a time), it is nevertheless true that the idea of blowing seven trumpets prior to judgment and destruction, which is about to happen here, is firmly rooted in the Old Testament. At this point the reader might expect the angels to blow the trumpets, but that does not happen yet.

"Another angel" comes and stands "before the altar" (8:3). Since "another" is indefinite, there is no reason to identify this angel with "another angel" in 7:2. Part of the furniture in the Tabernacle/Temple was the incense altar, upon which the priests were to burn incense continually (e.g., Exod 30:1-8; cf. Lev 16:12). The idea of a heavenly counterpart to the incense altar is found in Isa 6:6 (cf. Ezek 10:6). The angel is holding "a golden censer" (8:3). A censer is an instrument designed to place incense among the burning coals or to move the coals themselves (e.g., Lev 10:1). John has already seen in heaven golden crowns (4:4) and golden bowls (5:8); in this verse he sees a golden censer and a golden altar. The angel is given "much incense to mingle with the prayers of all the saints upon the golden altar before the throne" (8:3). Once again the spatial focal point of John's vision is the throne (4:2-6; 5:6-7; 7:9, 11, 15). For the second time in the book the incense in heaven is closely connected with "the prayers of all the saints" (cf. 5:8 [without "all"]). The mention of an incense altar reminds the reader of the altar mentioned in 6:9, where "those who had been slain" were crying out for God to avenge their blood (6:10). Given the connection of this scene to both passages, it is now confirmed that the "prayers" of the saints in Revelation are not prayers in general but specifically prayers that God will bring judgment upon those who have mistreated them. That the seven trumpets are connected with these prayers indicates that God is about to answer them.

The angel carries out his task: "the smoke of the incense rose with the prayers of the saints from the hand of the angel before God" (8:4)—i.e., God hears the prayers. Then the angel takes the censer, fills it "with fire [i.e., hot coals] from the altar," and throws it "on the earth" (8:5). The prayers for vengeance are about to be answered. The result is that the silence in heaven is broken: "and there were peals of thunder, voices, flashes of lightning, and a earthquake" (8:5; cf. 11:19). The first three of these John viewed coming from the throne in 4:5; the last was one of the results of the opening of the sixth seal (6:12). The seventh seal has been opened, the judgment of God has come to earth, the Day of the Lord is at hand (cf. 6:17). The question "How long . . .?" (6:10) is about to be answered. As for the opening of the scroll itself, the reader will have to wait a little longer.

"The rest of mankind . . . did not repent:" God's judgments and mankind's stubbornness
Revelation 8:7–11:14

Having introduced the inevitability of God's judgment, who is in control of it (the Lamb), and who can stand before it (the Great Multitude), the focus shifts to the precursors of the judgment itself and mankind's refusal to repent in the face of them.

"The . . . angel blew his trumpet": The plagues begin
Revelation 8:7–9:21

The announcement of the seven trumpets makes the reader think of the seven seals. Indeed, there are similarities between the seals and trumpets. First, of course, they both number seven. Second, the first four elements in each series are relatively brief and form a cohesive subunit in terms of content: four colored horses, four components of the created order (earth/sea/fresh water/heavenly bodies). Third, the fifth and sixth elements of each series move beyond the content of the first four (the slain under the altar/great earthquake; locusts/troops of cavalry). Finally, there is a literary separation of some length between the first six elements in each series and the seventh (144,000/great multitude; angel and little scroll/two witnesses). Given the similarities, the question naturally arises as to whether the correspondingly numbered elements in the seven seals and the seven trumpets are somehow related to one another. Are there really fourteen different elements, or just seven? To put it differently, do the first seal and first trumpet (and the second seal and the second trumpet, and so on down the line) "take place" at the same time?

A closer look, however, reveals that the formal similarities between the seals and trumpets are more than offset by their differences. For one thing, different agents control the two groups (the Lamb; seven angels). Along the same lines, while the seals are numbered individually, the trumpets are not; only the angels who blow them are so numbered (although for the sake of simplicity this commentary will speak, e.g., of the "third trumpet"). Third, there are brief breaks between the fourth and fifth trumpets and between the fifth and the sixth, while there are no such breaks in the seals. Fourth, the trumpets speak of the failure of people to repent, while the seals do not. Most importantly, the individual seals and trumpets simply do not "line up" with one another content-wise, as the following table indicates:

	SEAL	TRUMPET
#1	conquering	a third of the earth burns up
#2	men slaying one another	a third of the sea turns to blood
#3	inflation/famine	a third of the rivers and fountains turn bitter
#4	death	a third of the sun/moon/stars turn dark
#5	the slain under the altar	locusts
#6	a great earthquake	troops of cavalry
#7	silence in heaven	the kingdom becomes God's and Christ's

Hence, there is no reason to assume that the seven seals and the seven trumpets are related to one another in some simple and direct way. A careful examination of the seven trumpets is needed to determine how, if at all, they are connected to the seven seals.

The seven trumpets span a longer portion of the text than do the seals. Although the form of the first four trumpets (8:7-12) is not as repetitive as that of the first four seals, the descriptions of the first four trumpets are relatively short, and the contents are complementary. The descriptions of the fifth (9:1-11) and sixth (9:13-21) trumpets are much longer than those of the first four. There is a brief break between the fourth and fifth trumpet (8:13) and another between the fifth and sixth trumpet (9:12). The two breaks are connected thematically by the word "woe." In the first an eagle warns of three woes; the second warns that while one woe is past, two are still to come. Between the blowing of the sixth and seventh trumpets John describes a lengthy, highly complex vision in which he receives something like a second commission (10:1–11:13), which is followed by a warning that the second woe is past, but the third is coming soon (11:14). Finally comes the blowing of the seventh trumpet (11:15-19).

Like so much of Revelation, the seven trumpets draw deeply upon the Old Testament. Perhaps the most obvious parallels to the seven trumpets are the plagues associated with the exodus. As the following chart indicates, while some of the trumpets pick up the imagery of the exodus plagues, there is by no means simply a one-to-one correspondence between the two:

Exodus plagues (Exod 7:14–12:30)	Trumpets
#1: water turns to blood (7:14-22)	#2, #3
#2: frogs (8:1-15)	
#3: gnats (8:16-19)	
#4: flies (8:20-32)	
#5: plague on livestock (9:1-7)	
#6: boils (9:8-12)	
#7: hail (9:13-35)	#1
#8: locusts (10:1-20)	#5
#9: darkness (10:21-29)	#4, #5
#10: death of firstborn (11:1–12:30)	

Other Old Testament parallels will be noted throughout the discussion of the seven trumpets.

The blowing of the first trumpet affects the earth/land (8:7). Hail and fire mixed with blood are thrown (divine passive; RSV "fell") to the earth/land. The combination of hail and fire in judgment is an Old Testament image (e.g., Exod 9:23-25; Ezek 38:22; cf. Wis 16:22; Sir 36:29). Blood and fire are combined in Joel 2:30. The earth/land will also be affected by the first bowl (16:2). Hail will be mentioned again in connection with the seventh trumpet (11:19) and the seventh bowl (16:21), and blood in connection with the second trumpet (8:8), the second bowl (16:3), and the third bowl (16:4, 6). Fire, however, is the operative element here: the result is that "a third of the earth was burnt up, and a third of the trees were burnt up, and all the green grass was burnt up." "Fire" will be mentioned again in connection with the second trumpet (8:8), the sixth trumpet (9:17-18), and the fourth bowl (16:8), and "burning" in connection with the fourth bowl (16:8, 9). The reference to the land and the trees reminds the reader of the four angels standing at the four corners of the earth, ready to unleash the wind to "harm" the land and the sea and every tree (7:1-3). Here the sea is absent and the damage to the land and trees is limited to one third, though not so with the green grass. The division into thirds in connection with God's judgment comes from the Old Testament. In Ezek 5 the prophet is commanded to cut off his hair and beard, divide it into thirds, and dispose of each third in a manner corresponding to the fate awaiting the people of

Jerusalem: death by pestilence and famine, death by sword, and exile (Ezek 5:12 [twice]). Similarly, Zechariah speaks of two thirds of the people perishing and one third left alive (Zech 13:8-9; cf. *Sibylline Oracles* 3.544). For John only one third is struck, at least for now (cf. 16:2-9). The limitation of the damage to one third reminds the reader of the fourth seal, where Death and Hades were given authority to kill one fourth of the people (6:8). Does the increase from one fourth to one third here suggest an intensification of judgment?

The blowing of the second trumpet affects the sea (8:8-9). Something like a great mountain burning with fire is thrown (divine passive) into the sea. Jer 51:25 speaks of a "burnt mountain" (cf. *1 Enoch* 18:13). The reference to the sea reminds the reader of the element that was missing from 7:1-3 after the blowing of the first trumpet. The sea will also be affected by the second bowl (16:3). The effect upon the sea is threefold. First, one third of the sea becomes blood (8:8; cf. 16:3; Exod 7:20-21). Second, one third of the creatures of the sea die (8:9; cf. 16:3). Finally, a third of the ships are destroyed (8:9), which would signal an interruption in sea trade (cf. 18:19).

The blowing of the third trumpet affects the rivers and the fountains of water (8:10-11). A great star "blazing like a torch" (cf. *1 Enoch* 21:3) falls from the sky (8:10; cf. Isa 14:12; *1 Enoch* 86:1). The third bowl will also affect the rivers and fountains of water (16:4). "Wormwood," the name of the star (8:11), was a plant proverbial for its bitterness (e.g., Prov 5:4). The image is derived from Jer 9:15 (cf. Jer 23:15), where God warns the rebellious Israelites, "I will feed this people with wormwood, and give them poisonous water to drink." The effect of the falling star is to turn the waters into wormwood, thus making them bitter (8:11; cf. Exod 15:23), which is understood, as in Jer 9:15, as making them poisonous. The result is death for "many men" who drink from the waters (8:11). Once again, the plague is limited: the star falls upon one third of the rivers and fountains of water (8:10), and one third of the waters are turned into wormwood (8:11). Interestingly, "many"—not just one third—of the people die. John will speak of a fallen star again in 9:1.

The blowing of the fourth trumpet affects the celestial bodies—the sun, the moon, and the stars (8:12). The fourth bowl will also affect the sun (16:8). One third of the sun, one third of the moon, and one third of the stars are struck (divine passive). The result is that one third of their light is darkened (cf. Isa 13:10; Ezek 32:7-8; Joel 2:10, 31; 3:15; Amos 8:9): one third of the day does not shine, and, similarly, one third of the night (cf. Exod 10:21). The sixth seal affected the sun, moon, and stars, but in a different manner (cf. 6:12-14).

In 7:1-3 the four angels hold back the four winds so that they might not harm the physical environment. With the first four trumpets, that restriction has now been lifted; the four winds have started to blow.

The fifth trumpet does not follow immediately upon the fourth. Instead, John sees and hears "an eagle" flying "in midair [RSV "midheaven"]" (8:13). For an eagle as messenger, cf. *2 Baruch* 77:19-26; 87:1. Later John will see an angel flying in midair (14:6); also, the birds flying in midair will be invited to the great supper of God (19:17; cf. 19:21). The eagle speaks with a loud voice: "Woe, woe, woe to those who dwell on the earth, at the blasts of the other trumpets which the three angels are about to blow." The eagle's words serve four purposes. First, they bracket off the first four trumpets from the last three. Second, they provide a dramatic pause: the reader is already waiting for the last three trumpets; she must wait a little longer. Third, they characterize the last three trumpets with the word "woe," a word that foretells impending doom (e.g., Num 21:29; 1 Sam 4:8; Isa 3:11; Jer 48:1; Hos 9:12; Jdt 16:17; *1 Enoch* 99:13-14; Matt 11:21; Mark 14:21; Luke 6:25; Jude 11). In fact, the triple use of "woe" aligns in such a way with the three remaining trumpets that each will be characterized as a "woe" (9:12; 11:14). Fourth, they indicate that the woes are directed toward "those who dwell on the earth" (cf. Isa 24:17; 26:21; Hos 4:1). The reader recalls the hour of testing that "is coming" on those who dwell on the earth but from which those who keep God's word of patient endurance will be kept (3:10), as well as the cry of the slain for vengeance upon those who dwell upon the earth (6:10). In each case, the people of God were clearly distinguished from this group. It follows, then, that God's people will not be harmed by the last three trumpets. Why will they not be harmed? Because they have been sealed (7:3; cf. 9:4).

The description of the aftermath of the blowing of the fifth trumpet is much longer than that of the first four. The blowing of the fifth trumpet results in the unleashing of a hoard of stinging locusts. The structure of the passage is as follows: the unleashing of the locusts (9:1-3), the commission to the locusts (9:3-5), the effect of the locusts upon humans (9:6), a description of the locusts (9:7-10), the identification of the king of the locusts (9:11).

Following the blowing of the fifth trumpet John focuses his attention on the "bottomless pit" (9:1). The "bottomless pit," or the "Abyss" (*abussos*), is found seven times in Revelation, three times in this chapter. Here the "star fallen (perfect tense) from heaven to earth" (cf. *1 Enoch* 86:1) is given (divine passive) the "key" to the "shaft" of the Abyss (9:1), which he opens (9:2). A little later in this same section John will identify the "angel" of the Abyss (9:11). Twice later he will speak of the beast that "ascends" from the Abyss

(11:7; 17:8). Finally, he will again mention the "key" of the Abyss in chapter 20, where an angel holding the key will come down from heaven (20:1) and, after binding Satan, throw him into the Abyss, shutting and sealing it over him (20:3).

In the Old Testament the Abyss refers to the primordial "deep" sea (e.g., Gen 1:2; Ps 77:16; 104:6; Ezek 26:19; cf. *Jubilees* 2:2), the source of rivers (e.g., Deut 8:7; Isa 44:27; Ezek 31:4; cf. Pss 71:20; 78:15; *Jubilees* 3:24-27). It is the opposite of where God is: "Thy righteousness is like the mountains of God/Thy judgments are like the great deep" (Ps 36:6; cf. Ps 107:26). In the *Book of the Watchers* (*1 Enoch* 1–36) the fallen angels are imprisoned underground until the judgment (*1 Enoch* 10:4-6, 12; cf. Luke 8:31; 1 Pet 3:19; 2 Pet 2:4; Jude 6). In the *Book of Dreams* (*1 Enoch* 83–90) the Abyss is found in both of the dreams "Enoch" recounts. In the first, which depicts the coming flood, he sees the earth and everything in it swallowed up into the "great abyss" (*1 Enoch* 83:4; cf. *1 Enoch* 83:7). In the second, in an allusion to the story of the fallen angels in the *Book of the Watchers* (*1 Enoch* 6-8; 10:4-6, 12), he sees a star that had fallen from heaven (*1 Enoch* 86:1) being thrown into the Abyss (*1 Enoch* 88:1), following which other stars are bound and thrown into a chasm (*1 Enoch* 88:3). At the end of the vision "Enoch" once again witnesses judgment: the Watchers, the seventy shepherds, and the blinded sheep are thrown, one group at a time, into the Abyss (*1 Enoch* 90:24-27). John's understanding of the Abyss most closely parallels that of the these two Enoch booklets. John exhibits a threefold cosmology (cf. Pss 5:3; 135:6; Sir 1:3; *Testament of Levi* 3:9), with God in "heaven," people on earth, and nefarious creatures (locked) in the Abyss.

To the questions when and why the star fell John gives no answer. There is no reason to identify this fallen star with the fallen star of the third trumpet (8:10); there is no mention of this star "blazing like a torch." There is also no reason to view this star as a fallen angel. The connection between fallen stars and fallen angels in *1 Enoch* is directly related to the story of the fallen Watchers prior to the flood; John shows no interest in that story and displays no tendency to equate stars with angels. The star opens the shaft of the Abyss. Out of the shaft arises smoke like the smoke of a great furnace (9:2; cf. Gen 19:28; Exod 19:18). In the *Book of Dreams* the Abyss is said to be burning with fire (*1 Enoch* 90:24-27; cf. *1 Enoch* 10:12-14). Out of the smoke come locusts on the earth (9:3).

John draws upon both the eighth exodus plague (Exod 10:12-15) and the book of Joel for his description of a plague of locusts. Locusts were a major force of crop devastation in the Middle East, and Joel depicts his prophecy of the Day of the Lord in terms of a locust plague (Joel 1:2-2:27). Indeed, some of the bizarre details John records about the locusts are taken from Joel—e.g., they are like horses arrayed for battle (9:7; cf. Joel 2:4), and they have teeth like lions' teeth (9:8; cf. Joel 1:6). Similarly, both John and Joel mention the sound of chariots in battle (9:9; cf. Joel 2:5). Other details are John's own— i.e., having what looked like crowns of gold on their heads (9:7; cf. 4:4; 14:14), faces like human faces (9:7), hair like women's hair (9:8), scales like iron breastplates (9:9), and tails like scorpions with stings (9:10).

The locusts are under the ultimate control of God. Their commissioning centers on three divine passives. First, "power like the power of scorpions of the earth" is given to them (9:3). Scorpions were known for their ability to inflict painful—though rarely fatal—stings upon people (e.g., Deut 8:15; Ezek 2:6; Sir 26:7; 39:30; cf. 1 Kgs 12:11, 14). John will elaborate on the scorpion-like stinging abilities of the locusts in 9:5, 10. Second, they are told to harm only those people who do not have the seal of God upon their foreheads, and not to harm the grass or any plants or trees (9:4). The parallels with 7:1-3 are striking. Not only is there a reference to the sealing on the forehead (7:3), but also both passages use the word "harm" (7:2-3) and the expression "every tree" (7:1; cf. 7:3). But in 7:1-3 the reader has the impression that after the sealing, it is all right for the angels/winds to harm the trees; here the locusts may not. This is all the more noteworthy in that plants and trees are precisely what locusts would be *expected* to harm. Third, the locusts are allowed to torture them for five months, but not to kill them (9:5). As with the first four trumpets, there is a limitation here, though of a different sort. On the one hand, gone are the repeated references to "one third"; there is no limitation on how many people the locusts may torment. Yet the locusts are not allowed to kill them, and there is a set time period, which will be repeated in 9:10. Why five months? Perhaps because five months is the life cycle of a locust. But the number five can also symbolize "a few" (e.g., Lev 26:8; Isa 30:17; 1 Cor 14:19; cf. 1 Sam 17:40; *Testament of Simeon* 2:11 ["five months"]; Luke 12:6): the locusts' time to terrorize people will be brief.

In a pair of observations brought together in synonymous parallelism, John observes the locusts' effect upon humans: "And in those days men will seek death and will not find it;/they will long to die, and death will fly from them" (9:6). The future tenses of the verbs indicate that "those days" represents a time in the future, though John does not say how far. The first clause in each line indicates how terrible the locusts' torture will be; people do not under normal circumstances seek death or long to die. The last clause makes it clear that no escape will be possible; the "not" before "find" is emphatic, and the image of Death "fleeing" from people is most unexpected. Death is certainly acting out of character here (cf. 6:8). On the other hand, the whole tone of the verse reminds the reader of the desperate but futile attempt to escape the Day of the Lord on the part of those mentioned after the opening of the sixth seal (6:15-17).

Finally, John observes that the locusts have a leader: "the angel of the Abyss" (9:11). There is no reason to identify this angel with the fallen star in 9:1. The fallen star *unlocks* the Abyss; to be the locusts' leader the angel undoubtedly ascends *from* it. John gives the name of the angel of the Abyss in both Hebrew (Abaddon) and Greek (Apollyon). Both names mean "Destruction" (cf. 2 Thess 2:3), and *apoleia* regularly translates *abaddon* in the LXX. In the Old Testament Abaddon parallels Sheol (Job 26:6; Prov 15:11; 27:20; cf. 1QH 11[3].19), death (Job 28:8), and the grave (Ps 88:12). In 4Q504 7.8 it parallels the Abyss. John picks up this later tradition and develops it further: Abaddon/Apollyon is the name of the *angel* of the Abyss. John notes that the angel of the Abyss serves as the locusts' "king." John will later speak of God as "King of the ages" (15:3) and the Lamb as "King of kings" (17:14; 19:16). The "king" of the Abyss pales by contrast.

Once again there is a dramatic pause. There is no eagle this time; John simply comments that "the first woe has past; behold, two woes are still to come" (9:12). Since there were three woes before the blowing of the fifth trumpet and now one is past, it follows that the first woe must be the plague of locusts.

As with the fifth trumpet, the description of the aftermath of the blowing of the sixth trumpet is much longer than that of the first four. The blowing of the sixth trumpet results in the unleashing of a hoard of destructive cavalry. The structure of the passage is as follows: the release of the four angels (9:13-15), description of the cavalry (9:16-17), the impact upon a third of mankind (9:18), further description of the horses (9:19), the impact upon the rest of mankind (9:20-21).

Following the blowing of the sixth trumpet John hears "a voice from the four horns of the golden altar before God" (9:13). The reference to the golden altar reminds the reader of the golden altar "before the throne" in 8:3 (cf. 6:9); this is the same altar. For the first time John speaks of the "horns" of the altar (see on 6:9). The "voice" (John does not identify the speaker) commands the sixth angel, "Release the four angels who are bound at the great river Euphrates" (9:14). The command recalls 7:1-3, where the four angels standing at the four corners of the earth are forbidden from inflicting harm until the servants of God are sealed. The differences here are that the four angels are specifically said to have been "bound" and that they are at a different location—the great river Euphrates, rather than the four corners of the earth. In the Old Testament the "great" river Euphrates was seen as the eastern boundary of the land God promised to Abraham (Gen 15:18; Deut 1:7; cf. Exod 23:31; Deut 11:24; Josh 1:4; 2 Sam 8:3; 1 Kgs 4:21; *Jubilees* 14:18). It was later viewed in connection with the empire controlled by Babylon, through which the river ran (2 Kgs 24:7; Jer 46:2, 6, 10; 51:63; cf. Jdg 1:6). Later on it marked the eastern boundary of the Seleucid empire (1 Macc 3:32) and, by John's day, of the Roman empire. Hence, it is a standard symbol for a boundary and is so used here. Immediately John records that the angels "were released" (9:15). He further says that the angels "had been held ready for the hour, the day, the month, and the year" (9:15). The use of the divine passive here, along with the elaborate time signature, drives home God's orchestration of the entire scope of history, down to the very hour. The task of the four angels is to kill "a third of mankind" (9:15). The use of "one third" reminds the reader of the first four trumpets; that the angels are permitted to "kill" people is in direct contrast to the commission given to the locusts (9:5).

John abruptly shifts from the four angels to the troops of cavalry (9:16). Apparently these troops are the means by which the four angels are to carry out their task. The "number" (cf. on 7:4) of the troops is "two myriads of myriads [RSV "twice ten thousand times ten thousand"]"; John knows the number because he heard it (9:16). To calculate the number as two hundred million (a myriad = ten thousand) is to miss the parallel with 5:11. There John observed "a myriad of myriads" of angels; the number of troops is twice that amount—a large number indeed! John next describes the appearance of the horses and their riders as he saw them (9:17: "And this was how I saw … in my vision"): riders with breastplates (cf. 9:9) the color of red and sapphire and sulfur, and horses with heads like lions' heads (cf. 9:7-8) and with fire, smoke, and sulfur issuing from their mouths (cf. 1:16). If the reader wonders how fire, smoke, and sulfur relate to the mouths of horses, John adds in 9:19 that "the power of the horses is in their mouths." The parallel with 9:10 concerning the power of the locusts is clear. But John adds that the power of horses is also "in their tails; their tails are like serpents, with heads, and by means of them they wound" (9:19). Again, the parallel with 9:10 is obvious, but here it is as surprising as it is grotesque. Scorpions, to whom the locusts were compared, strike with their tails, but horses? Also, this is the first mention of the horses' tails; yet they are already described as having carried out their commission by using the weapons that come forth from their mouths—why do they also need tails to do harm? Indeed, why do they need to do "harm" at all when they are able to kill (9:17)?

In 9:18 John observes that the troops of cavalry indeed complete the task given to angels: a third of humanity is killed. John notes that the killing is carried out "by these three plagues . . . the fire and smoke and sulfur issuing from their mouths" (9:18; cf. 9:17). This is the first use—but not the last—of "plague" in the book.

A third of mankind is killed by the troops of cavalry; what about the remaining two thirds? John observes that "the rest of mankind, who were not killed by these plagues, did not repent of the works of their hands" (9:20). This is the first reference outside of the letters to the seven churches (2:5, 5, 16, 21, 22; 3:3, 19) to the need for repentance. The non-repentance of the rest of mankind will be repeated again in the next verse. Failure of people to repent will also be mentioned in connection with the fourth (16:9) and fifth (16:11) bowls (cf. 11:13). John clarifies the purpose of repenting as giving up the worship of "demons and idols of gold and sliver and bronze and stone and wood" (9:20). Demons will be mentioned again in 16:14 and 18:2. Though John will not mention idols again, he will speak of idolaters in 21:8 and 22:15. John's critique of idols—that they "cannot either see or hear or walk" (9:20)—stands in a long line of Jewish polemic against idol worship (e.g., Pss 115:4-7; 135:15-17; Dan 5:23; Ep Jer; Wis 14; *Sibylline Oracles* 3.11-35). Connecting demons to idol worship goes back to the Song of Moses (Deut 32:17). What "works" warrant repentance? John specifies these: "they did not repent of their murders or their sorceries or their immorality or their thefts" (9:21). John will bring together "murderers," "sorcerers," and "fornicators [lit., immoral people]," along with "idolaters" (cf. 9:20) and "liars" in 21:8 and the same three, along with "idolaters," "dogs," and "every one who loves and practices falsehood," in 22:15. "Harlotries" and "sorceries" are also juxtaposed in 2 Kgs 9:22 and Nah 3:4.

As with the seals, the question must be asked whether the trumpets depict successive events in human history. Like the seals, they are not portrayed as such. Any "chronology" that exists has to do with when they are blown, not when they "happen." A non-successive interpretation of the trumpets is confirmed at the fifth trumpet, where the locusts are instructed not to harm the grass (9:4). Yet the first trumpet resulted in all the grass being burnt up (8:7). If the trumpets represent a sequence of events, where did the grass in 9:4 come from? The point is that the trumpets, like the seals, do not represent a series of events that occur one after the other.

What do they represent? Certain details in the seven trumpets remind the reader of 7:1-3, where the four winds are restrained from harming the earth, sea, and "every tree" (cf. 8:7, 8-9; 9:4), the servants of God are sealed on their foreheads (cf. 9:4), and the four angels are waiting to harm the earth and sea (cf. 9:14); and of 6:17, where people seek an escape from the terror that is upon them (cf. 9:6). The natural inference is that what was still future in 7:1-3 and 6:12-17 is now present in 8:6–9:21. The sixth seal (6:12-17) leads up to the great day of wrath. The four angels standing at the four corners of earth are ready to let loose that wrath, but they are held back until the servants of God are sealed (7:1-9). The seventh seal brings in the great day of wrath (8:1-6), which is pictured from six different perspectives at the six trumpets (8:7–9:19). The angels are now released to do their terrible work (9:14-15). Awful things happen to the earth (and the cosmos) and to people, but not to those who have been sealed (9:4), who are kept from the hour of trial (3:10).

But a new element is introduced into the story. There remains, even in the face of these plagues, the possibility of repentance for those who are not sealed. But it is not to be (9:20-21). In spite of all that takes place, people prefer to worship demons and idols rather than the one seated upon the throne and the Lamb (cf. 5:13-14; 7:9-12).

"Take it and eat it":
The message of judgment
Revelation 10:1–11:14

Following the opening of the first six seals, the reader expects the opening of the seventh seal. Instead, she encounters a section that builds upon material introduced with the opening of the sixth seal. The same is true for the seven trumpets. The first six trumpets are blown; then follows not the seventh but a lengthy section that could well be called John's second commission. As we will see, this section too builds upon material introduced with the blowing of the sixth trumpet. The placement of the mention of the second woe being past is instructive here. In 8:13 the three woes are associated with the fifth, sixth, and seventh trumpets. The first woe follows immediately (9:12) upon the description of the effects of the fifth trumpet (9:1-11). But the second woe does *not* follow directly upon the blowing of the sixth trumpet (9:13-21). Rather, it is found at 11:14. It thus serves as a literary marker that ties the entire section 10:1–11:13 to the sixth trumpet.

The section consists of two main subunits: 10:1-11 and 11:1-13. In the first John sees an angel holding an open scroll (10:1-2), hears the seven thunders and is commanded not to write down what they said (10:3-4), describes the actions of the angel (10:5-7), takes the scroll from the angel and eats it (10:8-10), and is told to prophesy again (10:11). In the second he is directed to measure part of the Temple complex (11:1-2) and then relates the story of two witnesses who prophesy for 1,260 days (11:3-13). The section ends with an affirmation that the second woe is past and the third is coming soon (11:14).

The vision begins with John seeing "another mighty angel" (10:1). "Another" invites the reader to recall the first "mighty [RSV "strong"] angel," who, when John initially saw the sealed scroll in the hand of God, was "proclaiming with a loud voice, 'Who is worthy to open the scroll and break its seals?'" (5:2). A "mighty angel" will also be mentioned in 18:21. That this angel is said to be "coming down from heaven" (10:1) indicates that the setting for this vision will be the earth (cf. 10:2 , 5). That John gives further details about the angel is surprising, given that he has not commented on the appearance of angels up until now. What is so special about this angel? Is the angel Jesus? After all the angel has an open scroll in his hand (10:2), precisely what the reader expects from the Lamb, since the seven seals have now been opened. In addition, there are loose parallels between the description of this angel and previous descriptions of Jesus. For example, with respect to both John comments on their head, face, and legs (10:1; 1:14-16); indeed, both are said to have a face like the sun (10:1; 1:16). Similarly, both the angel and Jesus are associated with clouds (10:1; 1:7; cf. 14:14-16). But for the most part the descriptions differ. Even the words used for "face" are different (10:1: *prosopon*; 1:16: *opsis*), and Jesus is associated with clouds, while the angel is wrapped in a single cloud. Although there is no reason, then, to understand the angel to be Jesus, he is certainly impressive—a rainbow over his head (10:1), feet like fiery pillars (10:1; cf. Exod 13:21), a voice like a lion roaring (10:3; cf. Hos 11:10; Amos 3:8). That he stands with his right foot on the sea and his left foot on the land (10:2), a detail that is repeated in 10:5 and 10:8 and drives home the idea that what the mighty angel is about to do encompasses whole world (cf. 7:1-3), anticipates the beasts from the sea and the land in chapter 13 (13:1, 11 [RSV "earth"]). Presumably the detailed description is intended to make the reader realize the importance of what is about to happen.

The angel has in his hand an open scroll (10:2). Is this the scroll that had been sealed with seven seals (5:1)? The Lamb was given the scroll and opened the seals, but up to this point there has been no mention of him opening the scroll. Has the Lamb opened it behind the scenes and given it to the mighty angel to pass on to John (cf. 10:8-10), in the same way that the revelation itself has been passed on to John (1:1)? Or is this a different scroll? The Greek word used here is *biblaridion* (cf. 10:8, 9, 10 [Codex Sinaiticus: *biblion*]), which means "little scroll," rather than *biblion*, which is used in chapter 5. It is important to note that a voice "from heaven" calls this scroll a *biblion* in 10:8; hence, one must not press the distinction between *biblaridion* and *biblion* here. Yet *biblion* alone is used to characterize the scroll sealed with seven seals (5:1, 2, 3, 4, 5, 8, 9), while *biblaridion* is used only in 10:1-8.

The presence of a scroll in 10:1-11 can be explained perfectly well without recourse to the sealed scroll in 5:1 once the reader realizes that this section is based upon Ezek 2:8–3:3, where the Lord tells Ezekiel to open his mouth and eat what the Lord gives him (Ezek 2:8). Ezekiel sees a hand with a written scroll in it. The scroll, with writing on both sides, is opened for him; its words are of lamentation and mourning and woe (Ezek 2:9). Ezekiel eats the scroll and fills his stomach with it; in his mouth it is sweet as honey (Ezek 3:1-3). Here John is told to go and take the open scroll from the hand of the angel. John does so, and the angel responds with two commands: "Take it and eat" (10:9). The angel further explains what will happen when John eats it: "it will be bitter to your stomach, but sweet as honey in your mouth" (10:9). John obeys, and the angel's prediction is borne out: the scroll is indeed sweet in John's mouth, but his stomach turns bitter (10:10). Thus, John's use of Ezek 2:8–3:3 here explains the necessity of speaking of a second scroll. Presumably John's preference for *biblaridion* in 10:1-11 is designed to distinguish this scroll from the sealed scroll of 5:1.

Prior to the exchange of the scroll between the angel and John, the "seven thunders" sound (10:3). In the Old Testament thunder was often associated with the voice of God (e.g., Exod 19:19; 1 Sam 7:10; Job 37:2-5; Ps 29:3; cf. Sir 43:17; *Sibylline Oracles* 5.344). The Dead Sea Scrolls contain a fragmentary astrological text that includes dire predictions based upon the interpretation of thunder (4Q318 frag 2 2.6-9). Thunder is associated with judgment at several points in Revelation (8:5; 11:19; 16:18; cf. 4:5). John's response to hearing the seven thunders is to begin to write down what they say, but he hears a voice from heaven commanding him, "Seal up what the seven thunders have said, and do not write it down" (10:4). Three times Daniel was instructed to "seal up" his book because it was for the future (Dan 8:26; 12:4, 9). The angel provides John with no such explanation. Whatever the seven thunders are about the reader does not learn, but the fact that the seven thunders are sealed up does suggest that something important is about to happen.

In language reminiscent of Dan 12:7 (cf. Deut 32:40), the angel raises his right hand to heaven and swears by the one who lives for ever and ever (10:5-6). In John's opening vision of the throne he speaks of God as "the one who lives for ever and ever" (4:9, 10; cf. 15:3). Maintaining the connection with chapter 4 John describes God further in 10:6 as the one "who created heaven and what is in it, the earth and what is in it, and the sea and what is in it" (cf. 4:11; Gen 14:19; Exod 20:11; Neh 9:6; Ps 146:6; Ezek 12:28; Dan 12:7). Swearing oaths is a common Old Testament practice (e.g., Deut 6:13; Jdg 8:19; Ruth 3:13; 1 Sam 14:39; 2 Sam 4:9; 1 Kgs 1:29; cf. 1QapGen[1Q20] 2.14; *3 Baruch* 1:7; Matt 5:34-35; 26:63; Jas 5:12). The point of swearing an oath is to commit oneself to the absolute truthfulness of what is being said. This is the only act of swearing in the book, thereby heightening dramatically the significance of the oath itself. The content of the oath is that "there should be no more delay [*chronos*]" (10:6). The seventh angel is about to sound his trumpet, and "the mystery of God" is about to be fulfilled (10:7). The characterization of God's plan as a "mystery" is found in Jewish literature of this period (e.g., Wis 2:22; *3 Baruch* 1:6, 8; 2:6), especially among the Dead Sea Scrolls (e.g., 1QH 10(2).13; 1QpHab 7.5; 1Q27 1.3), and is picked up by Paul in the New Testament (Rom 16:25-26; Eph 3:4-6, 9-10; Col 1:26-27). John characterizes the "mystery" as something God "announced to his servants the prophets" (10:7). The language is reminiscent of Amos 3:7: "Surely the LORD God does nothing, without revealing his secret to his servants the prophets" (cf. Jer 7:25; 25:4; Dan 9:6, 10; Zech 1:6). The use of *chronos* here directs the reader back to the fifth seal, where the slain cried out for vengeance and were told that they must rest "a little longer [*chronos*]" (6:9-11). The obvious inference is that the mighty angel has announced the arrival of the time of vengeance upon "those who dwell upon the earth," who have shed the blood of God's servants (6:10). There will be no more delaying the judgment.

John returns to the little scroll. The voice from heaven that forbade John to write what the seven thunders said (10:4) speaks to John a second time (10:8). After taking the scroll from the hand of the mighty angel and eating it (10:9-10), John is told that he must "again prophesy about many peoples and nations and tongues and kings" (10:11). Two words cry out for further explanation: "again" and "about."

The use of "again" raises the question of what John has previously said about "peoples and nations and tongues and kings." John has mentioned peoples, nations, tongues, and *tribes* (but not kings) in 5:9 and 7:9. In both references people *from* these groups have been ransomed (5:9) or washed (7:9; cf. 7:14) by the blood of the Lamb. John has also spoken of "kings" twice: Jesus is the ruler of kings (1:5), and kings are among those groups that are terrified at the sixth seal (6:15-17). Neither grouping is necessarily positive in the book; after all, there are those from "peoples and nations and tongues" who have *not* been ransomed or washed. Although John will not mix "kings" with these other three groups elsewhere, he will speak of both "kings" (16:12, 14; 17:2, 10, 12 [twice], 14, 18; 18:3, 9; 19:16, 18, 19; 21:24) and "peoples and nations and tongues" (11:9; 13:7; 14:6; 17:15), always in ways that do *not* identify them as Christians. John's call is to prophesy "about" those who are not (yet?) part of the Church.

But what does "about" (*epi*) mean? Is John simply given a prophecy "concerning" these groups? To prophesy *epi* (cf. 14:6) is a common expression in the LXX that means to prophesy *against* (e.g., Jer 25[32]:30; Ezek 25:2; Amos 7:16). There will be no more delay (10:6): the time for judgment has come. But why, then, does the scroll taste as sweet as honey in John's mouth (10:10)? Does that not suggest a *good* message? Not at all. Ezekiel's experience was the same, yet God informed him that his message would not be heard by "rebellious" Israel (Ezek 2:3-7; 3:4-11). The scroll is "sweet" in the mouth because it is the message of God. John's addition that the scroll made his stomach turn bitter (10:10) simply underscores that the message is indeed one of judgment.

John is next given a measuring rod (11:1). What follows develops into what is, from a literary perspective, the most confusing section in the entire book. John is given four commands (11:1-2): (1) "Rise," (2) "measure" the Temple and the altar and the worshipers, (3) "do not measure" the outer court, and (4) "leave it [the outer court] out." So far so good. But the text abruptly shifts to the first person future indicative. The speaker (presumably God; cf. 10:4, 8), says, "I will grant my two witnesses power . . ." (11:3). Thus begins a story about the two witnesses that lasts all the way through 11:13. Unlike its beginning, however, the entire story is not cast as a simple prediction—it is not told in the future tense. In fact, the verb tenses change as John records the activities of the two witnesses: their power is described in the present tense (11:5-6), their encounter with the beast in the future tense (11:7), the events attending to their death in the future (11:8) and present (11:9) tenses, the joy over their death in both the present and the future tenses (11:10), and their "resurrection" and its aftermath in the aorist tense (11:11-12).

Adding to the confusion is the question of who is telling the story. The first person narration is found only in 11:3. Hence, given the verb tense changes, most scholars suggest that the one who speaks in 11:3 does not tell the entire story. The RSV, for example, closes the quotation marks at the end of 11:3. (The reader should note that the Greek language does not have quotation marks; quotation marks in English translations of the New Testament are always put in by the translators.) But if the speaker in 11:3 does not tell the entire story, then who does? Presumably John. But unlike everything the reader has seen so far in the book, 11:4-13 is not cast in the form of a vision. John claims to *see* nothing; he just tells the story. In a book characterized by the use of "And I saw . . ." over and over again, the lack of such an expression in this section is startling. If John is not recording a vision here, then where (and when) did he get his information? From a purely literary perspective, 11:4-13 reads like a commentary on 11:3. However the reader untangles all of these literary problems, one point needs to be emphasized: this passage is *not* a simple vision/prediction about the coming of two witnesses.

That conclusion is confirmed when the reader recognizes that John gives specific clues that this section is not to be taken literally. The most obvious clue is the explicit reference to an "allegorical" meaning in 11:8. But the reader must also consider the following: the two witnesses "*are*" (not "are *like*") two olive trees and two lampstands (11:4), fire pours out of the two witnesses' mouth(s) (11:5), the beast (!) "makes *war*" with *two* (!) people (11:7; see on 2:16), and their foes live to see the two witnesses ascend to heaven even though the witnesses previously had had fire pouring from their mouths by which their enemies were *doomed* to be killed (11:5, 12). To view this section as a literal description of the activities and fate of two individuals who will come at the end of time is simply to ignore all of the clues John gives to the contrary. Rather, John has dug deeply in the Old Testament to present a coherent, though non-literal, picture of something else.

In the opening subunit (11:1-2), John is given (divine passive) a measuring rod like a "staff." In John's vision of the new Jerusalem an angel will measure the city with a measuring rod of gold (21:15-16). "Staff" is used three other times in the book, always in connection with an allusion to Ps 2:9 (2:27; 12:5; 19:15—always translated in the RSV as "rod"), which is understood in Revelation in terms of judgment. The association of the measuring rod with a staff, therefore, indicates that the measuring is an act related to judgment.

John is commanded to measure three things: "the temple of God and the altar and those who worship there" (11:1). He is directed not to measure the court outside the Temple (11:2). The idea of "measuring" the Temple is drawn from Ezek 40:3; Zech 2:2 (cf. Zech 1:16; 11QTemple[11Q19-20] 38-40). "Temple" (*naos*) is used fourteen more times in Revelation. Most of the references are to the heavenly Temple (3:12; 7:15; 11:19; 14:15, 17; 15:5, 6, 8; 16:1, 17); two have to do with the lack of a Temple in the new Jerusalem (21:22). None refer to the earthly Temple in Jerusalem. "Temple of God" is used again only in 11:19 (cf. 3:12: "temple of my God"). Similarly, "altar" (*thusiasterion*) is used seven more times in the book, all in reference to the heavenly Temple (6:9; 8:3, 3, 5; 9:13; 14:18; 16:7).

The Jerusalem Temple had an outer court (11:2; 1 Kgs 7:12; Ezek 40:17-20; Mark 11:15-16; John 10:23; Josephus, *Antiquities* 15.396) into which Gentiles (nations) were permitted to enter (Philo, *Embassy to Gaius* 212; cf. Josephus, *Antiquities* 15.410-17). The idea that this court is given over (divine passive) to the nations is consistent with this practice but takes it a step further, since Jews were also allowed to enter this court. But the next clause shows that the "giving over" of the outer court to the nations is not really about the literal Temple at all; the action of the nations is that they "will trample over the holy city" (11:2), an idea firmly rooted in Jewish tradition (e.g., Ps 79:1; Isa 63:18; Dan 8:14; Zech 12:3; 1 Macc 3:51-52; *Psalms of Solomon* 17:22; *2 Baruch* 67:2; Luke 21:24). "The holy city" is a classic Jewish expression for Jerusalem (e.g., Neh 1:11; Isa 48:2; 1 Macc 2:7; 2 Macc 1:12; Tob 13:9; 3 Macc 6:5; Sir 36:12; 11QTemple[11Q19-20] 47.13; Matt 4:5; 27:53). In Revelation "the holy city" will be found again—explicitly identified as the "new" Jerusalem—in 21:2 (cf. 21:10; 22:19). Nowhere in the book is "the holy city" used to characterize the earthly Jerusalem.

The nations trample the holy city "for forty-two months" (11:2). This is the first of two occurrences of "forty-two months" in the book; the other describes the length of time the beast is allowed to exercise authority (13:5). The equivalent length of time—1,260 days—is found in the next verse and in 12:5. John is drawing upon the phrase "a time, two times, and half a time" in Daniel 7:25 and 12:7 (cf. Dan 9:27), an expression John himself will use in 12:14 as the equivalent of 1,260 days (cf. 12:6). Three and a half years (= forty-two months) eventually came to be associated with the drought during the time of Elijah (Luke 4:25; Jas 5:17; cf. 1 Kgs 17:1 and 18:1 ["the third year"]).

What is going on in this enigmatic scene? Since John nowhere else displays any interest in either the Jerusalem Temple (which had been destroyed by the Romans in AD 70 anyway) or the earthly city Jerusalem itself, we must look elsewhere for an understanding of 11:1-2. Given John's theological presentation of the Church as Israel (e.g., 1:5-6; 3:9; 7:4-14), it follows that "those who worship" in the Temple, who would normally be Jews, is another representation of the Church. This is supported by the fact that in Zech 2:5 measuring Jerusalem (Zech 2:1-2) is connected with protecting it: "I will be to her a wall of fire round about, says the LORD" (cf. 2 Sam 8:2). Previously in Revelation the 144,000, who represent the Church, were protected by being sealed (7:1-4). Like 7:1-4, then, 11:1-2 is best understood as another illustration of God keeping Christians from the hour of trial that is coming on the whole earth (3:10)—i.e., the day of wrath

(6:17). That "the nations" are not measured is a further indication that, by itself, "the nations" in Revelation is an expression characterizing those outside the Church (cf. 2:26). But keeping Christians from the day of wrath does not mean that they will escape persecution: the holy city (apparently another metaphor for the Church; cf. 21:9-10) will be trampled by the nations. Indeed, the earthly struggle between Christians and their enemies has been a theme throughout the book (e.g., 2:9-10, 13; 6:9-11) and will continue to be so.

The prediction concerning the nations is coupled with another about "my" (i.e., God's) two "witnesses" (11:3). Both Jesus (1:5; 3:14) and Antipas (2:13) have already been characterized as "the faithful witness"; in 17:6 the great harlot will be said to be drunk with "the blood of the saints, and the blood of the witnesses of Jesus." God will grant the two witnesses "power to prophesy for one thousand two hundred and sixty days" (11:3). 1,260 days is an alternate expression for 42 months. The point is clear: the period of the nations trampling the holy city is concurrent with the time of the ministry of the two witnesses. The two witnesses are clothed in "sackcloth" (11:3). Sackcloth, a rough, dark-colored fabric used for making sacks, was worn by people in the Old Testament as a symbol of mourning over distress (e.g., Gen 37:34; 2 Sam 3:31; Isa 15:3; Lam 2:10; Amos 8:10; cf. Jdt 8:5) and, especially, mourning over impending disaster or judgment (e.g., 1 Kgs 21:27-28; Esth 4:1; Jer 4:8; Joel 1:13; Jon 3:5-9; cf. 2 Macc 3:19; Jdt 4:10-14). In view of the latter, it was sometimes donned by penitents pleading for mercy (e.g., 1 Kgs 20:30-32; 1 Chr 21:16-17; Dan 9:3-19; cf. Matt 11:21). Given that John has just received a commission to "prophesy" (the only other use of the verb in the book) again "against" many peoples, nations, languages, and kings (10:11), it is clear that the message from God (see on 1:1-3) is one of impending judgment.

The two witnesses and their ministry are described further by John in 11:4-13. They are first characterized as "the two olive trees and the two lampstands which stand before the LORD of the earth" (11:4). This is the only use of "olive tree" in the book. John is drawing upon Zech 4 here. Zechariah sees "a lampstand all of gold, with a bowl on the top of it . . . . And there are two olive trees by it, one on the right of the bowl and the other on its left" (Zech 4:2-3). A little later an angel informs Zechariah that the two olive trees are "the two anointed who stand by the LORD of the whole earth" (Zech 4:11-14). "Lampstand" is used six times previously in Revelation, all in connection with the seven churches (1:12, 13, 20, 20; 2:1, 5). In 1:20, Jesus specifically identifies the seven lampstands as the seven churches. That the witnesses are called lampstands here serves to identify the witnesses with the Church. But previously there were seven lampstands, and here there are two. Does this imply that only a *part* of the church is meant— e.g., the *witnessing* church, or, more specifically, two of the seven (i.e., Smyrna and Philadelphia, the two that received no criticism)? Against this notion is the fact that nothing distinguishes one witness from the other; they are both characterized in the same manner. Also, there is no indication that they are part of a larger group. Finally, the "two" can be explained by the fact that Zechariah speaks of "two" olive trees (Zech 4:3, 11). It should also be pointed out that Deut 19:15 requires two (or three) witnesses in legal matters (cf. John 8:17), and the two witnesses speak a "legal message": the judgment of God. This is the only reference to "the Lord of the earth" in the book, though God has already been designated as the creator of the earth (10:6; cf. 4:11).

The two witnesses face opposition, characterized in 11:5 both as their "foes" (only here and in 11:12 in the book) and as those who desire to "harm" them (twice in this verse). But the two witnesses have a weapon: fire pours from their mouths and consumes their foes. The language is drawn from Jer 5:14: "behold, I am making my words in your mouth a fire, and this people wood, and the fire shall devour them" (cf. Gen 19:24; 2 Sam 22:9; 2 Kgs 1:10; Pss 11:6; 97:3). Indeed, those who desire to harm them "are doomed" to die in this manner: the fire is the message of judgment that none can escape (cf. 6:15-17). The fire coming out of their mouths reminds the reader both of the sharp sword coming out of the mouth of Jesus (1:16; cf. 19:15, 21) and of the fire, smoke, and sulfur coming out of the mouths of the horses at the sixth trumpet (9:17-18).

Twice John observes that the two witnesses have "power" (11:6). Power to shut the sky that no rain may fall recalls Elijah (1 Kgs 17:1), while power to turn the waters to blood (cf. 8:8; 16:3, 4) and to smite the earth "with every plague" (11:6; cf. 9:18, 20)—as often as they desire—recalls Moses (Exod 7:17, 19-20; cf. 1 Sam 4:8). The duration of the first power, and presumably the second, is said to be "the days of their prophesying" (11:6)— 1,260 days (11:3). The details must not be pressed literally—this is *not* a three-and-a-half-year drought. Nor should the two witnesses be identified as Moses and Elijah. Once again this is the Church described in terms of the Old Testament. Its power to speak for God, like that of Moses and Elijah, is great; its word of judgment is sure. The characterization of this work as "prophesying" picks up the initial statement in 11:3 that the two witnesses will "prophesy."

The verbs now shift to the future, to a time when the two witnesses are said to finish their testimony (11:7). At that time the beast that ascends from the Abyss (RSV "bottomless pit") will do three things: it will "war upon them and conquer them and kill them" (11:7). This is the first—and rather abrupt—reference in the book to the beast, who will take center stage in chapter 13, where it will be introduced as the beast rising out of the sea (13:1). In 17:8 John will be informed that the beast is to rise from the Abyss; the fact that he says so now is another indication that this section is not a vision, but John's commentary (after the fact) on 11:3. The reader has already encountered the Abyss in chapter 9, where it is the source of the torturing locusts at the fifth trumpet (9:1-3) and where its angel is named Abaddon or Apollyon (9:11). In 13:7 the beast is said to make war on "the saints" and, as here, to "conquer" them. In addition, those who oppose the beast in chapter 13 are said to be "slain" (13:10, 15). John is drawing on the language of Dan 7:21, where the little horn "makes war" with the saints and prevails over them. The reader should note that John, like Daniel, is applying "martyr" terminology to the entire Church.

John goes on to make three observations about the dead bodies of the two witnesses: they will lie "in the street of the great city which is allegorically called Sodom and Egypt, where their Lord was crucified" (11:8), men "from the peoples and tribes and tongues and nations" (cf. 5:9; 7:9; 10:11) will gaze at their bodies for three and a half days (11:9), and their bodies will be denied burial in a tomb (11:9). The language is reminiscent of Ps 79:2-3:

> They have given the bodies of thy servants
>   to the birds of the air for food,
>   the flesh of thy saints to the beasts of the earth.
> They have poured out their blood like water
>   round about Jerusalem,
> and there was none to bury them. (cf. Ezek 11:6)

The mention of the street of the great city anticipates the description of the street of the new Jerusalem in 21:21 and 22:2. Three and a half days is a period that corresponds numerically to 1,260 (days) = 42 (months) = 3 1/2 years, but is shorter.

The identity of the great city is puzzling. One might argue that since Jesus was crucified there, John must have Jerusalem in mind (cf. Jer 22:8). Indeed, despite all of the focus in Revelation on the death of Jesus, this is the only explicit mention of his crucifixion in the book. But given that John has made it clear that this section is not to be understood literally, such an identification should not be pressed. Further complicating the matter are the "allegorical" names given to the city. Along with Gomorrah, Sodom was destroyed by God in Gen 19:24-28 because of its wickedness, an event long remembered in Jewish, and eventually early Christian, literature (e.g., Deut 29:23; Isa 1:9; Jer 49:18; Amos 4:11; Zeph 2:9; 3 Macc 2:5; *Testament of Levi* 14:6; *Testament of Naphtali* 3:4; *Testament of Asher* 7:1; Matt 10:15; 11:23-24; Luke 10:12; Rom 9:29; 2 Pet 2:6; Jude 7). "Sodom" thus became a symbol for any wicked city. Indeed, Isaiah denounced Jerusalem as "Sodom" (Isa 1:10; cf. Jer 23:14; Ezek 16:46-49; *Ascension of Isaiah* 3:10). Egypt is not a "city" at all. It was, of course, the land out of which God brought the Jews through the exodus and was long remembered for its idolatry (e.g., Josh 24:14; Isa 19:1, 3; Ezek 20:7). "The great city" will be found seven more times in Revelation (16:19; 17:18; 18:10, 16, 18, 19, 22), where it is always identified as "Babylon," which will be characterized in terms of Rome. Since the wickedness of Babylon, not Jerusalem, will be the focus of attention as the book progresses (14:8; 17:1-6, 16-18; 18:2–19:2), there is no reason to view "the great city" any differently here.

The significance of bodies not permitted to be buried and, hence, lying in the street for all to see must be seen against the backdrop of the immense importance Jews placed upon burial of the dead (e.g., Gen 23; 35:20; 2 Kgs 23:17; Matt 23:29; Acts 2:29). In the book of Tobit, for example, it is precisely Tobit's dedication to burying dead Israelites that results in his property being temporarily confiscated by the Assyrians (Tob 1:16-20) and, ultimately, his accidental blindness (Tob 2:1-10). The death of the witnesses brings joy to "those who dwell on the earth" (see on 6:9-11), who were "tormented" by the two prophets (11:10; cf. 11:3, 6), who have now experienced the ultimate humiliation. The locusts at the fifth trumpet were permitted to "torment" (RSV "torture") people for five months (9:5). Apart from the use of the verb "torment" to describe the woman clothed with the sun being in labor (12:2), the noun and verb forms of "torment" will be used later always in connection with judgment—of those who worship the beast (14:10-11), of Babylon (18:7, 10, 15), and of the devil, the beast, and the false prophet (20:10).

The verbs now shift to the aorist. After three and a half days a breath of life from God "entered" them and they "stood" up on their feet (11:11). John draws here upon Ezekiel's vision of the dry bones, where "the breath came into them, and they lived, and stood upon their feet" (Ezek 37:10), which accounts for the shift in tense. That the dry bones represent Israel (Ezek 37:11) confirms the collective interpretation of the two witnesses as the Church. Again John notes the impact on those who see this: a "great fear" fell on them (11:11; cf. Exod 15:16). The noun "fear" is used twice more in the book, both in connection with people standing far off from fallen Babylon in "fear" of her torment (18:10, 15). The two witnesses "heard" a loud voice (cf. 1:10; 5:2; 7:2; 8:13; 10:3; 11:15; 12:10; 14:7, 9, 15, 18; 16:1, 17; 19:1, 17; 21:3) from heaven speaking to them (11:12). The invitation to "Come up hither!" is reminiscent of 4:1. The result is that the two witnesses "went up" to heaven (cf. 4:2) in a cloud (11:12; cf. 2 Kgs 2:11; Acts 1:9). John observes that their foes "saw" them (11:12).

John concludes his lengthy section on the two witnesses with a comment on the aftermath of their work: "at that hour there was a great earthquake" (11:13). "Hour" is used consistently in the book in connection with judgment (cf. 3:3, 10; 9:15; 14:7, 15; 17:12; 18:10, 16, 19). The great earthquake directs the reader's attention back to the sixth seal (6:12; cf. Ezek 38:19-20). The final mention of a great earthquake will be at the seventh bowl (16:18). The killing of 7,000 people is reminiscent of the killing of a fourth of the earth at the fourth seal (6:8) and of a third of mankind at the sixth trumpet (9:15, 18, 20). That one tenth of the city falls is a reversal of an occasional statement in Jewish literature of one tenth of a population *surviving* God's judgment (e.g., Isa 6:13; Amos 5:3; cf. *Jubilees* 10:9). Similarly, the killing of 7,000 people is a reversal of 1 Kgs 19:18, where God tells Elijah that there remain 7,000 faithful Israelites (cf. *Testament of Abraham* 17:14, where 7,000 people die when Death shows his ferocity to Abraham). The response of the survivors is intriguing: they became terrified and "gave glory" to "the God of heaven" (cf. Ezra 1:2; Dan 2:18, 19, 44; Jon 1:9). Giving glory to God will later be understood always in a positive sense: it will be used in connection with worshiping God (14:7; 19:7; cf. Jer 13:16) and synonymously with repenting (16:9). Thus, it would be tempting to suggest a similar interpretation here—that following the fall of a tenth of a city and the death of 7,000, the rest of the people repent and are saved from judgment—were it not for the fact that nowhere else in the book does John display any expectation of the masses repenting but, on the contrary, emphasizes the opposite (9:20-21; 16:10, 21; cf. 6:15-17). Thus, it is best to let the negative sense of being "terrified" (see on "fear" in 11:12) control the interpretation of this difficult passage. Having witnessed a demonstration of the judgment of God, the rest fear that they will experience the same thing (cf. 6:15-17).

Such an understanding of 11:13 is confirmed if John is consciously drawing upon Mic 7:8-17. This passage contains striking parallels to the end of the story of the two witnesses, including enemies rejoicing over the fallen (11:9-10; Mic 7:7), the fallen rising again (11:11-12; Mic 7:7), astonishment on the part of the enemies (11:12; Mic 7:10, 16), and subsequent fear on the part of the enemies (11:13; Mic 7:17). The final picture is one of terror at the prospect of judgment, not repentance:

> they shall come trembling out of their strongholds,
> > they shall turn in dread to the LORD our God,
> > and they shall fear because of thee. (Mic 7:17)

The numerous connections between the story of the two witnesses and previous sections of the book (e.g., the portrayal of the Church as Israel, the sixth and seventh seals, the fifth and sixth trumpets) confirm that the story of the two witnesses presents a different perspective on some earlier themes, along with some new ideas. The world stands under the certain judgment of God. The Church proclaims the message of that judgment. That which stands in opposition to God (the beast, introduced here for the first time in the book) seeks the destruction of the Church. It seems to succeed, to the delight of the world. But ultimately it does not, to the world's horror.

Once again there is a dramatic pause: "the second woe is past; behold, the third woe is coming soon" (11:14; cf. 8:13; 9:12). Since the first woe was the plague of locusts at the fifth trumpet, the second woe must include not only the horses of the sixth trumpet but everything up through the two witnesses. Themes running through the entire section (9:13–11:13) include judgment and the failure to repent. The third woe coming "soon" anticipates the blowing of the seventh trumpet, which follows immediately (11:15).

"The kingdom of the world has become the kingdom of our Lord and of his Christ": The judgment has arrived
Revelation 11:15-19

The seventh angel blows the seventh trumpet (11:15), after which John hears loud voices in heaven (11:15) and witnesses the response of the twenty-four elders (11:16-18) and the opening of the heavenly temple (11:19). This is the third woe (8:13), though John does not make it explicit.

When the seventh angel blows his trumpet, there are loud voices in heaven proclaiming the transfer of kingship from the world to the Lord and his Christ (11:15). "Christ" is used eight times in the book: four times in the expression "Jesus Christ" (1:1, 2, 5; 22:21), twice as "his [the Lord's, or God's] Christ" (11:15: "the Lord"; 12:10: God), twice by itself (20:4, 6). As a result, "he" shall reign for ever and ever (11:15; cf. Exod 15:18; Ps 10:16). That John does not specify whether the pronoun refers to the Lord or to

Christ is yet another indication of how he has blurred the differences between them (cf. 5:13). "Reign" is used seven times in the book: four times with respect to Christians (5:10; 20:4, 6; 22:5) and three times with respect to God (11:15, 17; 19:6). The inauguration of God's reign is set in the past (11:17 and 19:6 use the aorist); the kingdom has already been transferred. When it has been transferred John does not say, but the connections with 4:1–5:13 suggest that the Lamb's death is central to the transfer. The future is used here to signify the unending duration of God's/the Lamb's reign.

This is the third scene in which the twenty-four elders appear in the book (11:16; cf. 4-5; 7), reminding the reader that this is all a part of John's heavenly vision (4:1-2). Once again they fall on their faces and worship God (7:11; cf. 5:11). This is the only song of praise in the book that begins with the expression, "We give thanks to thee" (11:17; cf. 4:9; 7:12). God has already been designated "Almighty" in 1:8 and 4:8 (15:3; 16:7, 14; 19:6, 15; 21:22). Similarly, God has already been characterized as the one "who was and who is and who is to come" (1:4; 4:8; cf. 16:5). The deletion of the last phrase (cf. 16:5) is apparently an indication that since God has now begun his eternal reign, to call him "the one who is to come" is no longer necessary. The elders thank God "because" (RSV "that") he has taken his great power and has begun to reign (cf. 11:15). Drawing upon the language of the Psalms (e.g., Pss 2:1-2; 46:6; 98:1 LXX), the elders contrast the rage (*orgizo*) of the nations with God's wrath (*orge*), which they then explain in terms of judgment (11:18). They affirm that the time for the judgment of the dead (cf. Dan 12:2) has come. "Those who had been slain" who cry out for vengeance (6:9-11) will need to wait no longer (cf. 10:6). Further, they describe the two sides of that judgment (11:18). First, he will reward his servants the prophets. (For the expression used with respect to the Old Testament prophets, see 10:7.) If the two witnesses/prophets represent the entire church, then there is no reason to see prophets as a distinct subgroup of Christians here, any more than there is to see saints and those who fear his name as subgroups. Only the last part of the description—the small and the great—refers to different groups, and the point here is that God will reward *all* of the Christians, no matter what their stature is (cf. Ps 115:13). Second, and more briefly, God will destroy the destroyers of the earth (cf. Jer 51:21-25, where Babylon is said to destroy the whole earth). Elsewhere in Revelation "destroy" is used only in 8:9, with reference to the destruction of ships.

Finally, the blowing of the seventh trumpet is followed by the opening of the Temple of God in heaven (11:19). The ark of the covenant is seen in the Temple. The ark of the covenant was an ornate chest that represented

God's presence with Israel (Exod 25:8, 10-22). Inside of it were placed the two stone tablets Moses received on Mt. Sinai (Exod 24:16, 21; 1 Kgs 8:9). When the Israelites were on the move, the ark was carried by poles inserted through rings on its sides (Exod 25:12, 14-15; cf. Num 10:33; Deut 10:8; Josh 3:3). When they were settled, it was placed in the holy of holies, first in the Tabernacle (Lev 16:17) and later in the Temple (1 Kgs 8:1-6). As the unique place where God met Israel, the ark of the covenant took on a special significance on the Day of Atonement, the one day out of the year on which the high priest was permitted to enter the holy of holies (Lev 16:19-24; cf. Lev 16:1-2). There he would sprinkle blood upon the top of the ark, called the mercy seat (Exod 25:17-21), in order to make atonement for the people (Lev 16:11-16). 11:19 is the only mention in early Jewish or early Christian literature of a heavenly ark of the covenant.

John witnesses lightning, voices, thunder, an earthquake, and great hail (11:19; cf. Exod 9:24; Isa 29:6; 30:30; Ezek 13:11, 13). Coming out from the throne in 4:5 were lightning, voices, and peals of thunder; when the angel threw the censer to the earth just prior to the blowing of the first trumpet there were peals of thunder, voices, flashes of lightning, and an earthquake (8:5). At the sixth trumpet there will be all four of these (16:18) and, ultimately, great hailstones (16:21). The opening of the Temple in heaven sets the stage for a number of events that will be connected with the Temple (14:15, 17; 15:5, 6, 8; 16:1, 17).

The blowing of the seventh trumpet announces the climax of God's judgment. He has begun his rule. It is time for the judgment of the dead: wrath for the nations—for all who refuse to repent—and reward for God's people.

John's second "in the Spirit" experience is now over. He has been shown "what must take place after this." Much has been said about God's judgment, who is in charge of it, who can stand before it, and who will *not* be able to stand before it. But the story is not over yet. There remains to be fleshed out the opposition to God's work and to his Church—i.e., the beast, who is introduced in 11:7 and who is about to take center stage in the next section about the three signs in heaven. Furthermore, there remains to be fleshed out how the judgment (11:18) will take place, which will be the focus of John's third "in the Spirit" experience.

"I saw a great portent ...
And another portent appeared ...
Then I saw another portent"

Revelation 12:1–16:21

Between John's second and third "in the Spirit" experiences is a section in which John sees three "signs" (RSV "portent") in heaven: a woman clothed with the sun (12:1), a great red dragon (12:2), and seven angels with seven plagues (15:1). Between the second and third signs is a series of brief visions that highlight different aspects of the coming judgment (14:1-20). The mention of the first two signs sets up a confrontation that is developed in 12:1–13:18. The third sign, a third series of seven (seven seals, seven trumpets, seven bowls), is presented as the "last" of God's plagues, the completion of the wrath of God (15:1–16:17). The series of brief visions in the middle might well be the heart of John's message to his readers.

The section on the three signs in heaven also serves as the introduction to John's third "in the Spirit" experience (17:1–20:15). In a grand scheme involving those who oppose God and the judgment they will receive, John sets up a chiastic structure:

A. description of the dragon (ch. 12)
    B. description of the beast and the false prophet (ch. 13)
        C. description of Babylon (ch. 17)
        C'. judgment of Babylon (ch. 18)
    B'. judgment of the beast and the false prophet (ch. 19)
A'. judgment of the dragon (ch. 20)

"And the great dragon ... was thrown down to the earth ... and was angry with the woman": The first and second signs in heaven

Revelation 12:1–13:18

The first two signs in heaven, introduced one right after the other, mark out the parameters of a conflict that John develops throughout this section and that serves in many ways as a foundation for what follows. This section consists of two main subunits: the conflict between the woman and dragon (12:1-17) and the dragon's revenge (13:1-18).

"War arose in heaven":
The woman vs. the dragon
Revelation 12:1-17

12:1-17 consists of four parts: a confrontation between the dragon and the woman (12:1-6), a war in heaven between Michael and the dragon (12:7-9), a commentary by a great voice in heaven (12:10-12), and a continuation of the confrontation between the dragon and the woman and her offspring (12:13-18). While the section focuses on two key characters—the woman and the dragon, other characters play a role as well, most notably the woman's male child (12:4-5), Michael (12:7), and the rest of the woman's offspring (12:17).

The first sign in heaven is a woman. She is described in terms of astronomical phenomena: "clothed with the sun, with the moon under her feet, and on her head a crown of twelve stars" (12:1). Although a beautiful woman is described in terms of the moon and the sun in Cant 6:10 ("fair as the moon, bright as the sun"), John has moved beyond simile here; clearly the reader cannot press his details literally. John's description presents the woman in an exalted fashion and reminds the reader of earlier passages in the book. Jesus' face is like the sun shining in full strength (1:16; cf. 20:1). Jesus has promised the crown of life to the conqueror (2:10; cf. 3:11), the twenty-four elders have crowns of gold upon their heads (4:4; cf. 4:10), the rider on the white horse at the first seal is given a crown (6:2), and the locusts at the fifth trumpet had something like crowns of gold on their heads (9:7); in 14:14 one like a son of man will be said to have a golden crown on his head. The reader has learned that Jesus has seven stars in his right hand (1:16, 20; 2:1). Finally, twelve, of course, is the traditional number associated with Israel (see on 7:4-8).

The woman is described further as being pregnant and crying out "in her pangs of birth, in anguish for delivery" (12:2). Eventually she gives birth to a male child (12:5), after which she flees into the wilderness (12:6), an event upon which John elaborates in 12:13-16. There she finds "a place prepared by God, in which to be nourished" for 1,260 days (12:6, 14). The last detail, which John will confirm as a reference to Daniel in 12:14: "for a time, and times, and half a time" (cf. Dan 7:25; 12:5), reminds the reader of the two witnesses who prophesy for 1,260 days (11:3). The inference is obvious: the time the two witnesses prophesy and the time the woman is nurtured in the wilderness are one and the same. In 12:13 John observes that the dragon pursues the woman in her flight to her place in the wilderness. To aid her escape the woman is given (divine passive) "the two wings of a great eagle" (12:14). Endangered by a flood stirred up by the dragon, the woman is delivered when the earth opens its mouth and swallows the water (12:15-16). What will happen to the woman after her nurture in the wilderness for 1,260 days? John does not say at this point.

Who is the woman? The reader must resist a first impulse to infer from the woman giving birth to a male child (presumably Jesus) that she is Mary the mother of Jesus. John displays no interest in Mary anywhere else in the book; indeed, as will be made clear, the story is not about the birth of Jesus at all. The only specific "woman" John has mentioned so far is Jezebel (2:20), but the description of this woman hardly seems appropriate for a false prophet. Rather, John gives every indication that the woman is to be understood in terms of Israel. To begin with, the woman has a crown of twelve stars, the traditional number for Israel. In addition, his description of her as a woman in labor is reminiscent of similar Old Testament characterizations of Israel in distress as a woman about to give birth (e.g., Isa 26:16-18; Jer 4:31; Mic 4:9-10; cf. 1QH 11[3].7-12). Finally, what she does after the birth draws heavily upon the story of the exodus. Like Israel, she goes to the wilderness. Indeed, the motif of being taken to the wilderness on the wings of a great eagle while being pursued seems to be a direct allusion to Exod 19:4: "You have seen what I did to the Egyptians, and how I bore you on eagles' wings and brought you to myself" (cf. Isa 40:31). Even the river from the mouth of the dragon is reminiscent of the story of how Pharaoh commanded that all newborn Hebrew boys were to be cast into the Nile (Exod 1:22). Hence, the woman is not to be viewed literally as a specific woman, which is not surprising given that in books written near the same time as Revelation, women are used in visions to depict Jerusalem (4 Ezra 9:38–10:56) and the Church (Hermas, Visions 1–4). Here the woman is to be understood in terms of Israel. Is the woman therefore ethnic Israel? Given that John displays no interest in ethnic Israel elsewhere, it is difficult to see why he would picture ethnic Israel as being nurtured by God in the wilderness. Alternately, given John's ongoing characterization of the Church with language used in the Old Testament to describe Israel (e.g., 1:5-6; 7:4-7; 11:4-6, 11), is the woman here the Church? Given that the woman brings forth the Messiah, she cannot be the Church. Perhaps she represents true Israel—the Israel who brings forth the Messiah, who undergoes the (new) exodus, and whose "offspring" (the Church) is about to be attacked by the dragon. But the reader must be careful not to try to interpret the book allegorically, as if everything "stands for" something in the real world. What is important is that the woman serves as a foil for the dragon.

The second sign is "a great red dragon" (12:3). The reader has previously encountered a red horse at the second seal (6:4). This is the first mention of the dragon, who will play a significant role in this chapter and the next (12:4, 7, 9, 13, 16, 17; 13:2, 4; cf. 13:11). The word "dragon" will be found only twice more afterward (16:13; 20:2; cf. 20:7-10). "Dragon" (*drakon*) is used in the LXX to translate two words that have the connotation of a serpent or monster that inhabits the sea (or rivers): *lwytn* ("Leviathan"; Job 40:25; Pss 73(74):14; 103(104):26; Isa 27:1) and *tannim* (e.g., Exod 7:9-12; Deut 32:33; Job 7:12; Ps 73(74):13; Isa 27:1; Ezek 29:3; Amos 9:3). None of the Old Testament references identifies the "dragon" as red (cf. *Testament of Abraham* 17:14; 19:7-8). Similarly, nowhere in the Old Testament is this sea serpent/monster identified as the "serpent" (*nhs*; LXX: *ophis*, as in Rev 12:9; 14:15; 20:2) in the Garden of Eden (Gen 3:1-5).

John identifies the dragon further (note that this is John's comment; it is not revealed to him) in 12:9: he is "that ancient serpent, who is called the Devil and Satan." John will use a similar expression in 20:2. "Serpent" is probably an allusion to the serpent that deceived Eve in the Garden of Eden (Gen 3:1-5). For "Satan" and "the Devil," see on 2:9-10. Wis 2:24 speaks of the Devil in a way that ties him implicitly to the fall of Adam and Eve. The connection is made more clear in the *Apocalypse of Moses* 16:1-5, where Satan convinces the serpent to tempt Eve, and in the *Life of Adam and Eve* 33:3, where the Devil tempts Eve directly (cf. *1 Enoch* 69:6; *3 Baruch* 9:7). John uses "serpent" elsewhere in 12:14, 15; 20:2; "devil" again in 2:10; 12:12; and 20:2, 10; and "Satan" in 2:9, 13 (twice), 24; 3:9; and 20:2, 7.

John provides other details about the dragon. He has "seven heads and ten horns, and seven diadems upon his heads" (12:3). Beasts with extra appendages are not unusual in Jewish literature from the late Old Testament period through the first century AD. Daniel's third beast, for example, has four wings and four heads, and his fourth beast has ten horns (Dan 7:6-7, 20, 24; cf. *Sibylline Oracles* 3.397; *Testament of Naphtali* 5:6; *4 Ezra* 11:1). The diadem was a symbol of royalty. "Diadem" is used in Revelation initially in connection with the dragon, who has seven diadems, and the beast, who has ten (13:1); the rider on the white horse will wear *many* diadems (19:12). The seven diadems correspond to the seven heads (one diadem per head) of the dragon. The use of the number seven is probably intended to suggest the completeness of authority the dragon claims to possess. Ten horns, however, do not work well with seven heads. This is a clear indication that the numbers are not to be pressed literally; indeed, the reference to "ten horns" is drawn from the description of the beast in Dan 7:7, 20, 24. As noted previously, "horns" denote power (see on 5:6).

In addition, John observes that the dragon's tail "swept down a third of the stars of heaven, and cast them to the earth" (12:4). The reference to one third is probably intended as an indication of the constraints within which the dragon acts (cf. 8:7, 9, 11, 12, 15, 18). Any suggestion that John is speaking of fallen angels misses the clear allusion to Dan 8:10: "It [the little horn] grew great, even to the host of heaven; and some of the host of the stars it cast down to the ground, and trampled upon them."

Finally, the dragon is said to be "the deceiver of the whole world" (12:9). The "whole world" is also found in 3:10, with reference to the hour of testing that is about to come upon the whole world, and in 16:14, where the demonic spirits go out into the whole world to gather the kings for war. Elsewhere "deceiving" is done by Jezebel (2:20), the second beast/false prophet (13:14; 19:20; cf. 16:13-14), and the ancient serpent/devil/Satan (20:3, 8, 10; cf. 16:13-14). How and when the dragon deceives the whole world John does not say at this point.

A relatively minor character in the first part of this section (12:1-6), though one around whom the action swirls, is the "male child" (12:5, 13) with whom the woman is pregnant. The dragon intends to "devour" him when the woman gives birth (12:4). John's use of "male" (*arsen*) in 12:5 is odd, since he attaches it to "son" (*huios*; RSV "child"). It is probably intended as an allusion to Isa 66:7 LXX: "Before she was in labor she gave birth/before her pain came upon her she was delivered of a son [*arsen*]" (cf. Isa 66:8). The child is characterized as one who is to rule all the nations with a rod of iron (12:5). The same task, which is based on Ps 2:9, is given by Jesus to the conqueror in 2:27. In 19:15 Jesus is described in the same terms. Surely it is Jesus who is meant here. That this passage is not a reference to the physical birth of Jesus is clear from three considerations. First, the woman is not Mary. Second, the "birth" is followed directly—and most oddly—by the "ascension." Third, John nowhere else shows any interest in the birth of Jesus. Rather, that Jesus is "caught up to God and to his throne" (12:5) directs the reader to the first occasion in the book where Jesus is connected with the throne of God—i.e., when John sees the Lamb of God, looking as though it had been slain, standing between the throne and the four living creatures (5:6). Indeed, the focus throughout the book has been on Jesus' death, not birth, and so it follows that the confrontation between the woman and dragon must refer to the death and resurrection, rather than the birth and ascension, of Jesus.

An important character in the second part of this section (12:7-10), and one who is found only here in the book, is Michael (12:7). Michael is a major angelic figure in Second Temple Judaism. In Daniel he is identified as "one of the chief princes" (Dan 10:13)—specifically, the "prince" who contends on behalf of Israel (Dan 10:21; 12:1). In some writings he is listed among the four (e.g., *1 Enoch* 9:1; 40:9; *Apocalypse of Moses* 40:3; *Sibylline Oracles* 2:215) or the seven (e.g., *1 Enoch* 20:1-7; Tob 12:15) archangels. Elsewhere he is simply called an archangel (e.g., *3 Baruch* 11:8; *4 Baruch* 9:5; *Testament of Abraham* 1:4; *Life of Adam and Eve* 22:1; Jude 9) or "commander-in-chief" (e.g., *3 Baruch* 11:4; *Testament of Abraham* 1:4). In the Dead Sea Scrolls Michael seems to have been viewed as an angel who battles on behalf of his people against the forces of evil led by Belial—i.e., Satan (e.g., 1QM 17:6-8; 11QMelch[11Q13] 9-15). In an apparent reference to the lost ending of the *Testament of Moses*, Jude speaks of Michael rebuking the devil in a dispute over the body of Moses (Jude 9). The modern reader's surprise at finding Michael mentioned at all is perhaps surpassed only by the utter astonishment that it is Michael, and not Jesus, who wins the war in heaven! But, as John will make clear, Jesus is not, in fact, absent from the war. Moreover, the presence of Michael is precisely what one would expect from a writer who is indebted to Dan 12:1. The passage needs to be quoted in full: "At that time shall arise Michael, the great prince who has charge of your people. And there shall be a time of trouble, such as never has been since there was a nation till that time; but at that time your people shall be delivered, every one whose name shall be found written in the book." It is John's belief that the "time of trouble" predicted by Daniel is precisely that from which he and his readers, along with the rest of the Great Multitude, are to be delivered by the blood of the Lamb, who has taken possession of the book of life. Thus, it is only natural that Michael should have a role to play.

Finally, there is a brief mention at the end of the fourth section (12:13-17) of "the rest" of the woman's offspring (12:17). John further describes these as "those who keep the commandments of God and the testimony of Jesus" (12:17)—i.e., the Church. The reader will encounter those who keep the commandments of God (and the faith of Jesus) again in 14:12.

In terms of action, sections one (12:1-6) and four (12:13-17) constitute two parts to the same story. The dragon takes his stand before the laboring woman in order to consume her child when it is born (12:4). The woman gives birth to a male child (12:5), who is caught up to God and to his throne before the dragon can act (12:5). The woman then flees into the wilderness (12:6), pursued by the dragon (12:13), but God comes to her rescue by giving her the two wings of a great eagle (12:14). That the serpent's attempt to sweep the woman away in a flood by pouring water out of his "mouth" like a river (12:15) is incongruous with trying to stop a *flying* eagle demonstrates that the details of the story are not to be pressed literally. But the serpent's action is noteworthy on two counts. First, it is consistent with other "weapons" coming out of the mouths of characters in the book (the sharp, two-edged sword coming out of the mouth of Jesus [1:16; cf. 1:12; 19:15, 21]; fire, smoke, and sulfur issuing from the mouths of the horses at the sixth trumpet [9:17-18]; fire from the mouths of the two witnesses [11:5]; three foul spirits like frogs coming out of the mouths of the dragon, the beast, and the false prophet [16:13]). Second, in a moment of delicious irony the earth comes to the help of the woman by opening *its* "mouth" and swallowing the river that the dragon had poured out of *its* mouth (12:16). (For the earth opening for the opposite purpose (judgment), see Num 16:30-33 [cf. Deut 11:6].) Angry that the woman has escaped, the dragon goes off to make war with the rest of her offspring (12:17; cf. Gen 3:15). The dragon's intention to "make war" on the woman's offspring reminds the reader of the beast "making war" on the two witnesses in 11:7. The dragon takes his stand on the sand of the sea (12:18), presumably in preparation for his war with the rest of the offspring of the woman.

A different sort of action is found in the second section of the chapter (12:7-9). The scene is no longer the earth, but heaven. With a repetition of language John observes that "war" (*polemos*) arises in heaven, with Michael and his angels "making war" (*polemeo*; RSV "fighting") with the dragon; the dragon and his angels "make war" (*polemeo*; RSV "fought") in return (12:7). This is nothing if not a war! Yet for all of the "war" terminology the reader is reminded of how such terminology is not to be pressed literally in this book (see on 2:16 and 11:7). This section is the only place in the book that mentions the dragon's "angels." Presumably they are included here to counterbalance Michael's angels. Michael apparently initiates the war. Details of the war are not mentioned, but the result is that the dragon and his angels are defeated, and there is no longer "any place for them in heaven" (12:8). So the dragon is "thrown down": he is "thrown down" to the earth and his angels are "thrown down" with him (12:9; cf. Isa 14:12 [referring to the king of Babylon]; Ezek 28:16-17 [referring to the king of Tyre]). Parallel to the triple reference to "war" in 12:7 is the triple reference to being "thrown down" in 12:9: the certainty of a war in heaven is matched by the certainty of the dragon being thrown down from heaven. Yet the reader notes that if "war" is not to be taken literally here, then neither should "thrown down." The notion that this passage describes the primeval fall of Satan—a story that, contrary to what many people assume, is not found in the Old

Testament and, moreover, is of no interest to John elsewhere in the book—misses the point completely. Something else is going on here.

The third section of chapter 12 consists of a commentary provided by a loud voice in heaven (12:10). There are three parts to the loud voice's commentary: a statement of the present state of affairs (12:10), of what caused it (12:10-11), and of its implications (12:12). The present state is that "now the salvation and the power and the kingdom of our God and the authority of his Christ has come" (12:10). This statement bears a striking similarity to the proclamation (by loud voices in heaven) in 11:15. The reference to "salvation" is also reminiscent of the doxology in 7:10 ("Salvation be to our God who sits upon the throne and to the Lamb"; cf. the song of praise in 19:1). "Power" is given in praise to God in 4:11; 7:12; and 19:1, and to the Lamb in 5:12. Although this is the first time "authority" has been explicitly attributed to Christ in the book, it has been implied previously (e.g., in 5:7 the Lamb takes the sealed scroll and in 6:1 he begins to break the seals).

What has brought about this current state of affairs? The answer is that "the accuser of our brethren has been thrown down" (12:10). The verb connects this affirmation with 12:9, where the dragon was thrown down from heaven; hence, it is the throwing down of the dragon from heaven that has brought about the coming of the salvation, power, kingdom, and authority. The reference to "our" brothers is striking. The only previous use of the plural "brethren" in the book is in 6:11, where "those who had been slain" had been told "to rest a little longer, until the number of their fellow servants and their brethren should be complete, who were to be killed as they themselves had been." Is the loud voice coming from "those who had been slain"?

The accuser is further described as the one "who accuses them day and night before our God" (12:10). This is the only use of the noun "accuser" and the verb "accuse" in Revelation, though, as has been noted, "accusing" is precisely the task of Satan. Two things have happened to the accuser. First, he has been "thrown down" (from heaven). Second, "our brethren" have "conquered him" (12:11). Given the promise to the conqueror in each of the letters to the seven churches (2:7, 11, 17, 26; 3:5, 12, 21), the verb here can hardly be accidental. The reader is finally given the answer to the question that continually arises out of the seven letters: who (or what) does the conqueror conquer? *The conqueror conquers the accuser.* The conquerors are said to have conquered in two ways. First, they have conquered "by the blood of the Lamb" (12:11). "The blood of the Lamb" is also used in 7:14 (cf. 1:5; 5:9) with respect to the manner in which those who make up the Great Multitude have washed their robes and made them white. Second, the conquerors have conquered "by the word of their testimony" (12:11). John has previously said that he was on the island of Patmos on account of the word of God and the testimony of Jesus (1:9), "those who had been slain" are said to have been slain on account of the word of God and the testimony they held (6:9; RSV "witness"), and John observes concerning the two witnesses that they finished their testimony (11:7). There will be further references to those who bear the testimony of Jesus (12:17; 19:10 [twice]; cf. 20:4). The loud voice adds one final observation about the conquerors: "they loved not their lives [*psuche*] even unto death" (12:11). John's use of *psuche* once again connects this passage to the fifth seal (6:9: "the souls [*psuche*] of those who had been slain"; cf. 20:4). Is this an indication that conquering is reserved for martyrs? The seven letters hardly give that impression. Rather, John seems to be developing the notion that "martyr" terminology can be applied to the entire Church (see on 11:7).

Finally, the loud voice gives the implications of what has taken place. On the one hand, heaven and those "that dwell therein" are urged to rejoice (12:12; cf. Ps 96:11; Isa 44:23; 49:13). In 18:20 heaven, along with the saints and apostles and prophets, will again be invited to rejoice, this time over God's judgment of the great city. In 13:6 the beast will be said to blaspheme those who dwell in heaven. On the other hand, the loud voice pronounces woe (cf. 8:13; 9:12 [twice]; 11:14 [twice]; 18:10, 16, 19) to the earth and the sea (12:12). The earth and the sea are paired in 7:1-3 (along with every tree); 10:2, 5, 6, 8; and 14:7 (along with the sky and the fountains of water). The reason for the woe is that "the devil has come down to you" (12:12), a clear reference to the aftermath of the war in heaven (12:9). This solidifies the connection of section three (12:10-12) with section two (12:7-9). But now something new is added: the devil is "in great wrath, because he knows that his time is short" (12:12).

At first glance, the reader might be tempted to make a separation between the first and fourth sections, which are connected by the motif of the dragon opposing the woman, and the second and third, which describe and comment upon a war in heaven. But to make such a separation is to miss the fact that all four sections of chapter 12 function as a unified whole. For one thing, one character—the dragon/devil/serpent—is found in all four sections (12:3-4; 12:7, 9; 12:10-12; 12:13-17). But perhaps even more telling is that the reference to the dragon seeing that he had been thrown down to the earth in 12:13 inextricably cements the fourth section (the dragon's pursuit of the woman) with the second/third (the war in heaven/commentary). Indeed, the devil's/dragon's "great wrath" in 12:13 (third section) anticipates his "anger" in 12:17 (fourth section). To put it another way, 12:13 does *not* follow naturally upon 12:6. In fact, it makes no sense apart from 12:7-12.

Once the reader realizes this fact, the whole chapter comes together as a single story. 12:1-6 and 12:13-17 tell the story from the perspective of earth and 12:7-9 from the perspective of heaven, with 12:10-12 providing the commentary that ties everything together. The dragon—Satan, the "accuser"—stands ready to accuse sinners before God in heaven. It is the Lamb's task to silence the accuser. He accomplishes this through his death, which, however, is nothing without the resurrection (cf. 1:18; 5:6). The dragon, eagerly hoping to devour the dead Lamb so as to retain his role as accuser, is stunned to see the Lamb resurrected, which ends the dragon's role as accuser, thus forcing him out of heaven to earth. Enraged at the loss of his privileged position, the dragon decides to take revenge on the Lamb's followers on earth. Though he will "make war" on them, the Lamb's followers have already conquered him through the blood of the Lamb and through their testimony. Moreover, his time is short—"1,260 days." Dare the reader wonder at this point whether the "war" the dragon will wage against the followers of the Lamb will, in fact, be waged primarily by means of the very privilege of which he has been stripped by the Lamb—i.e., that of accusation?

"I saw a beast rising out of the sea":
The dragon's revenge
Revelation 13:1-18

Chapter 13 continues the vision of chapter 12. In 12:18 the dragon is standing on the sand of the sea, and in 13:1 John sees a beast rise out of the sea. The reader should note that chapter 13 is *not* cast in the future tense— i.e., as a prediction. It is a narrative of John's continuing vision told generally in the past (aorist) tense, though, as in 11:3-13, sometimes with varying tenses. 13:1-18 consists primarily of two visions: a first beast (previously introduced briefly in 11:7) that the world worships (13:1-8), and a second beast (heretofore unmentioned) that promotes the worship of the first beast (13:11-17). Each vision is followed by a brief exhortation (13:9-10 and 13:18).

13:1-18 focuses on the interaction among five characters/character groups: the first beast, the dragon, "the whole earth," "the saints," and the second beast. The first beast receives the most attention in John's narrative. John's description of the first beast draws heavily upon Daniel's vision of the four beasts in Dan 7. As with the four beasts in Daniel, John sees "a beast [*therion*] rising [*anabaino*] out of the sea" (13:1; Dan 7:3; cf. Isa 27:1). The language is similar to 11:7, which speaks of a beast rising (*anabaino*; RSV "that ascends") out of the Abyss. The natural inference is that this is the same beast, which will be confirmed in 13:7. *Therion* is a generic term for any kind of wild animal or beast, especially (but not always—cf. Acts 28:3-5) of the four-legged variety (cf. 6:8).

Like Daniel's fourth beast, the beast has "ten horns" (13:1; Dan 7:7, 20, 24). The further mention of "seven heads" (13:1) reminds the reader of the dragon in 12:3, which also has ten horns and seven heads and is reminiscent of Daniel's third beast, which has four heads (Dan 7:6). The beast also has "ten diadems" (13:1). The dragon, by contrast, has seven diadems (12:3). The difference in number is probably due to John's heavy dependence on Dan 7 in this section: the ten horns of Daniel's fourth beast are associated with ten kingdoms (Dan 7:24). John will elaborate on the beast's apparent "royal" authority, in conjunction with the dragon, in 13:2, 4, and 7, and he will return to the "seven heads and ten horns" in chapter 17 (17:3, 7, 9-10, 12, 16).

The placement of the diadems on the horns (13:1) rather than the heads, as with the dragon (12:3), supplies a grotesquely comic element to the picture and frees up the beasts' heads for something that is not found in the description of the dragon: it has "blasphemous names [RSV singular, with Codex Sinaiticus] upon its heads" (13:1). John returns to this motif in 13:5-6, where he says the beast "was given a mouth to utter haughty and blasphemous words" and "opened its mouth to utter blasphemies against God, blaspheming his name [cf. 16:9; see on 3:12] and his dwelling, that is, those who dwell in heaven [cf. 12:12]." Obviously this characteristic of the beast is important to John. The noun (*blasphemia*) and verb (*blasphemeo*) forms of "blasphemy" are found nine times in the book, four of them in these verses. Elsewhere the verb will be found three times in connection with the seven bowls (16:9, 11, 21; RSV "cursed"). The noun form, used with the sense of "slander" in 2:9, will be found again in 17:3 ("blasphemous names"; cf. 13:1). "Blasphemy" carries the connotation of speaking against someone (e.g., Matt 27:39-40; Mark 3:29; Luke 23:39), including the "name" of God (e.g., Isa 52:5; Rom 2:24; 1 Tim 1:6; Jas 2:7). Again, John is drawing upon Daniel: the fourth beast "shall speak words against the Most High" (Dan 7:25; cf. Dan 7:8, 11). Similarly, the "contemptible" (Dan 11:21) king "shall exalt himself and magnify himself above every god, and shall speak aston-ishing things against the God of gods" (Dan 11:36).

John's observation that the beast "was like a leopard, its feet were like a bear's, and its mouth was like a lion's mouth" (13:2) combines elements from the first four beasts in Daniel's vision. The first is "like a lion" (Dan 7:4), the second is "like a bear" (Dan 7:5), and the third is "like a leopard" (Dan 7:6), and while Daniel says nothing about a mouth "like a lion's," he does pay close attention to the mouth of the fourth beast (Dan 7:7-8). The importance of what John is doing here cannot be overstated. As in the case of the four living creatures (see on 4:7-8), John is not simply assembling Old Testament passages in a wooden manner so as to fit his own visions into a larger picture alongside those passages; he is *transforming* those passages into something fresh. John's "revelation" stands on its own.

John provides a final detail about the beast in 13:3: "one of its heads seemed to have a mortal wound, but its mortal wound was healed." This is the only detail that has no parallel in Dan 7. John returns to it twice more in his section on the second beast. In 13:12 he speaks of "the first beast, whose mortal wound was healed," and in 13:14 he mentions "the beast which was wounded by the sword and yet lived." There is no reason to press the reference to the "sword," since a sword would be a normal weapon for killing someone. Obviously the beast having a mortal would that was healed is important to John.

Following the focus on the story of the dragon in chapter 12, the reader might expect the dragon to play the central role in what follows; he has, after all, decided to make war on the rest of the woman's offspring (12:17). Rather, the reader learns that the dragon opts for a behind-the-scenes role in his quest for revenge. Hence, he is mentioned only twice in chapter 13. But his role is crucial: he gives the beast "his power and his throne and great authority" (13:2). John mentions this act again in an abbreviated form in 13:4: "for he [the dragon] had given his authority to the beast" (cf. 13:7: "authority was given [divine passive?] to it [the beast] over every tribe and people and tongue and nation" [for these groups see on 10:11]). John has previously mentioned the "throne" of Satan as being in Pergamum (2:13). While all of these elements in 13:2 are implied in the description of the dragon in 12:3, the reader knows that they are a sham. *True* power and throne and authority belong to God and Christ (12:10; cf. 5:13; 7:12; 11:15). As for the dragon, he has suffered a decisive defeat (12:7-8); he has been "thrown down" from heaven (12:9, 13)!

But enter the third character/character group in this chapter: "the whole earth" (13:3). They do not know what the reader knows. Although John mentions "the whole earth" only here in the book (cf. 3:10), he speaks again of "the earth" in the sense of people in 13:12. John will use several other designations for this group in this chapter: "all who dwell upon the earth" (13:8, 14 [without "all"]; see on 3:10), "every one whose name has not been written before the foundation of the world in the book of life of the Lamb that was slain" (13:8; see on 3:5), "its [the earth's] inhabitants" (13:12), and "all, both small and great [cf. 11:8, 19:5, 18; 20:12], both rich [cf. 6:15] and poor [the plural only here in the book], both free and slave" (13:17; cf. 6:15; 19:18). This group is taken in by the dragon's scheme. They follow the beast "with wonder" (13:3; cf. 17:8); they worship the dragon (13:4); they worship the beast (13:4, 8, 12); they ask, "Who is like the beast, and who can fight against it?" (13:4; cf. 18:18; Exod 15:11; Ps 89:8); they are deceived by the second beast (13:14; cf. *1 Enoch* 54:6); and they are marked "on the right hand or on the forehead" (13:16).

But the beast's authority over the whole world is not enough; its bene-factor, the dragon, seeks revenge on the rest of the woman's offspring (12:17). Thus, the beast makes war on the saints—the fourth character/char-acter group in the chapter—and conquers them (13:7). John has previously mentioned the prayers of the saints (5:8; 8:3, 4) and has spoken of the saints as those who are to receive a reward (11:18). He will also set forth an exhor-tation for the endurance and faith of the saints (13:10; cf. 14:12), speak of the blood of the saints (16:6; 17:6; 18:24), enjoin the saints to rejoice (18:20), speak of the righteous deeds of the saints (19:8), speak of the nations that are at the four corners of the earth surrounding the camp of the saints (20:9), and pronounce a benediction over the saints (22:21). That the beast makes war on the saints and conquers them reminds the reader of 11:7, where the beast makes war upon the two witnesses, conquers them, and kills them. Once again John is drawing upon the language and imagery of Dan 7: "this horn [of the fourth beast] made war with the saints, and prevailed over them" (Dan 7:21). John continues this theme in his description of the second beast. It causes those "who would not worship the image of the [first] beast to be slain" (13:15). Somewhat paradoxically, it causes people to be marked on the right hand or on the forehead "so that no one can buy or sell unless he has the mark" (13:16-17). This latter passage is telling. It is hard to imagine anyone worshiping the beast but refusing to be marked. So who would remain, after those who refuse to worship have been killed, to be prevented from buying or selling? The point, of course, is that the language is not to be pressed literally. This is yet another indication that while martyr language is used throughout the book, literal martyrdom is not its focus. But why speak of buying and selling here? Could it be that this is, in fact, a live issue for John's readers? We will return to this possibility after looking at the role of the fifth character in chapter 13: the second beast.

The second beast is described in terms of three characteristics and eight activities. As for characteristics, it "rose out of the earth," "had two horns like a lamb [or "ram"—see on 5:6]," and "spoke like a dragon" (13:11). The first is reminiscent of the first beast, who rose out of the sea (13:1). The second, reminding the reader of the centrality of the Lamb in the book, draws upon the language of Dan 8:3: "I raised my eyes and saw, and behold, a ram standing on the bank of the river. It had two horns." The third connects the second beast with the character who ties chapters 12 and 13 together: the dragon.

The eight activities of the second beast are all carried out in connection with—and sometimes in the presence of (13:12, 14)—"the first beast" (13:12). It "exercises all of the authority of the first beast" (13:13; cf. 13:2, 4, 5, 7), "makes the earth and its inhabitants worship the first beast" (13:12; cf. 13:4, 8), "works great signs" (13:13; cf. 16:14; 19:20), "deceives those who dwell on earth" by the signs (13:14; cf. 19:20; *Sibylline Oracles* 3.363-74), bids them "to make an image for the beast" (13:14), gives "breath to the image of the beast" (13:15), causes "those who would not worship the image of the beast to be slain" (13:15), and causes all "to be marked on the right hand or the forehead" (13:17).

Working signs is to be expected from one who will later be called "the false prophet" (16:13; 19:20; 20:10). Deuteronomy warns of false prophets who give "a sign or a wonder" and then say, "Let us go after other gods" (Deut 13:1-3). John understands the "great signs" in terms of making fire come down from heaven to earth (cf. 20:9) in the sight of men (13:13; cf. 1 Kgs 18:38; 2 Kgs 1:10, 12). Others in the book who "deceive" are Jezebel (2:20), Satan (12:9; 20:3, 8, 10), and Babylon (18:23). "Image," introduced here in the book, is found ten times in Revelation, always in connection with the beast (13:14, 15 [three times]; 14:9, 11; 15:2; 16:2; 19:20; 20:4). An "image" (*eikon*) was a cult statue set up to promote the worship of a god or of a deified emperor (cf. Dan 3:1 LXX: *eikon*). The idea that such statues could be animated through magical rituals was common in the ancient world (see the extensive evidence gathered by D. Aune, *Revelation*, 3 vols., Word Biblical Commentaries [Dallas: Word, 1997–1999]: 52B.762-64). Killing all who refuse to worship the image of the first beast is reminiscent of Dan 3:1-18. The mention of a "mark" is the first such reference in the book; the word will occur six more times, always in connection with the beast (13:17; 14:9, 11; 16:2; 19:20; 20:4). Having a mark on both the hand and the forehead will be found again only in 14:9 (cf. *Apocalypse of Elijah* 1:9). The great harlot will also have a name written on her forehead (17:5). The Old Testament speaks of marking on both the hand (Isa 44:5) and the forehead (Ezek 9:4). The practice of branding on the forehead was sometimes done to prisoners of war (e.g., Plutarch, *Pericles* 26) or to loyal followers of a god (e.g., Lucian, *De Syria Dea* 59). It marked the individual as belonging—either voluntarily or involuntarily—to someone else, as the marking here ties those marked to the beast. In addition, the mark prohibits those who do not have it from buying or selling (3:17). There is no precise parallel in the ancient world to this latter function of marking. Perhaps it has some association with trade guilds. It is worth repeating that the longest of the letters to the seven churches is written to the church at Thyatira, a city noteworthy for its large number of trade guilds and the home of the (false) "prophet" Jezebel. John identifies the mark as the name of the beast or the number of its name (13:17; cf. 15:2). From signet rings to stamps bearing the name of the emperor on deeds of sale, there are numerous ancient parallels to a mark as someone's name. The same cannot be said for a mark as the *number* of someone's name (see further below).

Each of the two visions in this section (of the first beast and of the second beast) is followed by a word of exhortation, presumably from John. The first exhortation—"If any one has an ear, let him hear" (13:9)—is reminiscent of, though not identical in form to, the exhortation at the end of each of the letters to the seven churches. Drawing upon the language of Jer 15:2 (cf. Jer 43:11), this exhortation affirms the inevitability of captivity and death by the sword (13:10). The exhortation concludes with a call "for the endurance [cf. 1:9; 2:2, 3, 19; 3:10] and faith [2:13, 19; 14:12] of the saints" (13:10). Almost the same expression (without faith) will be found in 14:12. This is the first of four *hode* ("Here is a call for . . .") statements to the reader (cf. 13:18; 14:12; 17:9). The first and the third such statements call for the endurance of the saints; the second and the fourth call for wisdom on the part of the reader. The exhortation drives home the seriousness of the first beast's assault on the Church (13:7), while at the same time laying out the appropriate response.

The second exhortation centers on the number of the beast. The challenge is for "wisdom" (cf. 17:9) to "calculate" the number (13:18). John gives two clues. The first is that it is "a human number," rather than a divine one (cf. 21:17): it can be calculated by a person. The second is that the number is 666 (13:18).

Probably nothing in Revelation has spawned a wider array of interpretations than 666 as the mark of the beast. The reader must keep two points in mind, both of which are often lost on modern interpreters. First, in Revelation the number is "six hundred sixty-six," *not* three sixes side by side. Second, as with everything else in the book, John expected *his readers* to make sense out of this number. But even keeping these two points in mind, it is not easy to grasp how John's readers would have understood the number.

A common approach to "calculating" 666 is to use gematria—a practice attested in John's day for assigning a number to a name. Each letter in a name is given a numerical equivalent based upon its position in the alphabet; the numbers are then added to produce the number of the name. Several early Christian fathers attempted to explain 666 by gematria, but there was no general agreement among them (e.g., Irenaeus, *Against Heresies* 5.30.3). A common scholarly interpretation of 666 is that it refers to the Emperor Nero. But the fact that this suggestion requires that the Greek form "Neron Caesar" be transliterated into Hebrew with a defective spelling, along with the fact that John wrote in Greek to readers who probably could not read Hebrew in the first place, renders this interpretation doubtful. Given the symbolic use of numbers throughout the book, however, perhaps this one is intended symbolically as well. Seven is the number of completeness throughout Revelation; perhaps six is intended to suggest incompleteness. But why six hundred sixty-six? The Christian editor of *Sibylline Oracles*, Book 1, observed that the number of the name "Jesus" (*Iēsous*) is 888 (I = 10, $\bar{e}$ = 8, s = 200, o = 70, u = 400, s = 200; *Sibylline Oracles* 1.324-29). Perhaps the idea is that 666 falls short of 888.

How would John's readers in the seven churches of Asia have understood the two beasts? As noted in the Introduction, the cult of emperor worship was especially strong in the province of Asia. Two of the seven cites to which John writes—Pergamum and Smyrna—were permitted to build temples devoted to the worship of the emperor prior to the time of Domitian; no other province had more than one. During Domitian's reign, the provincial council of Asia, made up of members of wealthy families from the various cities and towns of the province, was successful in receiving permission to construct a third temple. This temple, built in honor of the Flavian emperors—Domitian's father Vespasian, Domitian's brother Titus, and Domitian himself—was in Ephesus. There is little doubt that the Asian Christians would have understood the first beast in terms of the imperial cult—not so much Domitian himself as the institution of the emperor as representative of Rome. After all (slightly altering the words of those who worship the beast), "Who is like Rome, and who can fight against it?" Rome ruled the world. It was to be admired, feared, and worshiped by all. To John's readers, then, the second beast would represent all who promoted the imperial cult, such as the provincial council and the local imperial priesthood.

Archaeological evidence suggests that the temple in Ephesus served as a unifying force for the city of Ephesus and indeed throughout the entire province. Anyone who refused to participate in the cult would, at a minimum, be looked on with deep suspicion by his neighbors. Perhaps there were potential economic—and physical—consequences as well. The pressure upon Christians to participate in the imperial cult would be enormous.

But John's visions of the two beasts must be seen not only in the context of first century Asia, but also in the context of the rest of the book. One of the most striking features of chapter 13 is the similarities between the first beast and the Lamb. The first beast has ten horns and seven heads (13:1); the Lamb has seven horns and seven eyes (5:6). The first beast receives a throne and authority from the dragon (13:2); the Lamb takes the scroll from one seated upon a different throne (5:7; cf. 2:27) and comes to share that throne with the one seated upon it (7:9-12; 11:15-16). The first beast has a mortal wound that was healed (13:2, 12, 14), and it "lived" (13:14: *zao*); the Lamb was slain but stood again (5:6; cf. 5:9; 13:18): it died and "lived" (1:18 and 2:8: *zao*). Men worship the dragon and the first beast (13:4, 8); all of creation worships the one seated upon the throne and the Lamb (5:13-14). The first beast reigns for forty-two months (13:5); the Lamb reigns for ever and ever (11:15). The first beast has authority over every tribe and people and tongue and nation (13:7); the Lamb has ransomed people from every tribe and tongue and people and nation (5:9).

Similar, though not as extensive, are the parallels between the dragon and God. The dragon has a throne (13:2); God has a throne (e.g., 4:2-5, 9-10; 5:1, 7). The dragon gives his throne and authority to the first beast (13:2); God permits the Lamb to take the scroll from his hand (5:5:7; cf. 2:27) and shares his throne with the Lamb (7:9-12; 11:15-16). The dragon is worshiped alongside the first beast (13:4); God is worshiped alongside the Lamb (5:13-14). One might also note the that the first beast has a "name" (13:17), as does God (e.g., 3:12; 13:6).

But if the dragon corresponds in some sense to God and the first beast to the Lamb, then what of the second beast? Does it correspond to the Holy Spirit in some sort of "Unholy Trinity"? The reader must be careful not to read trinitarian theology into this chapter. It is clear that the second beast corresponds not to the Holy Spirit, but to the two witnesses. The duration of the reign of the first beast, and, hence, of the activity of the second beast, is 42 months (13:5); the duration of the activity of the two witnesses is 1,260 days = 42 months (11:3). The second beast does miracles (13:13, 15); the two witnesses do miracles (11:5-6). Specifically, the second beast makes fire come down from heaven (13:13); the two witnesses make fire come out of their mouths (11:5). The second beast causes the image of the first beast to speak (13:15); the two witnesses speak (prophesy) for God (11:3, 6). The second beast causes those who refuse to worship the first beast to be slain (13:15); the two witnesses kill their foes (11:5). Finally, the second beast will later be called the false prophet (16:13; 19:20); the two witnesses are called prophets (11:10).

Putting it all together, the reader recognizes that the dragon, the first beast, and the second beast are but cheap imitations of God, the Lamb, and the Church. It is God and the Lamb who are worthy of worship, not the dragon and the first beast. It is the Lamb who has truly died and come back to life, not the first beast. "Who is like the beast?" Why, he cannot even look into God's scroll, much less open it! But the Lamb . . . *he* can take it *and* open it. It is the reign of God and the Lamb, lasting for ever and ever, that is the authentic reign, not the first beast's reign that lasts for a mere 42 months. As the second beast pretends to be associated with the Lamb by having "two horns like a lamb" (13:11)—a paltry imitation of the Lamb's seven horns (5:6), it is the Church that is truly associated with him through his death (1:5; 5:9; 7:14; 12:11; cf. 2:26). And while God "seals" his servants on their foreheads (7:3-4; cf. 9:4; 14:1; 22:4), the second beast crudely "marks" his (13:15).

If all of this is but a cheap imitation of the real thing, John has carefully prepared the reader to understand why. The dragon has lost his position as accuser; he has been defeated by the blood of the Lamb. And he is now furious and desires revenge on the followers of the Lamb. So he props up an object of worship—a beast—as a rival to the Lamb. People will worship the beast because they refuse to repent of worshiping demons and idols anyway (9:20); they will willingly take his mark. The dragon will take revenge by uttering blasphemies against God, making war on the saints and conquering them, putting to death those who will not worship the image of the beast, preventing them from buying or selling without the mark of the beast. This is indeed the time of the trampling of the holy city (11:2), of the woman being nourished in the wilderness (12: 6, 14). It is the time in which the dragon has deceived the whole world (12:9) into worshiping the wrong god.

But the dragon is not in control. The dragon will indeed succeed in deceiving people, but only those whose names have *not* been written before the foundation of the world (on this expression see on 17:8) in the book of life (cf. 3:5; 20:12, 15; 21:27) of the Lamb that was slain (13:8), the Lamb who by virtue of that death received that book directly from the hand of the one seated upon the throne (5:7, 9-10). The first beast is "allowed" (divine passive) to make war on the saints, and the second beast is "allowed" (divine passive) to do signs to deceive those who dwell on earth and to give breath to the image of the first beast, but it is God who grants them the permission to do so. This is rather the time of the message of judgment against the world (10:11; 11:5-7), a message contained on a little scroll held by an angel who stands on both the sea, from which the first beast arises, *and* the land, from which the second beast arises (10:2, 5), thereby showing that the beasts are not in control of either.

And so there remains one question: Who is able to make war with the beast (13:4)? This question picks up the dragon's plan to make war with the rest of the woman's seed (12:17), as well as the description of the beast in 11:7 as making war with the two witnesses. The reader knows there is an answer, but she must wait a little longer for it.

"Here is a call for the endurance of the saints": Whom will you worship?
Revelation 14:1-20

John's visions of the first two signs in heaven (12:1–13:18) are not the most uplifting for his readers. True, the dragon has been thrown down from heaven. But he still takes revenge on the offspring of the woman; indeed, what the dragon and its cohorts do to the saints in 13:1-18 is hardly reassuring. It is most appropriate, then, that John's next vision is once again of the Lamb, who has been curiously inactive since he opened the seventh seal (8:1). 14:1-20 consists primarily of a series of brief visions: John sees the Lamb and the 144,000 (14:1-5), sees and hears three flying angels with messages of judgment (14:6-11), hears a voice speaking to him (14:13), and witnesses two visions of harvest (14:14-16, 17-20). In the center of it all, between the three angels and the voice, John gives an exhortation to his readers (14:12).

Several of the details in the opening vision in this section take the reader back immediately to 7:1-17: the Lamb (14:1, 4; 7:9-10, 14, 17), the 144,000 (14:1, 3; 7:4-8) with names on their foreheads (14:1; cf. 7:3), the throne (14:3; 7:9, 11, 15), and the four living creatures and the elders (14:3; 7:11). Two details confirm the identification of the 144,000 with the Great Multitude (see on 7:9). First, in 14:3 the 144,000 sing a new song "before the throne," while in 7:9-10 it is the Great Multitude that praises God "before the throne." Second, the 144,00 are "ransomed" (RSV "redeemed") from the earth (14:3; 14:5: "from mankind"), just as men from every tribe and tongue and people and nation—precisely the group that comprises the Great Multitude (7:9)—are "ransomed" (5:9). Finally, comparing the voice from heaven to the sound of many waters (14:2) recalls 1:15 (cf. 19:6), and comparing it to the sound of great thunder (14:2) recalls 6:1 (cf. 19:6), the sound of harps (14:2) recalls 5:8 (cf. 15:2), and "redeemed" (lit., "ransomed"; 14:3, 4) recalls 5:9.

John sees the Lamb standing upon "Mount Zion" (14:1). This is the only reference to Mount Zion in the book. David took Jerusalem from the Jebusites by capturing the "stronghold of Zion," which he renamed the City of David (2 Sam 5:6-10). Solomon built the Temple on a hill directly north of the City of David (1 Kgs 8:1-6). Hence, the site of the Temple, along with Jerusalem itself, came to be known as "Mount Zion" (e.g., Pss 48:2; 74:2; 78:68-69; Isa 8:18; 18:7; Lam 5:18; cf. Ps 2:6), or sometimes simply "Zion" (e.g., Ps 147:12; Isa 37:32; 62:1; Joel 3:17; Mic 3:12; 4:2). In the Old Testament the expression "Mount Zion" is identified further as a place that will experience future deliverance (Joel 2:32; Obad 17, 21) and blessing (Isa 4:2-6), to which gifts will be brought by foreigners (Isa 18:7), which God will defend (Isa 31:4-5), out of which will come a remnant of survivors (Isa 37:32), and to which exiles will come to be ruled by the Lord forever (Mic 4:6-7). John's choice of "Mount Zion," therefore, need not be pressed literally, as neither the references to the Lamb nor to the 144,000 are to be pressed literally; rather, it brings to the fore the rich Old Testament associations with future blessing.

That the 144,000 have "his [the Lamb's] name and his Father's name written upon their foreheads" (14:1) provides a stark contrast with those who follow the beast, who have the "mark" of his name upon their foreheads or right hands (13:16-17). Furthermore, it elaborates upon the "sealing" on the foreheads of the 144,000 in 7:3. In 3:12 Jesus promised the conquerors at Philadelphia that he would write upon them "the name of my God . . . and my own new name" (cf. 22:4). The writing of these names upon the foreheads of the conquerors/144,000 explains how they are sealed/protected by the Lamb.

John further characterizes the 144,000 in six ways. First, they sing "a new song" that they alone can learn (14:3). John will return to this song in 15:2-4. Second, they have been "redeemed" from the earth (14:3, 5). Third, they have not defiled (cf. 3:4: RSV "soiled") themselves with women, for they are chaste (14:4). As in 2:14, there is no reason to press the language literally here. Perhaps the 144,000 are to be contrasted with those who "commit adultery" with Jezebel (2:22). The image is drawn from the Old Testament provision that soldiers were to observe ritual cleanliness while serving in the army, which included sexual matters (Deut 23:9-10; 1 Sam 21:5; 2 Sam 11:8-11; cf. 1QM 7.3-6). For the 144,000 as an army, see on 7:4-8. Fourth, they follow the Lamb wherever he goes (14:4; cf. 19:14). Fifth, they were redeemed from mankind "as first fruits for God and the Lamb" (14:4). In the Old Testament the Israelites were commanded to bring the "first fruits" of the harvest as a offering to God (e.g., Exod 23:19; Lev

23:9-10; Num 28:26; Deut 26:1-2). The phrase could also be used metaphorically to describe Israel: "Israel was holy to the LORD/the first fruits of his harvest" (Jer 2:3; cf. Ezek 20:40-41). Clearly that is the sense here: the 144,000 (the totality of the true Israel) are the first fruits of God's harvest—i.e., they are offered to him. Although John speaks nowhere else in the book about "first fruits," the expression is quite appropriate here in anticipation of the two harvest scenes that are about to come (14:13-16, 17-20). Finally, John observes that in their mouths there is found no lie (cf. Ps 32:2; Isa 53:9; Zeph 3:13); they are blameless (14:5). The noun "lie" (*pseudos*) will be found again in 21:27 and 22:15. The verb form (*pseudomai*) occurs in 3:9, while "false prophet" (*pseudoprophetes*) is found in 16:13; 19:20; 20:10.

14:1-5 returns the reader to the 144,000/the Great Multitude/the conquerors. Despite all that the dragon may try to do, the Lamb has an army that is faithful to him; they do not take the mark of the beast on their foreheads. They belong to God and the Lamb, and they will be protected by the names of the Father and the Lamb.

At this point John sees three angels flying in midheaven (cf. 8:13; 19:17), one after another (14:6-12). The messages they bring direct the reader both backward and forward in the book.

There are several verbal connections between the activity of the first angel (14:6-7) and John's "second commission" (10:1-11): "proclaim" (*euaggelizo*: 14:6; 10:7 [RSV "announced"]); "proclaim *epi*" (RSV "to": 14:6, 6; cf. 10:11: "prophesy *epi*"); "nation and tribe and tongue and people" (14:6; cf. 10:11: omit "tribe"); "him who made heaven and earth, the sea and the fountains of waters" (14:7; cf. 10:6: omit "fountains of waters). On the combination heaven, earth, sea, and fountains of water, see also 7:17; 8:10; 16:4; 21:6. The angel proclaims the message of judgment that was also given to John.

The first angel (called "another [Codex Sinaiticus omits "another"] angel" by John) has "an eternal gospel" (14:6). The connections with 10:1-11 suggest that the "eternal gospel" is a message of judgment, which is confirmed by the next verse: "for the hour of his judgment has come" (14:7; cf. 6:17; 11:13; 18:10). Though the idea of the "gospel" (lit., "good news") as judgment might seem odd, Paul expresses a similar notion in 2 Cor 2:15-16: " For we are the aroma of Christ to God among those who are being saved and among those who are perishing, to one a fragrance from death to death, to the other a fragrance from life to life." John's combination in 14:6 of two expressions that he uses frequently—"those who dwell [here literally "sit"] upon the earth" and "every nation and tribe and tongue and people" (see on 6:10 and on 10:11)—underscores the universality of the proclamation. The proclamation is not without hope: those who hear it are called to "fear God and give him glory" and to "worship him" (14:7). The first suggests repentance (though see on 11:13). The second is the proper response to God (e.g, 4:8-11), as well as the *improper* response to the (first) beast (cf. 13:4, 8, 15).

The second angel also brings a message of judgment, this time of a specific nature: "Fallen, fallen, is Babylon the great" (14:8). The language echoes Isa 21:9 (cf. Jer 51:8). This is the first—but not the last—reference to "Babylon the great" in Revelation (cf. 16:19; 17:5; 18:2, 10, 21). The abrupt introduction of "Babylon the great" into the book, like the abrupt introduction of the beast in 11:7, serves to propel the reader forward. The latter tied the second "in the Spirit" experience with the next section of the book (the three signs in heaven), the former ties the section on the three signs in heaven with the next section (the third "in the Spirit" experience). Who is Babylon the great? What is its role in the story? What does it mean to say that it is "fallen"? Why has it fallen in the first place? The angel further characterizes Babylon the great as the one "who made all nations drink the wine of her impure passion" (14:8). The image is drawn from Jer 51:7: "Babylon was a golden cup in the LORD's hand, making all the earth drunken; the nations drank of her wine, therefore the nations went mad." The reference to "passion" (*porneia*) reminds the reader of the "immorality" (*porneia*) of Jezebel and those who commit adultery with her (2:20-22). For "nations" see on 10:11. Babylon's wine of her impure passion (see also 17:2 and 18:3, where the expression is repeated almost verbatim) will be contrasted soon with the wine of the fury of God's wrath (14:10; cf. 16:19; 19:15).

Like the second angel, the third brings a specific message of judgment, this time upon "any one who worships the beast and its image, and receives a mark on his forehead or his hand" (14:9; cf. 13:4, 8, 16-17). The same group is mentioned in 14:11: "these worshipers of the beast and its image, and whoever receives the mark of its name" (cf. 16:2; 19:20; 20:4). The language from chapter 13 has now become the language that depicts the "wrong" choice by humans—to worship the beast instead of God. Such a person "shall drink the wine of God's wrath" (14:10). Drinking from the cup of God's wrath is a common Old Testament image for receiving God's judgment (e.g., Ps 75:8; Isa 51:17, 22; Jer 25:15-17). Similar expressions will be found in 16:19 and 19:15 (cf. 14:19; 15:1, 7; and 16:1). The reader has already encountered references to the wrath of the Lamb (6:16), the great day of their (the one who sits upon the throne and the Lamb) wrath (6:17), and "your" (the one who sits upon the throne) wrath (11:18). Not to be missed is the deliciously ironic contrast with 14:8: those who have willingly drunk the wine of the impure passion of Babylon will find themselves (most unwillingly!) drinking the wine of God's wrath. Wine was typically mixed with water before drinking to dilute its potency. That the wine of God's wrath is "poured unmixed into the cup of his anger" (14:10) underscores the notion that God's wrath will be experienced in all of its strength.

Those who are to be punished "shall be tormented with fire and sulfur in the presence of the holy angels and in the presence of the Lamb" (14:10). Torment with fire and/or sulfur is another vivid Old Testament image (e.g., Gen 19:24; Ps 11:6; Isa 30:33; Ezek 38:22). The use of the verb "torment" directs the reader back to previous scenes of judgment (e.g., 9:5: locusts torment those who do not have the seal of God upon their foreheads; 11:10: the two witnesses/prophets torment those who dwell on the earth) and anticipates one final, climactic scene of judgment (20:10). See further on 11:10. Sulfur (always with fire) is found in connection with the locusts (9:17, 18) and the lake of fire (19:20; 20:10; 21:8). The "holy angels" are found only here in the book. The angel expresses the aftermath of their judgment vividly. First, the smoke of their torment goes up for ever and ever (14:11; cf. Isa 34:10). Second, there will be no rest day and night (14:11; cf. 14:13; 20:10) for the worshipers of the beast and its image and for those who receive the mark of its name. With this second, haunting reference to the mark of the beast (cf. 14:9), which brings this unit to a close, the horror begins to dawn upon the reader: those who took the mark of the beast upon themselves in order to buy and sell did not realize the mark would, in fact, identify them as those who were to receive the full judgment of God. *Psalms of Solomon* 15:9 expresses a similar thought: "They [the sinners] shall be overtaken as by those experienced in war/for on their forehead (is) the mark of destruction" (cf. *Psalms of Solomon* 15:6).

John follows the third angel's announcement with his third *hode* statement (14:12; see on 13:10). As in 13:10 there is a call for the "endurance" of "the saints." Here the saints are further characterized as "those who keep the commandments of God and the faith of Jesus." This forms an inclusion with 12:17, the only other place in the book where the commandments of God are mentioned, where the rest of the offspring of the woman were identified as "those who keep the commandments of God and the testimony of [RSV "and bear testimony to"] Jesus." That the saints and "the rest of the offspring of the woman" are to be equated with one another is not surprising. What is new is that the context of "keeping" (cf. 1:3) the commandments of God and the testimony/faith of Jesus is now made clear: the saints will be called upon to do this in the face of the activities of the two beasts. Any temptation to relax one's commitment to the Lamb and accommodate the beasts must be avoided, for those who follow the beast will suffer eternal torment. The reference to "the faith of Jesus" makes the reader realize that Jesus' praise of the church at Pergamum that they "did not deny my faith" even in the days of the martyr Antipas is not simply something from the past; keeping the faith of Jesus in the face of pressure to the contrary is an ongoing obligation for his followers.

John's call to endurance is followed by a voice from heaven telling John to write (14:13). John has previously been commanded to write to the seven churches (1:11, 19; 2:1, 8, 12, 18; 3:1, 7, 14) and been told not to write what the seven thunders said (10:4); he will be commanded again to write in 19:9 and 21:5. What he is directed to write here is the second of seven beatitudes in the book (1:3; 16:15; 19:9; 20:6; 22:7, 14): "Blessed are the dead who die in the Lord henceforth" (14:13). There has been a growing emphasis in the book on Christians who die or, better, are put to death (1:13; 6:9-11; 11:7-9; 12:11; 13:7, 10, 15); this theme will continue (16:6; 17:6; 18:24; 19:2; 20:4). Here, however, John does not explicitly speak of martyrdom. What is significant is that these people die "in the Lord"—i.e., as those who have kept the commandments of God and the faith of Jesus (14:12). At this point the Spirit voices his agreement (cf. 2:7; 22:17): "indeed" (*nai*; cf. 1:7 [RSV "Even so"]; 16:7 [RSV "Yea"]; 22:20 [RSV "Surely"]). He notes further that they will "rest from their labors [cf. 2:2], for their deeds follow [cf. 14:4] them." That the dead in the Lord will "rest" (cf. 6:11) forms a striking contrast to the plight of those who follow the beast, for whom there will be no rest (14:11). "Deeds" are found in a good sense in the book (2:2, 5, 19, 19, 15:3), as is the case here, in a bad sense (2:6, 22; 3:1; 9:20; 16:11; 18:6), in the neutral expression "I know your works" (3:1, 8, 15), and as a criterion for judgment (2:23; 20:12, 13; 22:12).

Having heard a message of judgment from the three flying angels, John now has a single vision (14:14: "Then I looked, and lo") of two parallel harvests: a harvest of grain (14:14-16) and a harvest of grapes (14:17-20). In each scene John sees someone with a sharp sickle (14:14, 17); "another angel" comes out of the Temple in heaven (14:15, 17); "another angel" gives the command, "Put in your sickle" (14:15, 18); and the figure swings his sickle and the harvest is duly noted (14:16, 19-20). The similarities suggest that the two scenes are visions of a single harvest. John draws upon the language of Joel 3:13, which also speaks of a dual harvest or grain and grapes:

> Put in the sickle,
>> for the harvest is ripe.
> Go in, tread,
>> for the winepress is full.
> The vats overflow,
>> for their wickedness is great.

The twofold harvest is one of judgment.

In the first harvest scene John sees a white cloud (cf. 1:7; 10:1; 11:12) with someone "seated" on it (14:14). John observes three things about the one seated on the cloud. First, he is "like a son of man" (14:14). This reminds the reader of John's opening vision, in which the one speaking to him was like a son of man (1:13). Second, he has a gold crown on his head (14:14; cf. 4:4). Third, in his hand is a sharp sickle (14:14). Only two sickles are mentioned in the book: this one (cf. 14:15-16) and the sickle in the next scene (14:17-19). Who is this figure? Does "another angel" in 14:15 imply that this figure is an angel? Or is it to be understood as referring back to the three angels flying in midheaven (14:6, 8, 9; cf. 14:17, 18) and therefore as distinguishing this figure from being an angel altogether? The latter seems more likely, given that the description of this figure as "one like a son of man" and the reference to him being seated on a cloud (cf. 1:7) would more naturally identify the figure as Jesus. Indeed, one would be hard pressed to explain why these details would have been included if the figure were anyone *other* than Jesus. That the angel "came out of the temple" (14:15) marks the first activity relating to the heavenly Temple since it was opened in 11:19 (cf. 14:17). The angel commands the one seated upon the cloud to send forth his sickle and reap "for the hour to reap has come, for the harvest of the earth is fully ripe" (14:15). The notion that the time has now arrived reminds the reader of 10:6: "There shall be no more delay." The one seated on the cloud swings his sickle on the earth, and the earth is reaped (14:16).

In the second harvest scene both figures involved are called "another angel" (14:17, 18; cf. 14:15). The first, who has a sharp sickle (cf. 14:14), comes out of the Temple in heaven (14:17; cf. 14:15). The second, who comes out "from the altar," is called "the angel who has power over the fire" (14:18). This is presumably the same angel as in 8:3-5. The second angel commands the first angel (14:18; cf. 14:15) to send forth his sickle "and gather the clusters of the vine of the earth, for its grapes are ripe" (14:18). The second angel does so and gathers "the vintage of the earth" (14:19). But unlike the "one like a son of man," this angel does more than just gather: grapes must be placed in a wine press. In keeping with the theme of divine judgment, the angel throws the grapes "into the great wine press of the wrath of God" (14:19), the appropriate place to make the wine of God's wrath (cf. 14:10). The concept is drawn from Isa 63:3 (cf. Lam 1:15), a passage to which John will return: "I have trodden the wine press alone, and from the peoples no one was with me; I trod them in my anger and trampled them in my wrath."

John makes two further observations about the vintage being cast into the great wine press of the wrath of God. First, "the wine press was trodden [*pateo*] outside the city" (14:20; cf. 19:15). Again the reader finds the irony of reversal: it was the nations who are said to "trample" (*pateo*) the holy city in 11:2. Now those who trampled are being trampled themselves. The allusion to 11:2 also answers the question of the city to which John is referring in 14:20: it is "the holy city" of 11:2. The trampling of the wine press "outside" the holy city indicates in yet another way (e.g., 3:10; 7:3-4; 9:4; 12:10) how the Church will be exempt from God's wrath. Second, "blood flowed from the winepress, as high as a horse's bridle, for one thousand six hundred stadia" (14:20). Again John draws upon Isa 63: "I trod down the peoples in my anger, I made them drunk in my wrath, and I poured out their lifeblood on the earth" (Isa 63:6). *1 Enoch* 100:3 contains a striking parallel: "The horse shall walk through the blood of sinners up to his chest" (cf. *6 Ezra* 15:35b-36). That the blood flows for 1,600 stadia (roughly 180 miles) is not to be pressed literally. Rather, it underscores the thoroughness of the judgment; that is a lot of blood!

14:1-20 brings together important elements from John's second "in the Spirit" experience (4:1–11:19) and his visions of the first two signs in heaven (12:1–13:18). In the face of the judgment of God, 4:1–11:19 introduced the reader to the Lamb, who has taken control over that judgment (5:5-7), and to those whom he has ransomed (5:9-10), who will not be harmed in any way by it (7:1-17). Over against them is the rest of mankind, who have everything to fear in the face of judgment (6:15-17), yet refuse to repent (9:20-21; cf. 11:3-10). The time for judgment has drawn near (6:12-14; 8:1–9:19; 11:15-19). 14:7 affirms that the hour of judgment has now come (cf. 14:8-9), and several pictures of that judgment follow (14:8, 9-11, 14-16, 17-20). John's vision of the first two signs in heaven gave a distinctive theological slant to what has gone before. The Lamb's victory is, in fact, a victory over the dragon (12:1-9), who has lost his right to accuse the Lamb's followers at the judgment (12:10-11). The dragon's response is to take revenge on the Church (12:13-17). He empowers two accomplices to deceive the world—that is why they do not repent—and, if possible, the followers of the Lamb (13:1-18). The stark contrast between the fate of the followers of the Lamb (14:1-5, 13) and that of the followers of the beast (14:9-11) brings home to the reader the question that is central to the entire book—Whom will you worship (14:12)?

"For with them the wrath of God is ended": The third sign in heaven
Revelation 15:1–16:21

The two harvests of 14:14-20, along with the reference to the "wrath" of God in 14:19, serve as an appropriate transition to the third and final sign in heaven: seven angels with seven plagues, which complete the wrath of God (15:1). This section consists of three units of unequal length: the song of the conquerors (15:2-4), the transferal of the seven bowls of wrath to the seven angels (15:5-8), and the pouring out of the seven bowls, one after another (16:1-21).

John introduces the sign in heaven as "great [cf. 12:1] and marvelous" (15:1; cf. 15:3). This is the third sign that John has seen, the first being the woman clothed in the sun (12:1) and the second the great red dragon (12:3). The third sign consists of seven angels holding the seven last plagues (15:1; cf. 15:6, 8; 16:9, 21 [twice]; 21:9). John has previously encountered seven angels to whom seven trumpets were given (8:2). John has mentioned "plagues" previously (9:18, 20; 11:6) and will do so again (18:4, 8; 22:18). These are the last plagues because "with them the wrath of God is ended [*teleo*]" (15:1; see on 14:10). *Teleo* was used previously in connection with the mystery of God (10:7; RSV "fulfilled") and the testimony of the two witnesses (11:7; RSV "finished"). It will be used again for the seven plagues (15:8; RSV "ended"), the words of God (17:17; RSV "fulfilled"), and the 1,000 years (20:3, 5, 7; RSV "ended").

Between the announcement of the seven last plagues and the unveiling of them, there is a dramatic pause: John has two more visions (15:2-4, 5-8). In the first, John describes what he sees (15:2), then what he hears (15:3). John sees two things. First, he sees "what appeared to be a sea of glass mingled with fire" (15:2). John previously mentioned a sea of glass in 4:6: before the throne was something like a sea of glass, like crystal. The significance of the sea of glass being "mingled with fire" is not clear, since in this same verse John mentions the sea a second time without reference to the fire. Given that fire is frequently used in the book in connection with judgment (e.g., 8:5, 7, 8; 9:17, 18; 11:5; 14:10; 16:8; 17:16; 18:8; 18:20; 20:9, 10, 14 [twice], 15; 21:8), perhaps it is another allusion to the impending judgment of God here.

Second, John sees "those who had conquered the beast and its image and the number of its name" (15:2). Although these images of the conqueror and the beast have been used previously in the book, this is the first time they have been combined. The conquerors conquer the dragon by the blood of the Lamb and by the word of their testimony (12:17), and they conquer the beast by not taking its mark (13:17; 14:9, 11) and by keeping the commandments of God and the faith of Jesus (14:12). Whether the conquerors stand "on" (*epi*; cf. 10:5, 8) or "beside" (RSV) the sea of glass (15:2) is not clear, but it certainly presents no barrier to them. That they are holding harps of God (15:2) reminds the reader of the 144,000 in 14:2 (cf. 5:8), as does the fact that they are singing (15:3). But whereas the 144,000 were singing a "new song" (14:3; cf. 5:9), the conquerors are singing "the song of Moses, the servant of God [cf. Num 12:7; Deut 34:5; Josh 1:2, 7; 14:7], and the song of the Lamb" (15:3). The "song of the Lamb" reminds the reader of 5:9-10 (cf. 7:9-10); that what follows is called "the song of the Lamb" is because of what he has done for them. The mention of Moses, the only such reference in the book, serves to underscore John's theme (note that this is John's commentary here) of the followers of the Lamb as the true Israel (see on 11:4).

The concept of "the song of Moses" is drawn from Deuteronomy. In Deut 31:19 God instructs Moses to "write this song, and teach it to the people of Israel; put it in their mouths, that this song may be a witness for me against the people of Israel" (cf. Deut 31:21). Moses complies (Deut 31:22) and speaks the song to the Israelites (Deut 31:30–32:47). While the song of Moses in Deuteronomy is a lengthy poetic composition that focuses to a large extent on Israel going astray and God's subsequent judgment, it does affirm the justice of God's judgments (Deut 32:4), with which the song here begins. Equally important is that it ends with an affirmation of God's judgment on those who *oppose* his people Israel: "Praise his people, O you nations/for he avenges the blood of his servants" (Deut 32:43). This verse is echoed at several key junctures in Revelation as a major theme that runs throughout the book (6:10; 16:6, 17:6; 18:20, 24; 19:2).

The song consists of an initial statement of praise, consisting of two lines in synonymous parallelism (15:3), followed by a rhetorical question and three causal clauses (15:4). The song of Moses and the Lamb is directed to the Lord God Almighty (15:3; see on 1:8). God's "deeds" and God's "ways," mentioned only here in the book, are praised as "great and wonderful" (cf. Exod 15:11; Pss 86:9-10; 92:5; 111:2-3; 139:14) and "just and true" (15:3; cf. Ps 145:17), respectively. The language is drawn from Deut 32:4: "The Rock, his work is perfect; for all his ways are justice. A God of faithfulness and without iniquity, just and right is he." God's judgments will be called "true and just" in 16:7 and 19:2 (cf. 16:5). While this is the only time that God is called "King" in the book, the expression "King of kings" is found in 17:14 (with reference to the Lamb) and 19:16 (with reference to the rider on the white horse). For "King of the ages" (RSV, following Codex Sinaiticus*), cf. *1 Enoch* 25:5; 27:3. The reading "King of the nations" (Codex Sinaiticus, Codex Alexandrinus; cf. Jer 10:7; Tob 13:11) fits well John's interest in the "nations" in the next verse and elsewhere (e.g., 2:26; 11:2, 18; 12:5; 14:8; 16:19; 18:3, 23; 19:15; 20:3, 8; 21:24, 26; 22:2).

The song asks, "Who shall not fear and glorify thy name, O Lord?" (15:4). The question both reminds the reader of the opening of the sixth seal, at which people were terrified of God (6:15-17; cf. 11:18; 16:9; 19:1, 5), and anticipates 21:24, 26. There follow three affirmations introduced by "for." First, God alone is holy (15:4; cf. 16:5). Second (RSV omits "for"), all nations (cf. 12:5; 14:8; 18:3, 23) will come and worship him (15:4). The idea of the nations coming to Jerusalem to worship God is a common theme in the Old Testament and in the Second Temple period (see on 21:24, 26). John will speak of the nations coming to the new Jerusalem (21:24, 26). Third, God's "judgments" (*dikaioma*) have been revealed (15:4; cf. Ps 98:2). *Dikaioma* is found elsewhere in the book only in 19:8 (RSV "righteous deeds").

In his second vision, during the "dramatic pause" between the announcement of the seven last plagues and the time that they are revealed, John witnesses the final preparation of the plagues (15:5-8). The "tent of witness"—i.e., the Tabernacle—was the precursor of the Solomonic Temple (e.g., Exod 38:21; 40:34). The terms should be seen in apposition here: "the temple—that is, the tent of witness" (15:5). The use of both expressions here and only here in the book serves to emphasize that these are the final plagues from God. The heavenly Temple was opened also in 11:19 (cf. 14:15, 17). Out of the Temple come the seven angels holding the seven last plagues (15:6; cf. 15:1). John describes their appearance in a twofold manner. First, they are "robed in pure bright linen" (15:6; cf. Dan 10:5). "Linen" (*linon*) is found only here in the book, but "fine linen" (*businnos*) will be mentioned later (18:12, 16; 19:8, 14). Second, their breasts are "girded with golden belts [RSV "girdles"]" (15:6). The "one like a son of man" in 1:13 had a golden belt girded around his breast. The priestly associations connected with linen (see on 19:8) and robes with gold decorations (see on 1:13), as well as the fact that the angels are coming out of the Temple, identify the seven angels as priests/mediators of God's final plagues upon the earth. One of the four living creatures (cf. 4-6; 7:11; 14:3; 19:4) gives the seven angels "seven golden bowls full of the wrath of God" (15:7; see on 14:10). The "bowls" are presumably incense bowls, as in 5:8. God is characterized further as the one who lives for ever and ever (15:7; cf. 4:9, 10; 10:6). The result is, first, that the Temple is filled "with smoke from the glory of God and from his power" (15:8; cf. 8:4; Exod 40:35; 1 Kgs 8:10-11; 2 Chr 5:13-14; Isa 6:4; Ezek 44:4). John will speak of "the glory of God" again in connection with the new Jerusalem (21:11, 23). Second, that no one is able to enter the Temple until the seven plagues of the seven angels are ended (15:8; cf. 15:1) anticipates the voice from the Temple in 16:17. But for the present, all of the heavenly focus will be on the last plagues.

The seven bowls present the reader with the third series of sevens in the book. As with the seven seals and the seven trumpets, there is a correspondence of the first four bowls with one another, but unlike the seals and the trumpets, there is no break between the sixth and the seventh bowls.

Several factors link the seven bowls much more closely to the seven trumpets than to the seven seals. First, once again the agents are angels rather than the Lamb. Second, once again the elements are not numbered—just the angels who control them (although once again for the sake of simplicity this commentary will speak, e.g., of the "fourth bowl"). Third, there are breaks in each series, although not exactly in the same places (after the fifth and the sixth trumpets; after the third bowl, in the middle of the sixth bowl). Fourth, both speak of the failure of people to repent (sixth trumpet; fourth and fifth bowls). Fifth, both draw upon the imagery of the exodus plagues. Finally, the individual trumpets and bowls line up fairly well content-wise, as the following table indicates:

	trumpet	bowl
#1	land	land
#2	sea, blood, death	sea, blood, death
#3	rivers and fountains	rivers and fountains
#4	sun	sun
#5	darkness, torment	darkness, anguish
#6	Euphrates/war imagery/mouth	Euphrates/war imagery/mouth
#7	loud voices in heaven/lightning, thunder, earthquake, hail	loud voice from the throne/lightning, thunder, earthquake, hail

Certainly there are differences between the trumpets and the bowls, as will be seen. But the strong parallels indicate some kind of association between the seven trumpets and the seven bowls.

As in the case of the seven trumpets, the seven bowls are rich in Old Testament allusions. The parallels with the exodus plagues can be set forth as follows:

Exodus plagues (Exod 7:14–12:30)	7 trumpets	7 bowls
# 1: water turns to blood (7:14-22)	#2, #3	#2, #3
# 2: frogs (8:1-15)		#6
# 3: gnats (8:16-19)		
# 4: flies (8:20-32)		
# 5: plague on livestock (9:1-7)		
# 6: boils (9:8-12)		#1, #5
# 7: hail (9:13-35)	#1	#7
# 8: locusts (10:1-20)	#5	
# 9: darkness (10:21-29)	#4, #5	#5
#10: death of firstborn (11:1–12:30)		

Other Old Testament parallels will be noted throughout the discussion.

16:1 provides one more introduction (15:1, 5-8) to the final plagues. A loud voice from the temple (cf. Isa 66:6) directs the seven angels to "go and pour out on the earth the seven bowls of the wrath of God" (16:1). On the wrath of God, see on 14:10 (cf. 6:16-17). The image of God "pouring out" his wrath in judgment is a familiar one in the Old Testament (e.g., Ps 69:24; Jer 10:25; Ezek 14:19; 22:31; Zeph 3:8; cf. Ps 75:8). Seven times an angel will pour his bowl, but each of the seven will pour his bowl onto (or into) something different: the earth (16:2), the sea (16:3), the rivers and fountains of water (16:4), the sun (16:8), the throne of the beast (16:10), the great river Euphrates (16:12), and the air (16:17). The recipients of the plagues are not all people, but only those who follow the beast (16:2; cf. 16:10). Unlike the seals and the trumpets, the pouring of the bowls is set forth as cumulative—e.g., the reference to the "sores" at the fifth bowl implies the first bowl (16:11; cf. 16:2).

The first angel pours his bowl on the earth: foul and evil sores come upon men who bear the mark of the beast and worship his image (16:2; cf. 13:15, 16-17; 14:9, 11; 19:20; 20:4). The sores will be mentioned again in 16:11. The plague is reminiscent of the sixth plague ("the plague of boils") God brought upon the Egyptians prior to the exodus (Exod 9:8-11; cf. Deut 28:35).

The second angel pours out his bowl into the sea. There are two results. First, it becomes "like the blood of a dead man" (16:3). At the second trumpet one third of the sea became blood (8:8). Second, every living thing in the sea dies (16:3). At the second trumpet one third of the living creatures in the sea died (8:8). Like the second trumpet, the second bowl picks up the imagery of the first exodus plague (Exod 7:14-21).

The third angel pours his bowl into the rivers and the fountains of water: like the sea, they become blood (16:4). At the second trumpet one third of the rivers and the fountains of water become bitter (8:11; cf. Exod 7:14-21).

At this point a heavenly commentary interrupts the flow of the narrative and explains the significance of the third bowl. John first hears "the angel of water" (16:5), a figure mentioned nowhere else in the book. This angel directs a word of praise to God, followed by two causal clauses and two indicative clauses. The angel praises God as "just" and identifies God as the one who is and was, the holy one (16:5). Although God's ways and judgments are said to be just (cf. Jer 11:20) and true in the book (15:3; 16:7; 19:2), this is the only time God himself is called just (cf. Pss 119:137; 145:17). For the one who is and who was, see on 11:17. For God as holy, see on 15:4. The first reason for praising God is that God has judged these things (16:5: RSV "in these thy judgments"). As in 11:18 God's acting in judgment, announced in 14:7, answers the question of "those who had been slain" at the fifth seal (6:9-10). The second reason is that those who "poured out the blood of the saints and prophets" now get their due (16:6). There is a double irony here. First, those who "poured out" (*ekcheo*—only in this chapter of the book) the blood of the saints and prophets (cf. Isa 26:21) are having judgment "poured out" (*ekcheo*) upon them from each of the seven bowls (16:1, 2, 3, 4, 8, 10, 12, 17). Second, those who have poured out blood deserve the blood that is given them to drink: "It is their due!" On the saints and the prophets, see on 11:18. On the blood of saints and prophets, see 18:24, where the order is reversed (cf. 17:6: the blood of saints and witnesses; 6:10: the blood of the souls under altar; 19:2: the blood of God's servants).

John then hears the altar speaking (16:7). The altar has previously been mentioned in 6:9; 8:3 (twice), 5; 9:13; 11:1; 14:18. Indeed, John has previously heard a voice from one of the horns of the altar (9:13). The altar agrees ("Yea"; see on 14:13), addressing the Lord God Almighty (cf. 15:3) and affirming his judgments as true and just (cf. 15:3; Deut 32:4).

The fourth angel pours his bowl on the sun. The sun "was allowed [divine passive] to scorch men with fire" (16:8). At the fourth trumpet a third of the sun, a third of the moon, and a third of the stars were darkened (8:12). The result is that people are "scorched by the fierce heat" (16:9). This contrasts sharply with the Great Multitude, who were promised in 7:16 that they would *not* be scorched by the sun. The people's response is twofold. First, they curse "the name of God" (16:9), which is consistent with their identity as those who follow the beast (16:2), about which John said the same thing in 13:6. John will provide similar observations after the fifth (16:11) and seventh (16:21) bowls. God is characterized further as the one who has power over these plagues (cf. 15:1, 7; 16:1). Second, they do not repent and give glory to God (16:9), a statement that will be repeated after the fifth bowl (16:11). John made a similar comment after the sixth trumpet (9:20-21). On giving glory to God, see on 11:13 (cf. 14:7; 19:7).

The fifth angel pours his bowl on the throne of the beast, following which the beast's kingdom becomes darkened (16:10). In 13:2 the dragon gave his throne to the beast; while there is no mention of a "kingdom" belonging to the beast at that point, it is certainly implied. The explicit reference here to such a kingdom anticipates 17:17, where the ten kings are said to give their kingdom (RSV "royal power") to the beast. That the beast's kingdom is "in darkness" recalls the fifth trumpet, where the sun and sky were "darkened" by the smoke from the Abyss (9:2). Once again the imagery is drawn from the exodus plagues, this time from the ninth plague—that of darkness (Exod 10:21-23; cf. Isa 8:22). John sets forth the results of the darkening of the beast's kingdom by using three third person plural verbs. The subjects of the verbs are presumably the "subjects" of the kingdom—i.e., the followers of the beast (cf. 16:2). First, "they" gnaw their tongues in anguish (16:10). "Anguish" is used twice in this sentence (cf. 16:11; RSV "pain"). By contrast, "anguish" is something that will *not* be experienced by those who make up the new Jerusalem (21:4; RSV "pain"). Second, they curse (cf. 16:9) the God of heaven for their pain and sores (cf. 16:2; cf. 11:13). Third, they do not repent of their works (16:11; cf. 2:22), which recalls the sixth trumpet (9:20-21) and the fourth bowl (16:9). That there is a repetition of the theme of cursing God, and not repenting at the fourth and fifth bowls, the first to follow the heavenly commentary that affirmed the justice of God's judgments, underscores the stark dichotomy between the beast and its followers on the one hand and God on the other (cf. 6:16-17).

The sixth angel pours his bowl "on the great river Euphrates" (16:12). At the sixth trumpet the four angels who were bound at the great river Euphrates were released (9:14). These are the only times that the Euphrates is mentioned in Revelation. The result is that its water is dried up "to prepare the way for the kings of the east" (16:12). God's drying up of water is a familiar theme in the Old Testament, dating back to the exodus (Exod 14:21-31; cf. Ps 106:9). In particular, Isa 11:15-16 speaks of God sending a scorching wind over the Euphrates so as to break it up into seven streams for people to cross in sandals (cf. Jer 50:38; 51:36) in preparation for the new exodus (cf. Isa 51:10). The mention of the kings "from the east" (literally, "from the rising sun") reminds the reader of the angel from the east who enjoins the four angels holding back the four winds not to release the winds until the servants of God are sealed (7:1-3). The divine passive ("the way was prepared" [RSV "to prepare]; cf. 9:7; 9:15; 12:6; 21:1), which is John's commentary, underscores the fact that God is in control. The expression "the kings from the east" (cf. Isa 41:2, 25; 46:11) is found only here in the book; elsewhere John mentions the kings of the earth (1:5; 6:15; 17:2, 18; 18:3, 9; 19:19; 21:24), the kings of the whole world (16:14), seven kings (17:10), ten kings (17:12, 12), and the kings whose flesh is eaten (19:18).

John next sees "three foul spirits like frogs" issuing from the mouths of the dragon, the beast, and the false prophet (16:13). This is the first mention in the book of the "false prophet," who is to be identified with the second beast of 13:11-17, and who will be mentioned again in 19:20 and 20:10. "Frogs," found only here in the book, is reminiscent of the second exodus plague of frogs (Exod 8:1-14; cf. Pss 78:45; 105:30). As with the sixth trumpet (the mouth of horses: 9:17-19), once again the mouth is a source (cf. the mouth of Jesus: 1:16; 2:16; 19:15, 21; the mouth of the two witnesses: 11:5; and the mouth of the serpent/dragon: 12:15, 16). "Foul spirits" is found only here in the book (cf. 17:4; 18:2 [twice]). John is probably drawing upon 1 Kgs 22:21-23, where God puts a lying spirit into the mouths of the (false) prophets (cf. Ezek 13:6-9, 19, 22). John goes on to describe these foul spirits as "demonic spirits, performing signs" (16:14; cf. 19:20). Demons are also mentioned in 9:20 and 18:2. The only other figure in the book who works "signs" is the second beast (13:13, 14). The signs "go abroad to the kings of the whole world" (16:14). There is no reason to differentiate these kings from the "kings from the east" at the beginning of this section (16:12): "east" is the correct directional word for "the great river Euphrates," while "the whole world" makes it clear that the seven bowls are about *universal* judgment. The purpose of the demonic spirits going abroad to these kings is "to assemble them for battle on the great day of God Almighty" (16:14). Assembling for war will also take place in 16:16; 19:19 (the beast and the kings of the earth and their armies); and 20:8 (the nations at the four corners of the earth). The great day (of wrath) has already been mentioned in 6:17 (cf. 9:15; 18:8). For "Almighty" see on 1:8.

16:15, apparently spoken by Jesus, serves as a parenthesis. It contains a promise/warning and a beatitude. Jesus promises/warns that he is coming (present tense) "like a thief" (see on 3:3). On Jesus' "coming," see 1:7; 2:5, 16; 3:11; 22:7, 12, 17 (twice), and 20 (twice). He then pronounces the third of seven beatitudes in the book (1:3; 14:13; 19:9; 20:6; 22:7, 14): "Blessed is he who is awake [see on 3:2-3], keeping his garments [cf. 3:4, 5, 18] that he may not go naked and be seen exposed" (16:15). "Keeping" one's robe, found only here in the book, is necessary to prevent one from going around naked (cf. 3:17; 17:16) and having one's "shame" (only here in the book) seen. The parenthesis serves two purposes. First, it provides a brief dramatic pause between the demonic spirits going out to assemble the kings (16:14) and the observation that they have completed their mission (16:16). Second, it reminds the reader one last time of similar statements in the letters to the seven churches: the coming of Jesus is a warning to all who are deceived by the demonic spirits, who do not repent (2:5, 26; 3:2-3), but it is a promise to all who are not deceived, who hold fast to what they have in Jesus (3:11).

The demonic spirits produce their intended result: they assemble the kings "at the place which is called in Hebrew Armageddon" (16:16). Only one other time does John call attention to a Hebrew word that he uses (9:11: Abaddon). What John means by "Armageddon" is one of the thorniest problems in Revelation. John specifically calls attention to the Hebrew, yet there is no Hebrew word "Armageddon." Therefore, it seems likely that John is inviting his readers (at least any who might know Hebrew) to dissect the word into its two component parts. The Hebrew word *har* means "mountain," and *megiddo* is a place name: Megiddo. Thus, "Armageddon" means "Mount Megiddo." The problem is that there was no Mount Megiddo in Israel, or anywhere else for that matter. There was, however, a *city* named Megiddo. Today the mound that marks the site has twenty levels that predate the book of Revelation, going all the way back to the Neolithic Age (sixth to fourth millennium BC). Megiddo became a fortified city prior to the Old Testament period and was a major Canaanite city before its destruction in the twelfth century BC. It was rebuilt by the Israelites during the time of King David and became a major administrative center under King Solomon (1 Kgs 4:12; 9:15). It was eventually conquered by the Assyrians in the late eighth century BC and was finally abandoned in the late fourth century BC. Megiddo was situated in the western part of the Jezreel Valley near the foot of Mount Carmel, where it controlled the main land route ("The Way of the Sea"—Isa 8:3) between Egypt and Syria. Hence, it had enormous strategic significance. As a result, "the plain of Megiddo" (Zech 12:11) was the site of numerous battles over the centuries—e.g., during the times of Pharaoh Thutmose III (1468 BC), Pharaoh Merneptah (1220 BC), the judges Deborah and Barak (Jdg 4:1-16; 5:19) and Gideon (Jdg 6:33–7:23), King Saul (1 Sam 29:1; 31:1), Pharaoh Shishak (924 BC), and Pharaoh Neco and King Josiah (2 Kgs 23:29-30; 2 Chr 35:22-24). Given this reputation, it is not surprising that John would tie the battle "on the great day of God the Almighty" (16:14) to Megiddo. But by adding "Mount" to it, John can hardly be doing anything other than alerting his readers to the fact that he is *not* talking about a literal place, since there was no literal "Mount Megiddo." Perhaps the addition of "Mount" is intended to make his readers recall Zech 14:4, where the Lord will stand on the Mount (*har*) of Olives and smite all of the nations who gather against Jerusalem to do battle (Zech 14:1-3, 12-15; cf. *Sibylline Oracles* 3.663-68). In *4 Ezra*, which is roughly contemporaneous with Revelation, the Messiah is pictured as dispensing final judgment from *Mount* Zion (*4 Ezra* 13:35-38).

The seventh angel pours out his bowl into the air (16:17). A great voice comes out of the Temple from the throne (16:17; cf. 16:1). "Out of the temple" reinforces the divine origin of the seven bowls (cf. 15:5, 8; 16:1), while "from the throne" underscores that fact. The voice says, "It is done" (16:17: *ginomai*), rather than "It is ended" (*teleo*), which might have been expected (cf. 15:1, 8). The use of *ginomai* anticipates a similar affirmation in 21:6. There are also lightning, voices, peals of thunder, and a great earthquake (16:18; see on 11:19). The earthquake is described as "such had never been since men were on the earth" (16:19; cf. Exod 9:18, 22-26; Dan 12:1; Add Esth 11:5-8; Mark 13:19; Josephus, *Jewish War* 5.10.5). The result is that "the great city was split into three parts, and the cities of the nations fell" (16:19; cf. 11:8, 13). The great city is identified in the next phrase as "great Babylon" (cf. 14:8; 17:5, 18; 18:2, 10, 16, 18, 19, 21). This is the only reference in the book to "the cities of the nations"; the judgment is universal. John comments that "God remembered great Babylon, to make her drain the cup of the fury of his wrath" (16:19; cf. 14:8). For the cup of the wine of the fury of God's wrath, see on 14:10. John's observation that "every island fled away, and no mountains were to be found" (16:20) reminds the reader of 6:14. The great hailstones (16:21) are reminiscent of 11:19 (cf. 8:7). John further describes the hailstones as being "heavy as a hundredweight"—i.e., weighing a hundred pounds—and as "dropped on men from heaven" (16:21). The result is that "men cursed God for the plague of the hail, so fearful was that plague" (16:21; cf. Num 11:33). As with the fourth and fifth bowls (16:9, 11), the response of men to the last of God's last plagues is to curse him (cf. 13:6). There is no repentance to the very end. The nations indeed raged (cf. 11:18).

The seven bowls portray a final, graphic picture of God's judgment that builds upon previous passages in the book (6:13-17; 8:1–9:21; 11:13, 15-18; 14:6-11, 14-20). As always, those who are judged stand firm in their opposition to God. Yet the story is not over: kings have been assembled at Armageddon for battle on the great day of God the Almighty. The story of that battle remains to be told.

Much more so than John's second "in the Spirit" experience (4:1–11:19), the section on the three signs in heaven (12:1–16:21) is replete with echoes of the letters to the seven churches. The conquerors return (12:11; 14:2; cf. 2:7, 11, 17, 26; 3:5, 12, 21), as does Satan (12:9; cf. 2:9, 13), and there are references, for example, to Jesus' coming (16:15; cf. 2:5, 16; 3:11), to a false prophet (16:13; cf. 2:20), to receiving power (13:2, 7; cf. 2:26-27), to ruling the nations with an iron scepter (12:5; cf. 2:27), to the book of life (13:8; cf. 3:5), and to the name of God and the name of Jesus/the Lamb (13:6; 14:1; cf. 3:12). In addition, there are exhortations to the reader (13:9-10, 18; 14:12; 16:15; cf. 2:7, 11, 17, 29; 3:6, 13, 22).

While there are certainly plenty of connections to 4:1–11:19, the echoes of the seven letters serve to provide a controlling perspective on 12:1–16:21. One might suggest that the section on the three signs serves to show how everything, especially the wrath of God, fits into God's grand scheme for his churches. Specifically, the story of the dragon's fall and the introduction of the two beasts—and the fate of those who follow the beast—serve to present the churches with the stark choice that they must make: in the face of all that confronts them in their various cities in Asia, will they choose to be faithful to Jesus or to follow Satan?

"The judgment of the great harlot"

Revelation 17:1–20:15

John's first "in the Spirit" experience introduced the situation of the seven churches of Asia and the call to conquer. His second "in the Spirit" experience introduced the Lamb who was slain, the Great Multitude, and the judgment of God. John's vision of the three signs in heaven clarified what it means to conquer by introducing the dragon, the beast, and the false prophet; it also brought the full force of the judgment to the forefront. But questions remain: Who can fight against the beast? What is this battle at Armageddon on the great day of God the Almighty? What is Babylon the Great, and how does it fall? What will happen to the dragon, the beast, and the false prophet . . . and, ultimately, to all who have chosen the beast over the Lamb? All of these questions will be answered in John's third "in the Spirit" experience, in which John will bring to completion the grand chiastic scheme that began in the section on the three signs in heaven involving those who oppose God and the judgment they will certainly receive.

John recounts his third "in the Spirit" experience in 17:1–20:15. One of the seven angels holding the seven bowls takes him in the Spirit (17:3) to see the great harlot Babylon (17:1-18), after which he hears a lament over the fall of Babylon the Great (18:1-19) and expressions of joy in heaven over the judgment of the great harlot (18:20–19:4) and the coming marriage supper of the Lamb (19:5-10). He then sees three final visions of judgment: of the beast and the false prophet (19:1-21), of the devil (20:1-10), and of the dead (20:11-15).

"I saw a woman sitting on a scarlet beast": The judgment of Babylon 1—The great harlot

Revelation 17:1-18

The angel invites John to come see the harlot (17:1-2), takes John in the Spirit to see the harlot (17:3-6), and then explains the mystery of the beast that carries the harlot (17:7-14), of the waters upon which she sits (17:15-17), and of the harlot herself (17:18).

The beginnings of John's third and fourth "in the Spirit" experiences (17:1, 3; 21:9-10) parallel one another. In each, "one of the seven angels who had the seven bowls [21:9 adds "full of the seven last plagues"] came and said to me, 'Come, I will show you . . .'" (17:1; 21:9: RSV "Then came . . . and spoke to me, saying, . . ."). In each John is to be shown a woman. Furthermore, in each John continues, "He took me in the Spirit to . . ." (17:3; 21:10). The identical terminology used to introduce the two experiences throws into sharp relief the differences. In chapter 17 John is taken to a "wilderness" (17:3), in chapter 21 to a "great, high mountain" (21:10); in chapter 17 he is to see "the great harlot" (17:1), in chapter 21 "the Bride, the wife of the Lamb" (21:9); in chapter 17 he is specifically told that he will see "the judgment" of the great harlot (17:1), in chapter 21 simply the Bride herself (21:9). Harlots are associated with barren places, brides with wonderful mountains (see on 21:10); harlots deserve judgment, brides honor.

One of the seven angels holding the seven bowls (cf. 15:1, 6, 7; 16:1) comes to John and speaks with him, inviting John to "Come" (17:1; cf. 21:9). The angel proposes to show (cf. 1:1; 4:1; 21:9-10; 22:1, 6, 8) John "the judgment [cf. 18:20; 20:4] of the great harlot who is seated upon many waters" (17:1). The great "harlot" (*porne*) is a new character in the book. "Harlot" is used again, always to describe the same woman, in 17:5, 15, 16; and 19:2 (great harlot). Both the verb (*porneuo*: RSV "commit fornication") and noun (*porneia*: RSV "fornication") forms are also used in connection with the harlot (verb: 17:2; 18:3, 9; noun: 17:2, 4; 18:3; 19:2; cf. 14:8). In addition, both the verb and the noun forms are used in connection with Jezebel (verb: 2:14, 20; noun: 2:21). The noun form is also found in 9:21 (cf. the adjective form *pornos* in 21:8; 22:15).

John's description of the great harlot, which he will identify as Babylon in 17:5, is replete with Old Testament allusions. The very idea of a city as a harlot is found, for example, in Isa 1:21 (Jerusalem), Isa 23:16-17 (Tyre), and Nah 3:4 (Ninevah). In addition, the ornate adornment of the harlot (17:4) is reminiscent of Ezekiel's description of the king of Tyre (Ezek 28:13), and being drunk with blood (17:6) echoes Ezek 39:19 (cf. Jdt 6:4). But the passage that has had the greatest impact on John's description of the harlot in chapter 17 is Jer 51, where Jeremiah speaks of God's impending judgment against Babylon: the harlot sits upon many waters (17:1; Jer 51:13), the nations have become drunk with the wine of her fornication (17:2; Jer 51:7), and she has a golden cup in her hand (17:4; Jer 51:7). John has drawn upon Jer 51 previously (e.g., 11:18) and he will do so repeatedly in chapter 18.

The angel emphasizes to John the influence of the great harlot on others. First, the kings of the earth (see on 16:12) committed fornication with her (17:2), a charge that will be repeated in 18:3, 9. Second, the dwellers on earth (see on 3:10) became drunk from the wine of her fornication (17:2), which reminds the reader of 14:8, where all the nations were said to have drunk the wine of the impure passion of Babylon (cf. 18:3).

The angel carries John away in the Spirit into a wilderness (17:3; cf. 21:10). Being carried to another place by the Spirit was something experienced frequently by Ezekiel (e.g., Ezek 3:14, 24; 8:3; 11:1, 24; 43:5). The reader has previously encountered "the wilderness" to which the woman clothed with the sun fled from the dragon (12:6, 14). Has the woman of chapter 12 become a harlot? Not at all. John makes this clear in two ways. First, the place to which the woman fled was "prepared by God" (12:6) so that she could be "nourished" (12:6, 14), hardly the kind of setting for producing a prostitute! Second, John has eliminated the definite article in 17:3: this is "a" wilderness, not "the wilderness." John has borrowed the notion of "wilderness" not from chapter 12 but from Isa 21:1, which speaks of Babylon (see 17:5) as the "wilderness of the sea."

John observes that "the woman" (cf. 2:20) is "sitting [cf. 17:1] on a scarlet beast" (17:3). The two characteristics of the beast that John notes—it is "full of blasphemous names" and has "seven heads and ten horns" (17:3)—serve to identify it as none other than the first beast of chapter 13 (cf. 13:1). John further describes the woman as "arrayed in purple and scarlet, and bedecked with gold and jewels and pearls" (17:4). In the next chapter Babylon will be characterized in virtually identical terms (18:16). The woman further holds "a golden cup" in her hand that is "full of abominations [cf. 17:5; 21:27] and the impurities of her fornication" (17:4). In accord with a theme that has been developing throughout the book, the harlot has a name written on her forehead (17:5; cf. 7:3; 9:4; 13:16-17; 14:1, 9; 20:4; 22:4). The name is a "mystery" (cf. 17:7; 1:20; 10:7): "Babylon the great, mother of harlots and of earth's abominations" (17:5). Babylon—always with "great"—is mentioned elsewhere in the book in 14:8; 16:19; 18:2, 10, 21. The reader realizes that now she will learn more about the enigmatic "Babylon" that was introduced in 14:8 (cf. 16:19). John sees the woman drunk from the blood of the saints and from the blood of the witnesses (RSV "martyrs") of Jesus (17:6; cf. 16:6), which is apparently to be identified with "the wine of her fornication" in 17:2 (cf. 14:8). John will again connect Babylon to the blood of the prophets and of saints (18:24) and to the blood of God's servants (19:2). John has previously mentioned Antipas "my witness" (2:13) and "my two witnesses" (11:3), all of whom were characterized as having been martyred (2:13; 11:7). Upon seeing the great harlot, John marvels "greatly" (17:6; cf. 17:7, 8; 13:3: RSV "with wonder").

Asking John why he marvels, the angel proposes to tell John "the mystery of the woman, and of the beast with seven heads and ten horns that carries her" (17:7; cf. 17:3). But he does not do so in that order. In a deliberate buildup of suspense, that which John has specifically been called to see—the harlot (17:1)—is left until the very end. The angel first identifies the beast (17:8), the seven heads (17:9-10), the beast again (17:11), the ten horns (17:12-14), and the waters (17:15). Only after explaining what the beast and the ten horns will do to the woman (17:16-17) does the angel finally identify the woman herself (17:18).

The angel identifies the beast ("that you saw"—cf. 17:3) in 17:8 and 11. He says four things about the beast. First, the beast "was, and is not, and is to ascend" from the Abyss (17:8). This phrase is repeated (with a slight variation in the third term) a second time at the end of the verse—"was and is not and is to come"—and (with the third term missing) a third time in 17:11: "was, and is not." Obviously, it is an important means of characterizing the beast. Second, the beast goes to destruction (17:8, 11: RSV "perdition"). "Destruction" (*apoleia*), a word found only in these two verses in the book, is related to the word Apollyon, the name of the angel of the Abyss (see on 9:11). The irony is clear: the one whose king is "the destroyer" will itself be destroyed (cf. 11:18).

Third, the angel informs John of the impact the beast will make: "the dwellers on earth" will "marvel" (17:8; see on 3:10; cf. 13:3). The angel further characterizes the dwellers on earth as those "whose names have not been written in the book of life [see on 3:5] from the foundation of the world" (17:8). A similar expression was used in 13:8: "every one whose name has not been written before the foundation of the world in the book of life of the Lamb." The phrase "from the foundation of the world" means "from the creation of the universe"—i.e., from the beginning of time (cf. Matt 25:34; Luke 11:50; Heb 4:3; 9:26). That peoples' names were written in the book of life *before* they actually lived is striking but not unique in the New Testament. Paul says God "chose us in him before the foundation of the world" (Eph 1:4; cf. Rom 8:29-30). The idea that there are heavenly tablets upon which God has written things before they happen is found in some Jewish writings of the Second Temple period (e.g., *Jubilees* 4:29; 32:21; *1 Enoch* 103:2-3). The dwellers on earth marvel "because" the beast was and is not and is to come (17:8). In 13:3 they marveled that the beast's mortal wound had been healed (cf. 13:12, 14). Presumably, these two characterizations of the beast mean the same thing.

Fourth, following the identification of the seven heads, the angel notes that the beast "is an eighth but it belongs to the seven" (17:11). Two observations are important here. First, in Christian writings of the first half of the second century, "eighth" becomes associated with the day on which Jesus was resurrected (e.g., *Epistle of Barnabas* 15:9; Justin, *Dialogue with Trypho* 41:4; 138:1; see on 1:10). Second, the angel does not say that the beast *is* one of the seven—i.e., that one of the kings actually reigns twice—but that it is "of" the seven. Presumably the point is that the beast reflects the same depraved nature as that of the other kings.

Though the language varies considerably in some cases, it is important for the reader to recognize that three of the four elements in the characterization of the beast in chapter 17 pick up the main points in the characterization of the beast in chapter 13. The reader who does not catch these allusions will struggle to understand the various details literally—e.g., that the beast literally existed at some point in time but did not exist in John's present or that the beast is literally an eighth king. Recognizing that chapter 17 alludes to chapter 13 reveals the following. First, to say that the beast "was and is not and is to come" (17:8; cf. 17:8, 11) is the same as saying that the beast had a mortal head wound that was healed (13:3, 12, 14), which is the same as saying that the beast is "an eighth" (17:11). All three expressions underscore the fact that the beast is a "cheap imitation" of Jesus, who was *truly* slain and raised from the dead (1:18; 5:6), and the first is also a parody of one of the characterizations of God in the book as "him who is and who was and who is to come" (1:4; cf. 4:8 and, with the last clause missing, 11:17 and 16:5). The main differences are that the beast, unlike God, is *not* and that it ascends from the Abyss (see on 9:1-2), which is how it is described in 11:7. The beast's point in trying to pass itself off as Jesus/God is to win the worship and allegiance of the dwellers on earth, which it succeeds in doing (13:4, 8; 17:8). The one new detail added in chapter 17, and mentioned twice for emphasis, is the fate of the beast: it goes to destruction, which anticipates 19:19-20.

17:9 begins with the fourth *hode* expression in the book (see on 13:10): "This calls for a mind with wisdom." As in 13:18, regarding the number of the beast, the reader is challenged to figure out what follows. To her astonishment, the angel identifies the seven heads of the beast in two different ways. First, they are "seven mountains on which the woman is seated" (17:9; cf. *1 Enoch* 24:1-3). That the woman was said in 17:1 to be seated upon many waters, not on seven mountains, suggests once again the fluidity of the imagery in the book. Given that the characterization of Rome as the city that sits upon seven hills is a commonplace among ancient authors (e.g, Virgil, *Aeneid* 6.782; Martial, *Epigrams* 4.64; Cicero, *Ad Atticum* 6.5; *Sibylline Oracles* 2.18; 11.109-16), it is scarcely possible, even though John consistently uses the number seven figuratively, that first century readers in Asia would not have made this connection. Such an allusion is indeed confirmed in 17:18.

But the seven heads "are also seven kings" (17:10). In the vision of an eagle with twelve wings and three heads in *4 Ezra* 11, both the wings and the heads are interpreted as kings (*4 Ezra* 12:14-16, 23-24). "Kings" have played a major role to this point in the book (see on 16:12). The angel says that five "have fallen, one is, the other has not yet come" (17:10). The language reverses the second of the three elements in the description of the beast, who "is *not*" (17:8, 8, 11). Again the reader thinks of God, the one who is, and who was, and who is to come (1:4).

At first glance, it might appear as if the identification of the kings—indeed, the date of the book itself—is a simple matter: one just needs to count Roman emperors. A list of emperors so designated by the Roman Senate through the time of Domitian is as follows:

31 BC–AD 14: Augustus (Octavius)
14–37: Tiberius
37–41: Gaius (Caligula)
41–54: Claudius
54–68: Nero
68–69: Galba
69: Otho
69: Vitellius
69–79: Vespasian
79–81: Titus
81–96: Domitian

The sixth (present) emperor would then be Galba. On the other hand, some ancient writers viewed Julius Caesar (d. 44 BC) as the first emperor (e.g., Suetonius, *Lives of the Twelve Emperors, Deified Julius* 76; Josephus, *Antiquities* 18.29-35; *Sibylline Oracles* 5.12-14), even though he was never designated as such by the Senate. The sixth emperor would then be Nero. Alternately, given the concern for emperor worship in the book, the angel might be counting as the "five" only those emperors who were deified by the Senate: Julius (if he is considered to be an emperor), Augustus, Claudius,

Vespasian, and Titus; Domitian would then be the sixth. Or, given the central focus of the book on the death of Jesus, perhaps the angel is counting only those who became emperor *after* that epoch-making event: the first would then be Gaius, and the sixth Vitellius. Finally, given that Galba, Otho, and Vitellius ruled only a few months apiece, perhaps the angel is not counting them at all: the sixth would then be Vespasian (if Augustus is reckoned first) or Domitian (if Gaius). That some of the above suggestions might be a bit fanciful does not render the situation any less of a mess!

But perhaps the whole approach of counting emperors is wrong-headed. Perhaps the "seven" is not to be pressed literally at all. John's consistent use of the number seven as a symbol for totality, the seven mountains in 17:9 notwithstanding, would certainly support this suggestion. The point then would not be to count the kings, but to understand that John's readers are nearer to the time of the last king than the first one.

The seventh is further characterized as follows: "when he comes he must remain only a little while [*oligon*]" (17:10). The reader is reminded that now that he has been thrown down from heaven, the dragon knows his time is short (12:12: *oligon*). Bad things in the book are always of limited duration.

Next, the angel identifies the ten horns ("that you saw"—cf. 17:3, 8): they are "ten kings" (17:12). The identification of horns with kings draws upon Daniel's vision of the fourth beast: "As for the ten horns, out of this kingdom ten kings shall arise" (Dan 7:24). Given the traditional language, there is no reason to press the number literally. He observes further that they "have not yet received royal power" (17:12; cf. 17:8, 10, 11)—i.e., their activity lies in the future. They have a specific relationship with the beast. First, they "are to receive authority as kings for one hour, with the beast" (17:12). "One hour" anticipates 18:10, 16, 19 (cf. 18:8). 17:17 makes it clear that the ten kings receive their authority, whether they realize it or not, from God. Second, they are "of one mind [cf. 17:17] and give over their power and authority to the beast" (17:13; cf. 13:2). These kings "will make war on the Lamb" (17:14; cf. Ps 2:2). On war imagery in Revelation, see on 11:7, where the beast makes "war" on the two witnesses. But unlike that war, where the beast conquers the two witnesses, in this war the Lamb will do the conquering (17:14; cf. 5:5; Isa 24:21). The angel gives the reason for the Lamb's victory: he is "Lord of lords and King of kings" (17:14). The title is derived from Dan 4:37 (LXX). In 19:16 the rider on the white horse will be called the King of kings and Lord of lords (cf. Deut 10:17; Ps 136:3; Dan 2:47; *1 Enoch* 9:4; 3 Macc 5:35). The angel adds that "those with him are called and chosen and faithful" (17:14; cf. 2:10, 13; 14:1-5). When will this "war" take place? What kind of "war" will it be? How will the Lamb "conquer" them? The reader will soon find out (19:11-21).

Finally, the angel identifies the waters ("that you saw"—cf. 17:3, 8, 12) upon which the harlot "is seated" (17:15; cf. 17:1): they are "peoples and multitudes and nations and tongues" (17:15). John draws upon an Old Testament tradition of identifying "many waters" with peoples and/or armies (e.g., Ps 144:7; Isa 17:12-13; cf. Isa 8:6-7; Jer 47:2). On "peoples . . .," see on 5:9. "Multitudes" is found only here in the book. Once again the angel explains the actions of the ten horns ("that you saw"): along with the beast, they will "hate the harlot; they will make her desolate and naked, and devour her flesh and burn her up with fire" (17:16). This verse draws upon Ezek 23:1-49, an allegory of two sisters, Oholah (Samaria) and Oholibah (Jerusalem). The sisters play the harlot—Oholah with the Assyrians and Oholibah with the Assyrians and the Babylonians—after which they are judged by God: "Behold, I will deliver you into the hands of those from whom you turned in disgust; and they shall deal with you in hatred, and take away all the fruit of your labor, and leave you naked and bare, and the naked-ness of your harlotry shall be uncovered" (Ezek 23:28-29; cf. Ezek 16:39; Mic 3:2-3). Similarly, according to Lev 21:9, if a daughter of a priest plays the harlot, she is to be burned with fire (cf. Jer 34:22). The angel explains the decision of the ten kings to hand over their royal power to the beast and to ravage the harlot as deriving ultimately from God: "God has put it into their hearts . . . until the words of God shall be fulfilled [*teleo*]" (17:17). God uses their own evil desires to carry out his purpose (cf. Gen 50:20): to bring judgment upon the harlot. For the use of *teleo* in the book, see on 15:1.

Finally, the angel identifies the woman ("that you saw"— cf. 17:3, 8, 12, 15): she is "the great city which has dominion over the kings of the earth" (17:18; cf. 1:5). The "great city" has previously been identified as Babylon (16:19; cf. 17:5; 11:8). The dominion of the "great city," which now lies desolate, over the kings of the earth is in stark contrast with that of the conquering Lamb, the King of Kings (17:4) and true ruler of the kings of the earth (1:5).

At the beginning of his third "in the Spirit" experience, John is told that he will see "the judgment of the great harlot" (17:1). In 17:1-18 he is intro-duced to the harlot, who is a new character in the book. He learns that the harlot is the great city Babylon (17:5, 18), with whom the kings of the earth have committed fornication, with the wine of whose fornication the dwellers on earth have become drunk (17:2), and who is herself drunk with the blood of the saints and the blood of the witnesses of Jesus (17:6). She is supported by the beast (17:3, 7), but that will not last, because the beast wants the whole world to follow itself (17:8-11). And so the beast will cooperate with the "ten kings" to destroy Babylon (17:12-13, 16-17). They will also make war on the Lamb (17:14). That war will be narrated (19:11-21), but first the judgment of the great harlot Babylon must be described in detail, which is precisely what will happen in John's next vision (18:1-19).

"Fallen, fallen is Babylon the great!": The judgment of Babylon 2— Lamentations on earth and rejoicing in heaven

Revelation 18:1–19:4

The brief but graphic depiction of the destruction of Babylon in 17:16 (cf. 17:18) is followed by a new vision (18:1: "After these things I saw . . ."), which centers on the fall of Babylon the great. First, an angel announces the fall of Babylon (18:1-3). Next, a voice from heaven exhorts God's people to come out of Babylon in view of her impending doom (18:4-8) and echoes the laments of the kings of the earth (18:9-10), the merchants (18:11-17a), and the seafarers (18:17b-19) over the fall of Babylon. At this point the vision shifts somewhat abruptly to a call to heaven to rejoice (18:20), followed by a mighty angel providing a stark description of the utter devastation of Babylon (18:21-24), after which John witnesses the heavenly joy as expressed by the Great Multitude in heaven (19:1-3) and by the twenty-four elders and the four living creatures (19:4).

For language and imagery to describe the destruction of Babylon (18:1-24) John has drawn heavily upon several key Old Testament passages against Babylon (especially Isa 13:1-22; 14:3-23; 47:1-5; and Jer 50:1–51:64) and Edom (Isa 34:1-17). Especially important is Ezekiel's oracle against Tyre (Ezek 26:1–28:19). The use of such "traditional" language has two important consequences. First, details should not be pressed literally. Second, John's "Babylon," though it would certainly be understood by his readers in terms of Rome, is bigger than any specific city or empire.

Yet 18:1-24 does not read like a patchwork of Old Testament passages. It is a seamless whole that exudes power and pathos. Moreover, it is filled with allusions to virtually every section that precedes it in the book. Indeed, this lengthy section of lament and, eventually, rejoicing is in many ways the climax of the entire book to this point. To be sure, important events will follow in the next two chapters. But they will be treated much more briefly before giving way to the true climax of the book: the vision of the new Jerusalem (21:1–22:6a).

The importance of the vision that is to take place can be seen from the introduction John gives to it in 18:1. First, "another angel" comes down "from heaven." The language is almost identical with 10:1 (which adds "mighty"). The reader remembers that the angel in 10:1 brought the message that there would be "no more delay" in God's avenging the blood of his servants (10:6; cf. 6:9-11). The inclusion with 10:1 suggests that that time has now arrived. Second, the angel has "great authority." "Great authority" is found previously only in 13:2, where the dragon gave "great authority" to the beast. Finally, the effect of the angel's descent is that "the earth was made bright [lit., "illuminated"] with his splendor." Elsewhere, "splendor" (lit., "glory") is connected only with God and the Lamb (1:6; 4:9, 11; 5:12, 12; 7:12; 11:13; 14:7; 15:8; 16:9; 19:1, 7; 21:11, 23, 24, 26); similarly, only God is said to "illuminate" (21:23; 22:5). The angel clearly has something important to do.

The angel calls out (cf. 10:3) "with a mighty voice" and begins with a stark announcement—"Fallen, fallen is Babylon the great!" (18:2). This announcement exactly repeats 14:8, where Babylon was introduced into the book for the first time (cf. Isa 21:9; Jer 51:8). The angel observes that Babylon "has become a dwelling place of demons, a haunt of every foul spirit" (18:2), reminding the reader of the sixth bowl, where three "foul spirits," characterized further as "demonic spirits," issue from the mouth of the false prophet (16:13-14; cf. 9:20). Baruch 4:35 speaks of desolate Jerusalem as being "inhabited by demons" (cf. Tob 8:3; Matt 12:43; Mark 5:10). Similarly, the city has become "a haunt for every foul [lit., "unclean"] and hateful bird" (18:2). The picture of a destroyed city as being inhabited by birds and animals (so Codex Alexandrinus) that are "unclean"—i.e., prohibited by the Jewish dietary laws (e.g., Lev 11:2-8, 13-19; Deut 14:4-8, 12-18)—is a staple of such passages in the Old Testament (e.g., Isa 13:21-22; 14:23; 34:11, 13-15; Jer 9:11; 50:39).

The angel concludes with three reasons for Babylon's fall (18:3). The first two have been mentioned previously; the third is new. First, that "all nations have drunk the wine of her impure passion" is virtually identical with 14:8 (cf. 17:2; Jer 51:7). Similarly, that "the kings of the earth [cf. 1:5; 6:15; 17:18] have committed fornication with her" is virtually identical with 17:2 (cf. 18:9; cf. Nah 3:4). This second statement once again underscores the metaphorical sense of "fornication" in the book (see on 2:20-22); cities cannot literally commit fornication. The new element is that "the merchants of the earth have grown rich with the wealth of her wantonness [*strenos*]." *Strenos*, which is found only here in the book, can mean to live in sensuality (so the RSV), or to live in luxury. The verb form (*streniao*) is found in 18:7

to describe, oddly enough, the kings rather than the merchants. Hence, there is merit to viewing the words in the sense of "sensuality." But given the focus in 18:11-16 on merchandise, the sense of "luxury" cannot be overlooked (cf. the harlot's lavish adornment in 17:4). Perhaps the word is intended to be deliberately vague here: Babylon's wealth has seduced people. Certainly the merchants will be mentioned again in this chapter (18:11, 15; cf. 18:23), as will the notion of growing rich (18:15, 19). The introduction of the theme of wealth so far into the book (cf. 3:17) might seem striking, yet it is hardly surprising for a description of a "great city," which would be expected to be a center of trade. Indeed, even this element of the description of Babylon is rooted firmly in the Old Testament. Ezekiel says of Tyre, "with your abundant wealth and merchandise you enriched the kings of the earth" (Ezek 27:33). Taken together, the three elements that constitute the reasons for Babylon's fall reveal a wealthy trade center that garners the admiration, if not envy, of kings, merchants, and nations, all of whom align themselves with her in one way or another. Conspicuous by its absence in this description is any mention of the city's gods—i.e., Babylon is not condemned for idolatry but for its influence on the rest of the world. Could this be an indication that one of most pressing concerns in the book is that of accommodation to the socioeconomic enticements of the Roman Empire?

John hears another voice from heaven (18:4; cf. 10:4, 8; 11:12; 12:10; 14:2, 13). The voice gives an exhortation to God's people to "come out" of Babylon (18:4), two reasons why they should do so (18:4), two observations about Babylon's ripeness for judgment (18:5), four commands to punish Babylon (18:6-7), Babylon's threefold boast (18:7), two observations about Babylon's destiny (18:8), and a final comment about God as judge (18:8).

Echoing the language of Jer 51:45, the angel exhorts "my people" to come out of Babylon (18:4). Once again, the call for God's people to leave a doomed city is a common Old Testament theme (e.g., Isa 48:20; 52:11; Jer 50:8; 51:6; Zech 2:6-7). There are two reasons for God's people to come out of Babylon: so as not to "take part in her sins" or "share in her plagues" (18:4; cf. Jer 51:6, 45). Given that "her sins" is undoubtedly a reference to the previous verse, the concern seems to be that Christians will be ensnared by the city's seductive wealth. The mention of "her plagues" (cf. 18:8) cements the connection between the fall of Babylon and the seven trumpets (9:18, 20) and the seven bowls (15:1, 6, 8; 16:9, 21; cf. 11:6). The reason why Babylon is to receive plagues is that "her sins are heaped high as heaven" (18:5; cf. Jer 51:9). Indeed, "God has remembered [cf. 2:5; 3:3] her iniquities" (18:5). Babylon is most definitely deserving of judgment, and God is ready to implement it.

The voice gives four commands for the execution of judgment upon Babylon. That an angel is apparently giving commands to God here should not trouble the reader; in 14:14-15 an angel commands "one like a son of man"—presumably Jesus—to "reap" the harvest. John's concern is not to explain how commands are given and received in heaven but to build a dramatic—indeed ironic—picture, based on Old Testament language and imagery, of Babylon's judgment. The command to "render to her as she herself has rendered" echoes Jer 50:15, 29. Similarly, the idea of repaying her "double for her deeds" (18:6) is reminiscent of Jer 16:18 (cf. Isa 40:2). On the idea of judgment according to one's deeds, see on 2:23. The third command essentially repeats the second, now employing the imagery of the cup used earlier. In the very "cup" Babylon used to seduce others (17:2; cf. 14:8), she will now drink her own judgment in a "double draught." The reference to "mixing" reminds the reader of the "cup" of God's anger, which is "unmixed" (14:10; cf. 16:19). The final command, too, plays upon the image of the high-living harlot (cf. 17:4; 18:3): "torment and mourning" are most appropriate for one who "glorified herself and played the wanton" (18:7). That Babylon glorified "herself" rather than God (cf. 15:4; see further on 18:1) is testimony to her arrogance, which will be elaborated upon in the lines that follow. The use of the noun "torment," which will be used twice more in this section (18:10, 15), echoes both the sixth trumpet (9:5) and the third angel's message of God's judgment (14:11; see further on 11:10). "Mourning" is used three times in this verse and the next.

The reason for Babylon's punishment is her arrogance (cf. Jer 50:31; Ezek 28:2; *Sibylline Oracles* 5.173). The reader has previously encountered arrogance in the church at Laodicea (3:17). Babylon's threefold boast—that she sits "a queen," that she is not "a widow," that she shall never see "mourning" (18:7)—along with the affirmation that "her plagues" will "come in a single day" (18:8) is modeled on God's message to Babylon in Isa 47:7-9:

> You said, "I shall be queen [RSV "mistress"] for ever,"
> so that you did not lay these things to heart
> or remember their end.
> Now therefore hear this, you lover of pleasures,
> who sit securely,
> who say in your heart,
> "I am, and there is no one besides me;
> I shall not sit as a widow
> or know the loss of children":

These two things shall come to you
in a moment, in one day.

What Babylon says "in her heart" cannot be secret from the One who
searches mind and heart (2:23). That she "sits" as queen reminds the reader
of the harlot being seated on the beast (17:1). Her emphatic, yet ironic,
boast that she will "never" see mourning is belied by the command just
given to give her mourning. She has no idea what is about to come upon
her!

That her plagues will come "in a single day," which will be repeated in
the ongoing description of her judgment as "in one hour" (18:10, 17, 19),
reminds the reader of the ten kings who ravage the harlot (17:16), being
given authority "for one hour" (17:12). There is no difference in meaning: "a
single day" picks up the traditional language of Isa 47:9. The point is that
the devastation will occur with breathtaking speed. Her plagues (see on 18:4)
are specified as "pestilence and mourning and famine" (18:8). Pestilence and
famine were linked together, along with the sword, after the opening of the
fourth seal (6:8). The addition of mourning here underscores the irony of
Babylon's third boast in 18:7. Pestilence (RSV "death") and mourning will be
so linked, along with crying and pain, in 21:4. The second observation about
Babylon's destiny—that "she shall be burned with fire" (18:8)—echoes a
classic Old Testament detail in descriptions of doomed cities (e.g., Isa 47:14;
Jer 34:22; 51:58; Ezek 28:18; cf. *Sibylline Oracles* 3.52-62), which were
frequently burned by those who conquered them (e.g., 2 Kgs 25:8-9). The
reader remembers 17:16, where the angel says that the ten horns and the
beast will burn up the harlot with fire. The reason for Babylon's judgment is
that the Lord God "who judges her" is "mighty" (18:8). For God as judge to
this point in the book, see 6:10; 14:7; 16:5 (cf. 19:11). Babylon's judgment
will be mentioned three more times in this section (18:10, 20; 19:2).

The announcement of Babylon's fate and the reasons for it are over.
Interestingly, there is no narrative of the actual destruction of Babylon,
which is another indication that this passage is not so much about a specific
city or empire—e.g., Rome—as it is about something deeper. Instead, the
reader finds three sections containing laments over the destruction of
Babylon: by the kings of the earth (18:9-10), by the merchants of the earth
(18:11-17a), and by the seafarers (18:17b-19). Each section begins with an
observation about the group's relationship with Babylon (18:9, 15, 17b).
Each group is said to stand "far off" (18:9, 15, 17b) and to "weep" over her
(18:10 [+ wail], 11 and 15 [+ mourn], 19 [+ mourn]). The kings and the
merchants are said to be "in fear of her torment" (18:10, 15), and the kings

and the seafarers are said to see "the smoke of her burning" (18:9, 18; cf. 17:16; 18:8; 19:3). The structure of each lament (18:19-10, 15-17a, 17b-19) is essentially the same: it begins with "Alas, alas, for the great city" (18:10 [RSV "thou great city"], 16, 19), continues with an observation about the city relevant to the group that is speaking (18:10, 16, 19), and ends with a reference to Babylon's destruction "in one hour" (18:10: "has thy judgment come," 17a: "all this wealth has been laid waste," 19: "she has been laid waste"). The section on the merchants is the longest of the three, containing a list of specific types of cargo (18:11-13) and a concluding observation about the fate of Babylon (18:14). In the final section, the seafarers precede their lament with a plaintive—and ultimately ironic—question. Whether these sections represent John's own commentary (so RSV) or are a continuation of the voice from heaven in 18:4 is unclear.

The very idea of people lamenting the fall of a great city is drawn from Ezekiel's oracle against Tyre, a coastal city renowned for being a center of trade:

> all the princes of the sea will step down from their thrones, and remove their robes,
> and strip off their embroidered garments; they will clothe themselves with trembling;
> they will sit upon the ground and tremble every moment, and be appalled at you.
> And they will raise a lamentation over you. (Ezek 26:16-17a)

Ezekiel goes on to recite their song of lament (Ezek 26:17b-18). Indeed, the prophet even mentions the responses of the three groups that are found in Rev 18 (cf. Ezek 27:29-32, 35-36). John will make good use of Ezekiel's prophecy against Tyre (Ezek 26:1–28:19) throughout this chapter.

"The kings of the earth" (see on 16:12; cf. Ezek 27:35) are characterized as those who "committed fornication and were wanton with her" (18:9; cf. 17:2; 18:3). The mention of smoke reminds the reader of the unending smoke of torment that rises from the punishment of those who worship the beast (14:11; cf. Isa 34:10). The kings stand far off (18:10; cf. 18:15, 17b) because they are "in fear of her torment" (cf. 18:15). One can mourn the destruction of a city; just do not get too close! On "torment" see on 18:7. The kings lament that Babylon was "the mighty city" (18:10). It is precisely a city's power that attracts kings to enter into alliances with it in the first place. The reference to the "judgment" (*krisis*) of the city forms an inclusion with the beginning of John's third "in the Spirit" experience: "Come, I will show you the judgment [*krima*] of the great harlot" (17:1).

The lament of "the merchants of the earth" (cf. Ezek 27:36) is similar to that of the kings. The merchants are characterized in terms of their own relationship with Babylon: they are those "who gained wealth from her" (18:15). Merchants are mentioned only in this section of the book (cf. 18:3, 11, 23); material wealth here (18:3, 17, 19; cf. 5:12) and in 3:17. The merchants describe the great city as the one "that was clothed in fine linen, in purple and scarlet, bedecked with gold, with jewels, and with pearls" (18:16). The language is virtually identical with the description of the harlot in 17:4. Fine linen, not found in 17:4, is one of the cargo items listed in 18:11-13 and will be mentioned again (19:8 [twice], 14), as will precious stones (21:11, 19) and pearls (21:21). True to their professions, the merchants lament the swift ruin of "all this wealth" (18:17; cf. Ezek 27:33; 28:4-5).

Prior to the merchants' lament is a unit that has no parallel in the section on the kings or, for that matter, on the section on the seafarers that is to follow. The merchants of the earth are said to "weep and mourn" for Babylon (18:11), a statement that is repeated in 18:15. The self-centered, though understandable, reason—that "no one buys their cargo any more" (18:11)—matches the self-centered orientation of Babylon herself (18:7). The reader remembers that no one could buy or sell unless he had the mark of the beast (13:17). Once again John echoes Ezekiel's oracle against Tyre by listing the various kinds of cargo in which the merchants deal (18:12-13; cf. the similar, though not identical, list in Ezek 27:12-24). The diverse list, which consists primarily of luxury items affordable only by the rich, reveals not only some items that were produced in Italy itself (e.g., wine, olive oil, fine flour), but also an extensive network of trade—e.g., central Europe (iron), Spain (gold, silver, iron, wine, olive oil), North Africa (citron [RSV "scented"] wood, olive oil, ivory, wheat), Egypt (fine linen, fine flour, wheat), East Africa (cinnamon, myrrh, frankincense), Arabia (cinnamon, myrrh, frankincense), the Persian Gulf (pearls), the Indian Ocean (pearls), India (precious stones, ivory, cinnamon, *amomon* [RSV "spice"]), China (silk), Scythopolis (fine linen), Tyre (purple dye, silk), Phrygia (marble), Corinth (bronze), Greece (iron, wine), and Sicily (wine). The merchants lament the fate of Babylon: it has lost forever "the fruit for which thy soul longed" and "all thy dainties and thy splendor" (18:14; cf. Ezek 27:27, 34). The fleeting "splendor" (*lampra*) of Babylon stands in stark contrast to the unending "splendor" (*lampros*: RSV "bright") of the pure linen of the seven angels (15:6), the fine linen of the Bride of the Lamb (19:8), the river of the water of life (22:1), and Jesus himself (22:16). The last phrase, "never to be found again," anticipates a recurring refrain in 18:21-23: "shall [be found, be heard, be found, be heard, shine, be heard] in thee no more."

Finally, the seafarers bring their lament. Specifically, they are identified as "all shipmasters and seafaring men, sailors and all whose trade is on the sea" (18:17b; cf. Ezek 27:29). These are the people who make possible all of the trade that comes by ship. The merchants—and the city—would be much the poorer without them. But unlike the kings and the merchants, the seafarers preface their lament with a question: "Who is [RSV "was"] like the great city?" (18:18). The seafarers in Ezekiel's oracle against Tyre raise a similar question: "Who was ever destroyed like Tyre in the midst of the sea?" (Ezek 27:32). But perhaps more importantly, the question in 18:18 takes the reader back to the first question in 13:4: "Who is like the beast?" If such a question can be raised about the great city, which has now been destroyed, can there be any doubt that the same fate awaits the beast, who goes "to destruction" (cf. 17:8, 11)? Like their predecessors in Ezek 27:30, the seafarers throw "dust" on their heads (18:19). Like the merchants in 18:17a, the seafarers lament the sudden demise of that which deprives them of their livelihood—of the city "where all who had ships at sea [cf. 8:9] grew rich by her wealth" (18:19; cf. Ezek 27:9).

The announcement of the destruction of Babylon and the subsequent laments (18:1-19) bring to fruition what John was promised in 17:1—that he would see the judgment of the great harlot. The dominant—though by no means only—element in the description of Babylon in this section has been the economic element. To be sure, this emphasis could be explained in terms of John's heavy dependence in this section on Ezekiel's prophecy against Tyre. In addition, one could argue that to describe a great city in terms of its being a center of trade would be only natural. And so once again, one should not press the details literally here. But at the same time one cannot help but notice the parallels between the arrogance of Babylon and that of the church at Laodicea, which prided itself on its prosperity. There are also strong parallels to the situation in the church at Thyatira, where "Jezebel's" false teaching might be connected with participation in trade guilds. The reader also remembers the mark of the beast, without which one cannot buy or sell. Add to these virtually no interest in this section on military prowess or idolatry, and the reader can infer only that the economic emphasis must be more than simply traditional. John's readers are, at least in part, being enticed by the socioeconomic system of Rome. Hence, they need to "come out" of her. Perhaps this is why the "judgment of the great harlot" takes precedence even over the judgment of the beast, the false prophet, and the dragon in this section, both in terms of space allotted and in terms of

John's initial orientation to his third "in the Spirit" experience in 17:1. It is the temptation to accommodate to the surrounding culture, as much as (more than?) the threat of outright persecution, that is the most serious problem faced by the seven churches of Asia.

From the perspective of all who have engaged themselves on earth with the great city Babylon, her destruction is a disaster to be lamented. But from God's perspective, it is to be celebrated. With no indication of a change of speaker there is an abrupt shift in tone in 18:20. In words echoing Jer 51:48, heaven is invited to "rejoice" over Babylon (18:20; cf. Deut 32:43). This is the second time in the book that heaven has been called upon to rejoice; the first time was after the dragon was thrown down from heaven (12:12). Also invited to rejoice are the saints and apostles and prophets. There is no reason to see these as three distinct groups. On saints and prophets see on 11:18. The presence of "apostles" is somewhat surprising, since it is used elsewhere only in 2:2, referring to the apostles whom the church at Ephesus found to be false, and in 21:14, where it refers to the twelve apostles. Yet if the word "apostle" were restricted to the Twelve, then there would be no reason for the church at Ephesus to have "tested" those who called themselves "apostles." As in the case of "saints" and "prophets," then, "apostles" must be a word that is applicable to all Christians. The reason to rejoice is that "God has given judgment [cf. 14:7; 16:7; 17:1; 19:2; 20:4] for you against her" (18:20). This statement will be defined more clearly in 18:24 and 19:2.

Following the abrupt shift from lament to rejoicing, John sees "a mighty angel" (18:21; cf. 5:2; 10:1), who carries out a symbolic act (18:21) and then explains its meaning (18:21-24). The angel's act—taking up "a great millstone" and throwing it "into the sea"—and the first part of the explanation that follows it (18:21) is reminiscent of Jer 51:63-64 (cf. Ezek 26:12; 27:27). Millstones were used in pairs, one being rotated on top of the other to make flour or oil. The largest millstones were turned by animals and could be called "the millstone of a donkey" (Matt 18:6; Mark 9:42: RSV "a great millstone"). The idea of having a great millstone hung around one's neck and being cast into the sea is found in Matt 18:6 and Mark 9:42. The angel explains his action in terms of the utter and final destruction of "the great city" (cf. 18:2, 10, 16, 19, 20; cf. 16:19) Babylon. That Babylon is "thrown down" is reminiscent of the dragon being "thrown down" from heaven (12:9 [three times], 10, 13; cf. 8:7, 8) and anticipates what will happen to the beast and the false prophet (19:20) and the devil (20:10). The refrain "shall . . . in thee no more" occurs six times in 18:21-24.

There follows a list of things that will be forever absent from the city in the aftermath of her destruction (cf. Isa 13:20): the sound of harpers and minstrels; the sound of flute players and trumpeters; a craftsman of any craft; the sound of a millstone; the light of a lamp; and the voice of bridegroom and bride (18:22-23). Once again, this is a common theme in Old Testament passages that describe the utter destruction of a city. The absence of music is mentioned, for example, in Isa 14:11; 24:8; Ezek 26:13 (cf. 1 Macc 3:45). Jer 25:10 mentions the millstone, the lamp, and the bride and bridegroom. Jeremiah also speaks of the absence of the voices of bride and bridegroom (Jer 7:34; 16:9; 33:11; cf. Bar 2:23). It is worth noting, in light of the emphasis on economics in 18:1-19, that the absence of craftsmen is not found in such passages in the Old Testament. The traditional language has been supplemented by that of commerce.

The pronouncement of three reasons for the destruction of Babylon in 18:23-24 forms both an inclusion and a chiasm with 18:3. Though rejoicing in heaven will continue for a few more verses, the scene is set to shift now from Babylon to heaven. The first two reasons are given in the second person, while the third is in the third person. The first reason—that "thy merchants were the great men of the earth" (18:23)—parallels the third reason given in 18:3. The language is drawn from Isa 23:8. Though it is not specified exactly what the merchants have done wrong, the point seems to be that through the economic prosperity of the city, its merchants have achieved an influence beyond what they deserve. True power is not economic power. The second reason—that "all nations were deceived by your sorcery" (18:23; cf. Isa 47:9; Nah 3:4)—parallels the second reason given in 18:3. "Sorceries" were previously mentioned after the blowing of the sixth trumpet as something from which "the rest of mankind" did not repent (9:21); "sorcerers" will be found in 21:8 and 22:15. Up to this point in the book Jezebel (2:20), the dragon (12:9; cf. 20:3, 8, 10), and the false prophet (13:14; cf. 19:20) have been associated with the act of deceiving. To that list is now added Babylon. The third reason—that "in her was found the blood of prophets and of saints, and of all who have been slain on earth" (18:24)—seems at first glance to parallel only loosely the first reason in 18:3, which speaks merely of the kings of the earth drinking the wine of Babylon's impure passion (cf. 17:2). But in 17:6 that wine is identified as the blood of the saints and the blood of the witnesses of Jesus, so the parallel is real. Given the parallel, then, between 17:6 and 18:24, "prophets" parallels "witnesses" (cf. 11:3, 10), which once again demonstrates that "saints," "witnesses," and "prophets" are all interchangeable terms that can be used for Christians in general. The further identification of those who have shed their blood as all who have "been slain" on earth (18:24) takes the reader back immediately to the fifth seal, where those who had "been slain" for the word of God cried out for God to avenge their blood (6:9-10). Given the use of "all" in 18:24, it is clear that "the number of their fellow servants . . . who were to be killed as they themselves had been" is now complete (6:11). God's promise has been fulfilled. Their blood has been avenged on Babylon (cf. Jer 51:35, 49).

In 19:1 the focus shifts ("After this . . .") from earth (and Babylon) to heaven. John hears "the loud voice of a great multitude in heaven." Is this group the same as the Great Multitude in 7:9? Four points favor this identification. First, the language is identical with 7:9. Second, the Great Multitude in 7:9 was in heaven, as is this group. Third, as the introduction of the Great Multitude in 7:9 followed the question of "those who had been slain" in 6:9-10, so also the mention of this group follows the answer to their question in 18:24. Finally, in both songs "Salvation . . ." dominates the opening of the song. Following the lengthy section on the fall of Babylon, the Great Multitude, not heard from since chapter 7 but waiting in the wings, reappears with its characteristic song of salvation, but now in a higher key.

The song begins with "Hallelujah!" (19:1), which will be repeated in 19:3, 4, 6. "Hallelujah," from the Hebrew *halelu yah*, literally means "Praise Yah(weh)." Yahweh is the Old Testament name for God (cf. Exod 3:14). "Hallelujah" is frequently used in the Psalms (e.g., Pss 106:1; 111:1; 112:1; 113:1; 117:1; 146:1; 147:1; 148:1; 149:1; 150:1; cf. 3 Macc 7:13; Tob 13:18). To "our God" they render "salvation [cf. 7:10; 12:10] and glory [cf. 1:6; 4:9, 11; 5:12, 13; 7:12; 19:7] and power [cf. 4:11; 5:12; 7:12; 11:17; 12:10]."

The reason for the praise is threefold (19:2). First, God's "judgments are true and just," an expression found also in 16:17 (cf. 15:3). Second, he "has judged the great harlot" (cf. 17:1; 18:9, 20). They characterize the great harlot further as one "who corrupted the earth with her fornication" (cf. 17:2, 4; 18:3). Third, "he has avenged [*ekdikeo*] on her the blood of his servants." The use of *ekdikeo* here cements once and for all the connection with 6:9-10, the only other place in the book where *ekdikeo* is found. This will be the last mention in the book of the theme of avenging the blood of God's servants (cf. 16:6; 17:6; 18:24), a theme drawn from Deut 32:43 (see on 15:3; cf. 2 Kgs 9:7; Ps 79:10; Joel 3:21).

The reintroduction of the theme of the blood of God's servants in 18:24 and 19:2—and of Babylon's responsibility for it—raises the question of whether the "economic" interpretation of the sins of Babylon as characterized in 18:1-19 is sufficient. Have we not returned once more to the problem of persecution and martyrdom? Indeed, the theme of blood comes as the third, and (dramatically) last, of three observations about Babylon in 18:23-24 and is one of only *two* such observations made in 19:2. Certainly it would be foolish to say John was unaware that God's opponents ever perse-cute and kill God's people (cf. 2:13; 6:9-10; 11:7-12; 13:15). But that is quite different from saying God has a special concern for literal martyrs in this book or even that his primary concern is with literal persecution and martyrdom. The theme is drawn from Deut 32:43, from which John quotes virtually verbatim in his final comment on the issue (19:2), and which is part of the Song of Moses, to which John refers in 15:3. These observations lend support to the notion that persecution/martyrdom is part of a "traditional" theme in the book, rather than a primary point of interest for John and, hence, the seven churches of Asia. John has already given several clues to this effect (see, e.g., on 11:7-12 and on 13:15-17) and will give one final—and unmistakable—one in 20:4-6.

The Great Multitude speaks for a second time, again beginning with "Hallelujah!" (19:3). Echoing the words of Isa 34:10, they affirm the utter destruction of the great harlot: "the smoke from her goes up for ever and ever" (19:3; cf. 17:16; 18:8, 9, 13). Responding to the Great Multitude, the twenty-four elders and the four living creatures (cf. 4:1–5:13; 7:11; 11:16; 14:3) fall down and worship (cf. 5:8, 14; 7:11; 11:16) "God who is seated on the throne" (19:4; cf. 4:2, 3, 4, 9, 10; 5:1, 7, 13; 6:16; 7:10, 15), assenting to all that the Great Multitude has said. Their words are simple: "Amen. Hallelujah!" (19:4). For "Amen" see on 1:6. This is the last reference in the book to the twenty-four elders and the four living creatures.

When she comes to the end of the section on the judgment of Babylon (18:1–19:4), the reader has encountered several "lasts" in the book—the last reference to the great city Babylon, to the great harlot, to the need to avenge the blood of the servants of God, and to the twenty-four elders and the four living creatures. It is clear that this section marks a significant climax of sorts in the book. But several questions remain. What will happen to the dragon? to the beast and the false prophet? What about the battle of Armageddon? And what about the question of 13:4: who can fight against the beast? The reader might also ask, what will the kings of the earth, the merchants, and the seafarers do after the destruction of Babylon? To put it differently, is the fall of Babylon an event in history to be followed by other events throughout the course of the rest of history? Does "time" as we understand it continue?

"The Bride has made herself ready":
The announcement of the wedding of the Lamb
Revelation 19:5-10

In a manner similar to 8:1-6, 19:5-10 serves as a key transition passage in Revelation: both are brief passages set in heaven, both are closely connected with what precedes them, and both introduce new elements into the book (the arrival of judgment, the Bride of the Lamb). John first hears a voice from the throne praising God (19:5) and something like the voice of the Great Multitude announcing the wedding of the Lamb (19:6-8). There follows the fourth beatitude, spoken by the angel (19:9) and an interchange between the angel and John (19:10).

The voice from the throne (19:5; cf. 16:17; 21:3) serves to set the tone for what is to follow. The invitation to "Praise our God" (cf. Pss 106:48; 134:1; 135:1) is found only here in the book. That those invited are "his servants, you who fear him, small and great" (19:5) directs the reader back to 11:18, where all of those groups are mentioned. That verse announced the arrival of "the time for the dead to be judged, for rewarding thy servants, the prophets and the saints, and those who fear thy name, both small and great." The reader is ready: it is time for judgment and reward.

John then hears a longer announcement. The piling up of phrases used to introduce the announcement (19:6)—"what seemed to be the voice of a great multitude, like the sound of many waters [cf. 1:15; 14:2], and like the sound of mighty thunderpeals [cf. 6:1; 14:2]"—serves to build suspense and heighten the dramatic effect of what is about to be said. Given John's insertion of "what seemed to be" before "a great multitude," there is no reason to believe that he is restricting what follows to the lips of the Great Multitude (cf. 7:9; 19:1). All three phrases suggest volume: this is a loud—and, hence, very important—announcement!

Once again the song begins with "Hallelujah!" (19:6; cf. 19:1, 3, 4). The reason for the praise is that "the Lord our [Codex Alexandrinus omits "our"] God the Almighty has begun to reign [aorist of *basileuo*: RSV "reigns"]" (19:6; cf. 1 Chr 16:31; Pss 93:1; 97:1; 99:1). For "Lord God Almighty" see 1:8; 4:8; 11:17; 15:3; 16:7; 21:22 (cf., without "Lord," 16:14; 19:15). Once again (cf. 19:5) there is an allusion to 11:17, which says that "the Lord God Almighty . . . hast . . . begun to reign [aorist of *basileuo*]". The storyline that was left off in 11:17-18 has now been picked up again. The voice calls for "us" to "rejoice [*chairo*] and exult and give him the glory" (19:7; cf. 1 Chr 16:28-29). Elsewhere, *chairo* is used only in 11:10. In yet another allusion back to chapter 11, the reader recognizes the irony. Those who dwell on the earth rejoiced over the death of the two witnesses; now it is time for the two witnesses—the Church—to rejoice. On giving glory to God, see on 11:13 (yet another allusion to this section).

The reason for the joy is that the "marriage of the Lamb has come" (19:7). The marvelously mixed metaphor of a lamb getting married catches the reader completely unawares: nothing in the book has prepared her for "the marriage of the Lamb." But not only does the reader learn for the first time about such a marriage, she also learns that it "has come." The announcement speaks not only of the Lamb's marriage, but also of "his Bride [*gune*—lit., "woman"]" (19:7). The Bride is the fourth woman mentioned so far in the book, after Jezebel (2:20), the woman clothed in the sun (12:1, 4, 6, 13, 14, 15, 16, 17), and the great harlot (17:4, 6, 7, 9, 18). As there is a certain correspondence between the first and the third, so also there is a certain correspondence between the second and the fourth. Is the Bride, in fact, to be identified with the woman clothed with the sun? After all, the Bride "has made herself ready" (19:7), which could be an allusion to the woman being nourished in the wilderness for 1,260 days (12:6, 14). Weighing against this identification, however, is that, apart from the reference to a "woman," there are no clear allusions here to chapter 12. Similarly, the great harlot is not simply Jezebel. What *is* important about the Bride is that she is the counterpart to the great harlot. As the beast is content with a harlot, the Lamb chooses a Bride. Evil is always a "cheap imitation" of what is true and right.

Who is the Bride? 19:8 equates the "fine linen" that "was granted her" to wear with "the righteous deeds of the saints." Clearly the Bride is not a literal woman. The association with the saints (cf. 5:8; 8:3, 4; 11:18; 13:7, 10; 14:12; 16:6; 17:6; 18:20, 24; 20:9; 22:21) suggests that the Bride is to be identified with the Church. The non-literal use of the image of a bride has its roots in the Old Testament: Isa 48:18, for example, speaks of Jerusalem as a bride adorning herself (cf. Isa 61:10). Similarly, in the New Testament Paul speaks of the Church as the Bride of Christ (e.g., 2 Cor 11:2; Eph 5:31-32).

The Bride's preparation for the marriage is explained in two ways that at first glance might seem to be in tension. On the one hand, the Bride "has made herself ready" (19:7; cf. 21:1)—i.e., she seems to have taken the initiative. On the other hand, "it was granted her to be clothed with fine linen, bright and pure" (19:8)—i.e., she seems to be the beneficiary of someone else's (presumably God, since "was granted" is best understood as a divine passive) actions. But then the fine linen is defined as "the righteous deeds of the saints" (19:8), which seems to support the first option. As has been the case throughout the book, precedence should be given to the second option.

It is the Lamb who has loved, freed, and made (1:5-6), ransomed and made (5:9-10; cf. 14:5), and shed the blood to be used in the washing of robes (7:14). Yet the Lamb's followers are not off the hook: they are expected to live appropriately as conquerors (2-3), hold to the word of their testimony (12:11), keep the commandments of God and the faith of Jesus (14:12; cf. cf. 12:17), and "come out" of Babylon (18:4). But such deeds are possible only because of what the Lamb has done first. All brides make themselves ready for their wedding; the Bride of the Lamb has received her wedding garment from the Lamb.

In contrast to the gaudy adornment of the great harlot (17:4), the Bride's wedding attire is simple and straightforward (19:8). The great harlot Babylon was "clothed" in fine linen, purple and scarlet, and gold, jewels, and pearls (18:16; cf. 17:4); the Bride will be "clothed" simply in fine linen. The great harlot was renowned for its "splendor" (*lampros*); the Bride's fine linen is "bright" (*lampros*). Babylon will become a haunt for "impure" (*akatharos*: RSV "foul") spirits, birds, and beasts; the Bride's fine linen is "pure" (*katharos*). Fine linen was worn by priests (e.g., Exod 28:5, 6, 8, 15, 39, 42; Lev 6:10 [LXX Lev 6:3]; 16:4, 22). It could also be part of the adornment, along with jewelry and other fine clothing, of a woman dressed for beauty (e.g., Ezek 16:10-14). Given the fact that fine linen is the only part of such adornment specified here, it is likely that another reference to the priestly role of the Church is intended (cf. 1:6; 5:10; 20:6).

19:9 begins rather abruptly: "And the angel [lit., "he"] said to me." Who is "he"? Presumably an angel (so RSV). Does "he" refer to the last angel mentioned (18:21)? the angel who mediated the revelation to John (1:1)? The latter has been strangely absent from the book up until now, though John will mention him in 22:8. Given that what will take place at that point is remarkably similar to what happens here, John is probably speaking here of that angel. John's account of the revelation that God gave to Jesus Christ to make known to him by an angel (1:1) has paid no attention to this mediating angel up to this point in the book, but that does not mean that the angel has not been present all along. It is noteworthy that the angel makes his first explicit appearance in the book at the point of the announcement of the marriage of the Lamb. He makes his second, and final, appearance in 22:8, thus framing the narrative of the marriage supper (19:17-21) and the appearance of the Bride herself (21:9–22:6a). The timing of these appearances by the "featured guest" can only heighten the reader's sense that, despite all that has gone before in the book, the best is about to come.

As in the case of the second beatitude (14:13), John is specifically commanded here to write another (the fourth; cf. 1:3; 14:13; 16:15; 20:6;

22:7, 14): "Blessed are those who are invited to the marriage supper of the Lamb" (19:9). The marriage supper, a normal part of a wedding celebration, was not mentioned in 19:7, where the marriage of the Lamb was announced. The reference to the supper here, especially in the form of a beatitude, underscores the importance of the impending wedding of the Lamb. To ask questions about the relationship of the invited guests to the Bride—e.g., since the Bride represents the Church, who else would be invited?—is to press the language too literally and, hence, to miss the point. This is all a picture. The marriage of the Lamb has arrived, and it far surpasses everything else in importance.

The angel speaks again to John, affirming that he speaks "the true words of God" (19:9). This expression, introduced here in the book for the first time, anticipates a similar expression in 21:5 and 22:6. John's response is startling. In an action that will be repeated in 22:8-9, John falls before the feet (see on 4:10) of the angel and worships (19:10; cf. 22:8). But the angel stops John, identifying himself as "a fellow servant [cf. 6:11] with you and your brethren [cf. 1:9; 6:11; 12:10] who hold the testimony [cf. 1:2, 9; 12:17; 20:4] of Jesus" (19:10; cf. 22:9). This is a rather remarkable statement for an angel, if that is indeed who is speaking here; there is nothing to distinguish him ontologically from a human. He then commands John, "Worship God" (19:10; cf. 22:9), a most appropriate command for this book (see on 22:9).

This passage is odd, to say the least. After all of the worship directed toward God and the Lamb that John has witnessed in this book, one would think he would know better than to worship an angel! Is he really so slow to catch on? Alternately, is it possible that the passage is aimed at a problem of angel worship in the churches of Asia (something of which John has made no mention to this point)? This passage is best understood as a literary device designed to underscore emphatically that God alone is to be worshiped. A similar incident occurs in the apocryphal book of Tobit. In Tob 12:16, near the conclusion of the book, Tobit and his son Tobias fall down before the angel Raphael, who, while disguising who he really is, has been the source of the solutions for the various problems that drive the plot of the book and who has now revealed his true identity. Raphael's response is to deflect the attention from himself and to direct the father and son to praise and give thanks to God, which they do (Tob 12:17-22). John wants to make sure his readers get the point—indeed, so sure that he will repeat the story in 22:8-9.

This section concludes with a final explanatory observation: "for the testimony of Jesus is the spirit of prophecy" (19:10). Is this John's observation (so RSV) or the angel's? The latter is certainly possible, but given that this observation is missing from the almost identical passage in 22:8-9, the former is more likely. "Prophecy" is used six times elsewhere in the book. Since five of these references are to John's book itself (1:3; 22:7, 10, 18, 19; cf. 11:6), it is reasonable to infer that this observation is also about the book—it is the testimony Jesus gives that inspires John's prophecy (cf. 1:1).

The little section 19:5-10 serves several purposes. First, by introducing the Bride of Christ, it anticipates John's fourth "in the Spirit" experience, which will focus on the Bride of Christ, just as the introduction of the beast in 11:17 anticipated the section on the three signs in heaven and the introduction of Babylon in 14:8 anticipated the third "in the Spirit" experience. Second, through its allusions to 11:15-18 it picks up the storyline of God beginning his rule and establishing the time for judgment and reward: judgment will follow in 19:11-21 and 20:1-3, 7-15, and reward, anticipated in 20:4-6, in 21:1–22:6a. Finally, the interchange with the angel, along with John's subsequent observation, anticipates the end of the book and its intended effect upon the reader (22:6b-21).

"And I saw the beast and the kings of the earth with their armies gathered to make war against him who sits upon the horse and against his army": The judgment of the Beast and the False Prophet
Revelation 19:11-21

The judgment of the great harlot Babylon has taken place. Now what about the beast and the false prophet? The reader need wait no longer. This section consists of three scenes, each introduced by "And I saw . . . ." John sees a rider on a white horse and his armies (19:11-16), an angel inviting the birds to the great supper of God (19:17-18), and the defeat of the beast and the false prophet, along with the kings and their armies (19:19-21).

19:11-21 is a mosaic of images from previous sections of book. For example, the armies of heaven (19:14) recall 7:4-8 and 14:1-5; treading the wine press (19:15) recalls 14:20; "King of Kings and Lord of Lords" (19:16) recalls 17:14; "God Almighty" (19:15) recalls 16:14; kings, captains, mighty men, the free, and the slaves (19:18) recall 6:15; "the kings of the earth" (19:19) recalls 17:2, 18; 18:2, 3, 9; the horses and those riding upon them (19:18) and the armies of the kings (19:19) recall 9:16; the kings as "gathered to make war" (19:19) recalls 16:14, 16 (and anticipates 20:8); making war against the rider (19:19) recalls 17:14 (the ten kings against the Lamb);

the false prophet (19:20) recalls 16:13; and the juxtaposition of the beast and the false prophet with miraculous signs (19:20) recalls 16:14.

But above all, this section recalls the first seal. The figure whom John sees is initially described in words that are identical in 6:2 and in 19:11: *kai idou hippos leukos kai ho kathemenos ep' auton* (lit., "and behold a white horse and one sitting upon it"). That the same nine consecutive Greek words are found in both passages leaves no doubt that the reader is intended to connect them. Furthermore, unless there is some good reason to distinguish between the two riders—which there is not—the reader has no choice but to see them as one and the same. To recall the opening of the first seal is to recall the scroll that was transferred from the one seated upon the throne to the Lamb (5:1, 7). Is the reader about to encounter that scroll again?

John sees heaven opened (19:11; cf. 4:1; Ezek 1:1), as well as a white horse and someone sitting on it (19:11). Once again the reader thinks of the "hear/see" pattern that John has used to identify the conquering Lion with the slain Lamb (cf. 5:5-6) and the 144,000 "Jews" with the Great Multitude from every nation, tribe, people, and tongue (7:4-9). John has just heard an invitation to the marriage supper of the Lamb (19:9); is he now about to see the supper itself?

In addition to his being seated upon a white horse, John characterizes the rider in nine ways. Once again it is worth noting how much of the characterization is John's commentary, rather than part of the vision (e.g., what he is called [19:11], the fact that he alone knows the inscribed name [19:12], that he "will" tread the wine press [19:15]).

First, the rider is called "Faithful and True" (19:11). This first detail is a good indication of what will be made clear as the description continues— i.e., that the rider is Jesus. Jesus is called the "faithful and true witness" in 3:14 (cf. 1:5). In addition, God affirms his own words to be "faithful and true" in 21:5 (cf. 3:7).

Second, the rider "judges and makes war" in righteousness (19:11). That God will come to judge in righteousness is a common theme in the Old Testament (e.g, Pss 9:8; 72:2; 96:12-13; 98:9; cf. *Psalms of Solomon* 17:29). Zechariah uses the image of a war to depict the confrontation between God and "the nations": "then the LORD will go forth and fight against those nations as when he fights on a day of battle" (Zech 14:3; cf. Isa 30:30-33). Isa 11:4 combines both concepts: "with righteousness he shall judge the poor, and decide with equity for the meek of the earth; and he shall smite the earth with the rod of his mouth, and with the breath of his lips he shall slay the wicked." Elsewhere in Revelation only God is said to judge (6:10; 11:18; 16:5; 18:8, 20; 19:2; 20:12, 13). "Making war" is a common theme throughout the book (e.g., the beast vs. the two witnesses [11:7 + *poieo*], Michael and his angels vs. the dragon and vice versa [12:7], the dragon vs. the rest of the offspring of the woman [12:17 + *poieo*], the beast vs. the saints [13:7 + *poieo*], the kings of the whole world assembling on the great day of God the Almighty [16:14 + *sunago*], the ten kings vs. the Lamb [17:14], and the gathering of Gog and Magog [20:8 + *sunago*]). In 2:16 Jesus threatens to make war with those who hold to the teachings of the Nicolaitans in Pergamum. Against whom does the rider come to make war? The answer is given in 19:19, where the reader learns that the beast and the kings of the earth with their armies are gathered (*sunago*) to make war (+ *poieo*) against the rider and his army.

As has been the case throughout Revelation, the war imagery must not be pressed literally. Instructive in this regard is Joel 3:2, where God says, "I will gather all the nations and bring them down to the valley of Jehoshaphat, and I will enter into judgment with them there." A few verses later there is a shift to war imagery; God says,

> Proclaim this among the nations:
> Prepare war,
> stir up the mighty men.
> Let all the men of war draw near,
> let them come up.
> Beat your plowshares into swords,
> and your pruning hooks into spears;
> let the weak say, "I am a warrior."
> Hasten and come,
> all you nations round about,
> gather yourselves there. (Joel 3:9-11)

Yet the very next verse returns to the theme of judgment:

> Let the nations bestir themselves,
> and come up to the valley of Jehoshaphat;
> for there I will sit to judge
> all the nations round about. (Joel 3:12)

Joel is not speaking of a literal war here, but of judgment. The language of war is simply used to depict in a vivid fashion the hatred toward God of those who are to be judged by him.

Similar is *4 Ezra* 13, a passage that has striking similarities to John's vision and that is roughly contemporary with it. The Jewish author records a vision in which he sees the Messiah and "all who had gathered together against him, to wage war with him" (*4 Ezra* 13:8). The Messiah defeats his opponents using weapons that come forth from his mouth (*4 Ezra* 13:9-11). God then interprets the vision for the author: the weapons from the mouth symbolize words of judgment that the Messiah will speak against his enemies (*4 Ezra* 13:27-38). As in Joel, war imagery serves the larger theme of judgment.

Given so many popular interpretations of Revelation as a book that predicts literal wars on earth, most notably Armageddon, *the importance of recognizing the use in Judaism of war imagery as a graphic depiction of judgment can scarcely be overstated.* John has given clues throughout the book that this is his intention, as we have seen. He provides perhaps the clearest statement of all in 19:11 by prefacing "makes war" with the verb "judges." 19:11-21 is a picture of judgment, *not* of a literal war.

Third, the rider's eyes are "like a flame of fire" (19:12). The same language is used for Jesus in 1:14 and 2:18.

Fourth, the rider has "many diadems" upon his head (19:12). Elsewhere in the book only the dragon (12:3) and the beast (13:1) are said to be wearing diadems. That the rider is wearing "many" diadems is telling: the dragon has only seven and the beast only ten. In addition, the dragon and the beast were limited to one diadem per head. The rider has *many* diadems on *one* head. The rider—not the dragon or the beast—is the one with true and complete royal authority.

Fifth, the rider has "a name inscribed which no one knows but himself" (19:12). Elsewhere the conqueror (2:17; 3:12), the 144,000 (14:1), and the great harlot (17:5) have names written on them (cf. 13:1). The conqueror's name is a "new" name that no one knows except the one who receives it (2:17).

Sixth, the rider is "clad in a robe dipped in blood" (19:13). Whose blood is on the robe? One possibility, given the centrality of the theme of the blood of Jesus/the Lamb in the book (1:5; 5:9; 7:14; 12:11), is that it is Jesus' own blood. Another is that it is the blood of the righteous (cf. 6:10; 16:6; 17:6, 6; 18:24; 19:2). The image is drawn from Isa 63, which speaks of God coming "in crimsoned garments" (Isa 63:1-2). The reason they are so stained is that God has trodden the winepress of his wrath: the blood is that of the nations, who have been trampled by God (Isa 63:3-6). That the rider is said to tread "the wine press of the fury of the wrath of God the Almighty" (19:15) confirms the picture in Isaiah and recalls the harvest of grapes in 14:17-20, where blood flows out of the wine press of God's wrath (14:19-20). The blood belongs to those who receive the wrath of God—those who follow the beast (14:9-11). Only here and in 16:16, which speaks of "the battle on the great day of God the Almighty," is "God Almighty" used without the title "Lord" (cf. 1:8; 4:8; 11:17; 15:3; 16:7; 21:22).

Seventh, the rider's name is "The Word of God" (19:13; cf John 1:1, 14; 1 John 1:1). "The word of God" is used elsewhere in 1:2, 9; 6:9; and 20:4, always in connection with "testimony" (of Jesus: 1:2, 9; 20:4; of "those who had been slain": 6:9).

Eighth, the rider has a weapon: "from his mouth issues a sharp sword" (19:15). The sword, which recalls the sharp two-edged sword issuing from Jesus' mouth in the opening vision (1:16; cf. 2:12, 16), will be mentioned again in 19:21. That the rider will use the sword from his mouth to "strike" (*patasso*) the nations recalls Isa 11:4 (LXX), where the Branch from Jesse (Isa 11:1) will "strike" (*patasso*) the earth with the rod of his mouth (cf. *Psalms of Solomon* 17:35; 1QSb[1Q28b] 5:24-25). The rider will also "rule" the nations "with a rod of iron." This allusion to Ps 2:9 has been found previously in 2:27 as a promise to the conqueror and in 12:5 as a description of the "male child."

Finally, the rider has "a name" (cf. 19:12) inscribed "on his robe [19:13] and on his thigh": "King of kings and Lord of lords" (19:16). In 17:14 the name in reverse order—Lord of lords and King of kings—is applied to the Lamb. Whether the name is written in two places—the robe and the thigh—is unclear, since "and" could be epexegetic—"on his robe, that is, on his thigh." In any event, "thigh," which is used only here in the book, might seem an odd place for a name. Elsewhere in the book names are written on foreheads (2:17: the conqueror; 14:1: the 144,000; 17:5: the great harlot) or, simply, heads (13:1: the beast). Perhaps more important is the repetition of "a name written" from 19:12. The name no one knows but the rider himself is none other than "King of kings and Lord of lords."

In 19:14 John interrupts his description of the rider to speak of those who accompany him. He describes them in four ways. First, they are "the armies of heaven," forming a counterpart to the "armies" of the beast and kings in 19:19. Second, they "follow" the rider, which reminds the reader of the 144,000 who "follow" the Lamb (14:4). Third, they are, like the rider himself, on white horses. Finally, they are wearing "fine linen, white [*leukos*] and pure," reminding the reader of 19:8, where the Bride of the Lamb has been given fine linen, bright (*lampros*; cf. 18:16) and pure, to wear. White robes (*himation*) are promised to the conqueror in 3:4-5 (cf. 3:18) and are worn by the twenty-four elders (4:4). White robes (*stole*) are given to "those who had been slain" in 6:11 and are worn by the Great Multitude (7:9, 13). The members of the rider's "armies" are not angels, but Christians. The census of the Lamb's army was taken in 7:4-8: 144,000 "out of every tribe of the sons of Israel" (7:4). The Lamb's army was mustered in 14:1-5. Now is the time for battle.

In the second scene John sees an angel standing in the sun (19:17; cf. 10:1; 12:1). The angel cries out in a loud voice (cf. 6:10; 7:2, 10; 10:3; 14:15; 18:2) to all of the birds (*orneon*) flying in midair (19:17; cf. 8:13; 14:6). The same word is used in 18:2. Here the focus is on scavengers. The angel invites the birds to gather together for "the great supper [*deipnon*] of God" (19:17). Nowhere else does John mention "the great supper of God." On the other hand, the wedding supper of the Lamb, the only other use of *deipnon* in the book, has just been announced (19:9). Once again the "hear/see" pattern plays out: the wedding supper of the Lamb and the great supper of God are one and the same. The menu is delineated by five uses of "flesh" (19:18). First is the flesh of kings; 19:19 will identify these kings as "the kings of the earth" (cf. 1:5; 6:15; 17:2, 18; 18:3, 9; 21:24). Second is the flesh of "captains" (elsewhere only in 6:15: RSV "generals"). Third is the flesh of "mighty men" (elsewhere only in 6:15). Fourth is the flesh of "horses and their riders," which form an obvious contrast to the rider on the white horse and his armies (19:11, 14). The only other mention of horses and their riders is in 9:17, which describes the troops of cavalry who are identified closely with the four angels who are released from the great river Euphrates to kill a third of mankind following the blowing of the sixth trumpet (9:14-16). Fifth is the flesh of "free and slave, both small and great." Both pairs were previously connected, along with the rich and the poor, in 13:16 as those who receive the mark of the beast. The free and the slaves are also mentioned in 6:15, and the small and the great in 11:18 and 19:5 (both times in a positive sense). The mention of five groups (the kings of the earth, the chiliarchs, the strong, the free, and the slaves) from 6:15 directs the reader to believe that the great day of the wrath of God and the Lamb (6:16-17) is at hand.

The entire scene is strongly reminiscent of Ezek 39:17-20, where God instructs Ezekiel to call the birds and the wild animals to gather for a great sacrificial feast that God is preparing from the flesh and blood of mighty men, princes of the earth, horses and riders, and warriors of every kind (cf. Jer 7:33; 16:4; 19:7; 34:20). In Ezek 39:4 God specifies that this prophecy is directed against Gog, who is earlier identified as "Gog, of the land of Magog" (Ezek 38:2). What makes this parallel particularly striking, and indeed what suggests that it is not accidental, is that in 20:7-10, a section with strong ties to 19:11-21, John will specifically mention Gog and Magog (20:8).

In the third scene John sees the rider's opponents and, ultimately, their defeat. He sees the beast, most recently mentioned in chapter 17 and by now a familiar character in the book, and "the kings of the earth with their armies" (19:19). The only armies mentioned in the book besides those aligned with the rider on the white horse (19:14) are the mounted troops mentioned in 9:16. The enemies are "gathered [*sunago*] to make war [lit., "the war" (*ho polemos*)] against him who sits upon the horse and against his army" (19:19). Prior to this point in the book, the only time that kings are "gathered" to make war is in 16:14, where the kings of the whole world—the kings of the east (16:12)—gather (*sunago*: RSV "assemble") at Armageddon (16:16) to make "the war" (*ho polemos*) on the great day of God the Almighty. In 17:14 an angel tells John that ten kings, functioning alongside the beast, will make war (*polemeo*) against the Lamb, who will conquer them. By now it is clear that there is but one "war." Armageddon, the war against the Lamb, and the war against the rider on the white horse are one and the same. And there is but one set of enemies. The kings of the earth, the kings of the whole world, the kings of the east, and the ten kings are also one and the same.

With an economy of words John portrays the war and its aftermath in 19:20 (contrast the many words of the *War Scroll* [1QM]!). No description of the war is given, no tactics, no account of its progression; John simply says that the beast "was captured." The sheer brevity of the statement takes the reader's breath away. After all, here is the beast that conquers and kills the two witnesses (11:7); that receives power and a throne and great authority from the dragon (13:2); that has the whole world following it (13:3) and worshiping it (13:4, 8); that makes war (not "the war") with and conquers the saints (13:7); that is given authority over every tribe, people, language, and nation (13:7); that will hate the great prostitute, bring her to ruin, leave her naked, eat her flesh, and burn her with fire (17:16); that will gather the kings of the earth and their armies together for "the war" (19:19). Everything to this point in the book has suggested that to the question simmering since 13:4—Who can make war against the beast?—there can be only one answer: no one. But the reader now learns the correct answer to the question: there is one who can make war against the beast, and his victory is so effortless that all that needs to be said is "the beast was captured!" As the beast is a cheap imitation of the Lamb (ch. 13), so also is he a cheap imitation of the *real* war-maker: the rider on the white horse.

Captured along with the beast is the false prophet, the second beast of chapter 13 (cf. 16:13; 20:10). John reminds the reader that the false prophet worked signs in the presence of the beast (13:13-14) and that by them "he deceived [cf. 13:14] those who had received the mark of the beast and those who worshiped its image" (cf. 13:15-17; 14:9, 11; 16:2; 20:4). Elsewhere in the book Jezebel "deceives" "my servants" (2:20), Satan deceives "the whole world" (12:9) and "the nations" (20:3, 8, 10), and Babylon deceives "the nations" (18:23).

The punishment of the beast and the false prophet is to be "thrown alive into the lake of fire that burns with sulfur" (19:20). The promise in 17:11 that the beast goes to "destruction" is now fulfilled. This is the first mention of the lake of fire in the book, though it will be found five more times, with slight variations in language: the lake of fire (20:14, 14, 15), the lake of fire and sulfur (20:10), and the lake that burns with fire and sulfur (21:8). In Dan 7, John's main source for his language about the beast (see on ch. 13), Daniel eventually sees the beast slain and "its body destroyed and given over to be burned with fire" (Dan 7:11; cf. Isa 30:33). Here the beast is thrown into the lake of fire *alive*. In Ezek 38:22 fire and sulfur (RSV "brimstone") are among the elements of judgment (along with torrential rains and hailstones) promised to Gog. The association of fire with judgment is common in Jewish literature of the period (e.g., *1 Enoch* 10:6; 54:1; 90:26; 103:7; 108:3-6; *2 Enoch* 10:2; *4 Ezra* 7:36), as well as in the New Testament (e.g., Matt 13:42, 50; 18:8-9; 25:41; Mark 9:47-38; Luke 16:23-24).

With the beast and the false prophet out of the way, John turns to the fate of "the rest" (cf. 19:9): they are "slain by the sword of him who sits upon the horse, the sword that issues from his mouth" (19:21; cf. 19:14; Isa 11:4). That "the rest" are slain with the weapon that was to be used to strike down "the nations" (19:15) serves to identify "the rest"—"the kings of the earth and their armies" (19:19)—with the nations. All the birds gorge themselves on the "flesh" (19:21) that was promised to them in 19:18. The great supper of God (19:18), the marriage supper of the Lamb (19:9), has arrived!

Through his use of allusions in this section, John ties together a number of key passages from earlier in the book. 19:11-21 is first and foremost a picture of judgment and presents a brief, but vivid, portrait of the great day of wrath (6:12-17; cf. 14:14-20), which was otherwise anticipated in the images of the war of Armageddon (16:12-16) and the war against the Lamb (17:13-14). The question of 13:4—Who can make war against the beast?—has been answered. The rider on the white horse, accompanied by his army of "144,000" Israelites—the Church (7:1-17; 14:1-5)—has defeated the beast and his associate, the false prophet, and thrown them into the lake of fire. The fears of those who were terrified at the prospect of the great day of wrath (6:15-17), who viewed the rider as an enemy, have materialized: they have been slain by him and have become a feast for the scavenging birds. But this is still just a prelude. The birds' feast is in fact the marriage supper of the Lamb. There is still a wedding to perform. And there is still that vengeful dragon, who went off to make war on the woman's offspring . . . .

"The nations . . . marched up over the broad earth and surrounded the camp of the saints and the beloved city": The judgment of the devil
Revelation 20:1-10

One by one John has witnessed the destruction of the enemies of God in the reverse order of their status. The dragon props up the beast, which in turn supports Babylon; yet John sees first the destruction of Babylon, then that of the beast. Could it be the dragon's turn next? This reversal leads to a dramatic buildup from least powerful enemy to most powerful. Will *any* of God's enemies be able to resist destruction?

20:1-10 unfolds in three scenes, all of which are tied together by references to "1,000 years" (20:2-3, 5-6, 7). First, John sees the binding of the dragon by an angel for 1,000 years (20:1-3). He then sees those who reign with Christ for 1,000 years (20:4-6). Finally, he recounts the release and subsequent defeat of Satan after the 1,000 years are completed (20:7-10). 20:1-10 is strongly reminiscent of chapter 12, where the dragon was first introduced. As before, the first and third scenes, which focus on the dragon's activities before and after a particular event, are sandwiched around a central scene, though this time the dragon is absent from the central scene.

The first scene begins with John seeing an angel coming down from heaven. Given that the other times that John has seen such angel led to important developments—the announcement that judgment would be delayed no longer (cf. 10:1, 6) and the announcement of the fall of Babylon (18:1)—the reader senses that something important is about to take place. The angel holds two things in his hand (20:1). One is "the key" of the Abyss (RSV "bottomless pit"). The Abyss is first mentioned in 9:1-2, where a star fallen from heaven to earth is given the key of the shaft of the Abyss; out of the Abyss comes smoke (9:2), and out of the smoke come torturing locusts (9:3-10). Elsewhere the beast is said to ascend from the Abyss (11:7; 17:8). In the same way that the key of (the shaft of) the Abyss can be used to unlock the Abyss and let evil out, as in 9:1-2, it can be used to lock the Abyss and keep evil in, as will be the case in 20:3. Second, the angel holds a "great chain."

John next uses five aorist verbs to describes the angel's actions, which form the heart of the scene. First, he "takes" the dragon (20:2). Second, the angel "binds" him (20:2; cf. 9:14), presumably with the great chain. Third, he throws (*ballo*) him into the Abyss (20:3). Four times in chapter 12 John observes that the dragon was "thrown" (*ballo*) down from heaven to earth (12:9, 9, 10, 13). Finally, the angel "locks" the Abyss and "seals" it over the dragon (20:3). Clearly, the dragon is not going to get out on his own! In *1 Enoch*, a book that contains numerous references to the Abyss (and similar places), the fallen angel Azazel is bound and cast into darkness (*1 Enoch* 10:4; cf. *1 Enoch* 10:4-6, 12-13; 88:1-3; 90:25; 54:1-6).

After just reading about the destruction of Babylon and the casting of the beast and the false prophet into the lake of fire, the reader might be inclined to believe that this is the end of the dragon. But John notes, perhaps surprisingly and certainly cryptically, that the dragon's stay in the Abyss is not permanent. Rather, he is bound (and, hence, imprisoned in the Abyss) for 1,000 years (20:2). However long 1,000 years might seem to the reader, it is obviously a *limited* period of time for the dragon. John observes that the dragon will—indeed, he must (*dei*)—be released at the end of that period "for a little while" (20:3; cf. 6:11). Why he must be released is not explained here. The reader is left in suspense.

John observes that the purpose of the binding and imprisonment of the dragon is "that he should deceive the nations no more till the thousand years were ended" (20:3). That deceiving is inherent to the dragon's nature is clear from 12:9, which has already been alluded to in 20:2 and which characterizes the dragon as the deceiver of the whole world. The clear implication is that when the 1,000 years are over, the dragon *will* deceive the nations, which is precisely what happens in 20:7. But why is there a period of time during which the dragon does *not* deceive the nations? What goes on during that period of time? And why must he be released at all? How long is the "little while" that follows the 1,000 years? Why is the length 1,000 years in the first place? The reader who ponders these questions is aware that every other use of "must" (*dei*) in the book refers to the perspective of God (1:1; 4:1; 10:11; 11:5; 13:10; 17:10; 22:6). Thus, she is sure of one thing: this, too, is under God's control. John may well be drawing upon Isa 24:21-22: "On that day the LORD of heaven will punish the host of heaven, in heaven, and the kings of the earth, on the earth. They will be gathered together as prisoners in a pit; they will be shut up in a prison, and after many days they will be punished." If so, then the obvious question is, Is the purpose of the eventual release of the dragon so that he can be "punished"?

It is important to recognize that a good portion of 20:1-10 is John's commentary—i.e., there is much that John does not actually "see" in this section (e.g., the entire unit 20:7-10). Certainly one thing John does not experience—nor is he told about it—is the 1,000 years. Where did he come up with the number? The answer is not altogether clear, but it is possible that John's source is Ps 90:4: "For a thousand years in thy sight/are but as yesterday when it is past." This passage is alluded to in both *Jubilees* 4:30 and 2 Pet 3:8. Indeed, on the basis of this passage *Jubilees* predicts a time of blessing when people's ages will reach 1,000 years (*Jubilees* 23:27-28). During that period of blessing "there will be no Satan and no evil [one] who will destroy" (*Jubilees* 23:29). To be sure, the parallel is not exact; *Jubilees* is speaking of people's longevity, not of the length of the period of blessing itself. But the point is that there was speculation on the significance of 1,000 years in this time period.

The second scene begins with John seeing two things: thrones and "the souls of those who had been beheaded" (20:4). Although John has spoken of God's "throne" (3:22 and frequently), Jesus' "throne" (3:22), and even the "throne" of the Satan (2:13; cf. 13:2), only once has he spoken of "thrones" in the plural: in 4:4, where he saw the "thrones" of the twenty-four elders. John says obliquely that "they" sat upon the thrones and speaks of "them" as "those to whom judgment was committed" (20:4). The entire verse draws upon Dan 7, a passage that has influenced John over and over again. The first part reflects Dan 7:9, where Daniel speaks of seeing "thrones" that "were placed." Later Daniel observes that "the court shall sit in judgment" (Dan 7:26), presumably upon those thrones. The second part echoes the end of Dan 7:21-22, a most important passage for John: "As I looked, this horn made war with the saints, and prevailed over them, until the Ancient of Days came, and judgment was given for the saints of the Most High, and the time came when the saints received the kingdom."

John has already drawn upon Dan 7:21 at two key junctures in the book: in 11:7, where the beast makes war with the two witnesses and conquers and kills them, and in 13:7, where the beast makes war on the saints and conquers them. But up until now John has not completed the story told in Dan 7:21-22. Now he does. The saints are not defeated at all. Rather, God renders judgment on their behalf and gives them the kingdom, complete with thrones for them to sit upon and with judicial power to exercise. Indeed, 20:4 directs the reader back to 2:26-27, where Jesus promises to share his power over the nations with the conqueror, and to 3:21, where he promises to let the conqueror share his throne. "Judgment" has been used twice previously in the book, both times with reference to the judgment of the great prostitute Babylon (17:1; 18:20), who spilled the blood of the saints (17:6; 18:24; 19:2). The irony is clear: those who seemed to have been "judged" by Babylon will now sit in judgment alongside the Lamb and God.

Second, John also sees "the souls of those who had been beheaded" (20:4). That John sees the "souls" is yet another tie to the fifth seal, where it is the "souls" of "those who had been slain" that speak (6:9). It is unlikely that the change from "slain" in 6:9 to "beheaded" here is intended to distinguish the two groups of "souls" from one another. The significance of "beheaded" (*pelekizo*: from *pelekus*, a double-edged axe—found only here in the New Testament) is that it was the method of execution reserved for Roman citizens. While it is likely that only a small percentage of the Christians in the seven churches of Asia possessed Roman citizenship, they lived in a province that was, on the whole, fully supportive of the Roman Empire. A close identification with the Empire and its culture was, of course, one of their main problems, as the seven letters make clear. The emphasis in the book on allegiance to the Lamb (rather than to the emperor), which is repeated in this verse, reaches its graphic climax here: the followers of the Lamb who are "slain" might even be Roman citizens! The ones who are seated upon the thrones—the beheaded souls—are therefore none other than the souls under the altar who had cried out for vengeance. The connection with the fifth seal is confirmed.

John characterizes the "beheaded" in two additional ways. First, he gives the reason for their beheading: "the testimony [*marturia*] of [RSV "their testimony to"] Jesus and the word of God" (20:4). The combination of these two phrases is given prominent display (in reverse order) twice at the beginning of the book. In 1:2 they encapsulate that which John saw and to which he testifies in the book, and in 1:9 they provide the reason for John's being exiled on Patmos. Thus, these phrases (cf. 12:17) encompass what allegiance to the Lamb is all about and, hence, why the followers of the Lamb might be "beheaded." Indeed, the followers of the Lamb have been characterized precisely as two "witnesses" (11:3: *martus*) who have a "testimony" (11:7: *marturia*) to complete and as those who conquered the accuser by the blood of the Lamb and the word of their "testimony" (12:11: *marturia*).

Second, John says the "beheaded" had not "worshiped the beast or its image and had not received its mark upon their foreheads or upon their hands" (20:4). John has described the followers of the beast variously as those who worship the beast (13:4, 8, 12), those who worship its image (13:15), those who receive/have the mark [on the right hand or the forehead] (13:16;

17), and those who receive/have the mark and worship its image (16:2; 19:20). The only other place where all of these are combined is 14:9 (cf. 14:11), which is the first clear statement about the judgment that awaits the followers of the beast. The combination of all of them here underscores the complete faithfulness of the "beheaded."

John further characterizes the "beheaded" with two aorist indicatives: they came to life and reigned (or "began to reign") with Christ. "Come to life" (*zao*) is repeated in 20:5 with reference to the rest of the dead (cf. 2:8: Jesus; and 13:14: the beast). "Reign" (cf. Dan 7:27) will be found again in 20:6 in the future tense. Elsewhere in the book it is said that God will reign (11:15) or has begun to reign (aorist: 11:17; 19:6) and that Christians will reign (1:6; 5:10; 22:5). Reigning with Christ is also the final promise to the conqueror in the seven letters: "I will grant to him to sit with me on my throne" (3:21). "Christ" stands alone in the book only four times: twice in this section (here and in 20:6) and in two passages that speak of "the kingdom of our Lord and of his Christ" (11:15 and 12:10 [+ authority]). As is the case here, in both of these passages the coming of the "kingdom" is described with an aorist indicative (*egeneto*: "has come"). John observes that the "beheaded" come to life and reign with Christ "for a thousand years" (cf. 20:6)—i.e., the length of time during which the dragon is bound (20:2; cf. 20:7) and cannot deceive the nations (20:3; cf. 20:8).

John now introduces a parenthetical statement concerning the "rest of the dead." In contrast to the "beheaded," who came to life at the *beginning* of the 1,000 years, "the rest of the dead did not come to life until the thousand years were ended" (20:5). This parenthetical statement anticipates the judgment scene in 20:11-15, where the sea and Death and Hades give up their dead (20:13 [twice]) so that "the dead" can stand before the great white throne (20:12, 12; cf. 11:18).

After the parenthesis John returns to the "beheaded." He calls their coming to life "the first resurrection" (20:5), an expression that will be repeated in 20:6. Nowhere else in the book is there any mention of a "second" (or any other) resurrection, but given the use of "came to life" for both the "beheaded" and the "rest of the dead," it follows that the "rest of the dead" coming to life after the 1,000 years constitutes the second resurrection.

John now sets forth the fifth of seven beatitudes in the book: "Blessed and holy is he who shares in the first resurrection" (20:6; cf. 1:3; 14:13; 16:15; 19:9; 22:7, 14). This is the only beatitude that adds a second adjective to "blessed." Christians have frequently been characterized as "saints" (lit., "holy ones") in the book—with reference to their prayers (5:8; 8:3, 4), as those to be rewarded (11:18 [+ servants and prophets]), as those with

whom the beast makes war (13:7), as those called to faithful endurance
(13:10 [+ patience]; 14:12), as those whose blood has been shed (16:6
[+prophets]; 17:6; 18:24 [+ prophets]; cf. 18:20 [+ apostles and prophets]),
and as those who have righteous acts (19:8); they will also have a camp that
will be surrounded by the nations (20:9), and they will be the recipients of
the final benediction of the book (22:21). We now learn that they share in
the first resurrection.

John goes on to explain why such people are blessed and holy: "over
such the second death has no power" (20:6). Later the second death will be
explicitly identified as the lake of fire (20:14; 21:8). One of the promises to
the conqueror is that he shall not be hurt by the second death (2:11). The
reader now learns *why* the second death will not hurt the conquerors:
because they share in the first resurrection. The mention of the "second"
death naturally raises the question of what the "first" death is. John never
speaks directly of the "first" death, but previous references to death in the
book make it clear that he would understand the "first" death to be physical
death (e.g., 1:18; 2:10, 23; 6:8; 9:6; 12:11; 13:3, 12; 18:8; 20:13, 14; 21:4).

Finally, John contrasts the second death having no authority over these
blessed and holy ones with two final observations about them (20:6). First,
"they shall be priests of God and of Christ" (cf. Isa 61:6). "Priest" has been
used twice in the book, both times as a description for Christians (cf. 1:6;
5:10). In both passages the verb used is in the aorist tense—Christians have
already been made priests. Here the future tense is used. Also, in both
passages Christians are priests "to God." The addition of "Christ" here (cf.
20:4) is consistent with John's merging of Christ with God throughout the
book. Second, "they shall reign with him a thousand years." The language
reminds the reader of 20:4 (cf. 1:6; 5:20; 22:5), though once again there is a
shift from the aorist in 20:4 to the future here.

One final question about the "beheaded" remains: are they literal
martyrs? The reader who insists on interpreting Revelation "literally" has no
choice but to say that the only people who experience the benefits of the first
resurrection are those who have been literally "beheaded" (technically, killed
with the double-edged axe). To counter that one does not have to press the
literal meaning of "beheaded" in order to claim that these are all martyrs is to
beg the question. John did not need to use the word "beheaded" if he simply
wanted to say these people are martyrs; he has already used more general
expressions elsewhere (e.g., 6:9). Surely the very specificity of "beheaded" is
an indication that John does not intend for the reader to take the expression
literally. After all, the twin promises of being priests and reigning given to the
"beheaded" are elsewhere given to *all* Christians (1:5; 5:10). So if "beheaded"

is not to be taken literally, then why should "slain" in 6:9 or, for that matter, any of the rest of the "martyr" terminology in the book? It is precisely the recognition that the "beheaded" in 20:4-6 are really *all* Christians that vitiates the martyr motif elsewhere. Revelation is not primarily about literal martyrdom, but about "martyrdom" of a different sort.

With what kind of "martyrdom" is Revelation concerned? Given the "judgment" theme that permeates the book, the answer would seem to be that it is a "martyrdom" of accusation. Through his various henchmen, Satan the Accuser will bring accusation against Christians. These accusations might create economic difficulties for them or even cost them their lives. But such earthly "judgments" are nothing compared to the heavenly judgment, and through the death of the Lamb Satan has lost his place in the heavenly Throne Hall. Therefore, those who have been ransomed by the Lamb have nothing to fear from the heavenly judgment. This changed status is the "first resurrection." Indeed, they have already begun to reign with God and the Lamb and will share in dispensing that judgment from the thrones that they have been given. For the followers of the Lamb, Satan is locked away in the Abyss.

In the final scene John returns to the theme of the binding of Satan (cf. 20:1-3). He describes no vision as such. Rather, he begins with two future indicatives relating what will take place when the 1,000 years "are ended" (cf. 20:3, 5): "Satan will be loosed from his prison" (20:7), and he "will come out to deceive the nations" (20:8). John then shifts his attention from Satan to the nations themselves, using two aorist indicatives to relate the actions of the nations: they "marched up over the broad earth," and they "surrounded the camp of the saints" (20:9). Continuing his focus on the nations, John uses two more aorist indicatives to tell what happened to them: "fire came down from heaven and consumed them" (20:9). John then turns his attention back to the devil, "who was deceiving [present participle; RSV "had deceived"] them," with one last aorist indicative: he was "thrown into the lake of fire and sulfur" (20:10). Finally, he returns to the future tense: Satan, the beast, and the false prophet "will be tormented day and night for ever and ever" (20:10).

John's begins with the activities of Satan (20:7-8). That Satan is released from his prison and that he deceives the nations constitute nothing new: both were anticipated in 20:3. The difference is that now, with the 1,000 years over, these actions are actually carried out. John uses two infinitives to express the purpose of Satan's "going out" from his prison: to "deceive" the nations and to "gather" them (20:8). Presumably the first is to be understood in terms of the second: Satan deceives (aorist) the nations precisely by gathering (present) them. The reader now understands Satan's necessary (20:3:

"must") task after the completion of the 1,000 years: to gather the nations for "the war [RSV "battle"]."

"The nations" are described in two ways. First, they are "at the four corners of the earth" (20:8). In 7:1 John speaks of four angels standing at the four corners of the earth, holding back the four winds of the earth. Second, they are "Gog and Magog" (20:8), a clear allusion to Ezek 38–39. In Ezek 38:2 God tells Ezekiel to prophesy against the mysterious Gog, of the land of Magog. At some point in the future, after Israel has returned from exile and is living in peace, Gog will come from the north with many nations and a mighty army to attack Israel (Ezek 38:4-16; 39:2). But God will destroy Gog, along with his armies, and Magog (Ezek 38:17-22; 39:2-20). God tells Ezekiel that he will accomplish all of this in order to show the nations that he is the Lord (38:23; 39:7, 21-22, 28). John has already alluded to this passage in 19:18 (cf. 19:20). As has been his practice throughout the book, once again John draws upon Old Testament imagery while reworking it at the same time. This is immediately clear from the fact that he speaks of Gog *and* Magog, rather than Gog *of* Magog (though perhaps *Sibylline Oracles* 3.319, 512 attests to a tradition of speaking about Gog *and* Magog). But it is also seen in that John no longer restricts Gog and Magog to the north, but rather identifies them with the nations "at the four corners of the earth." A similar universalizing of Gog and Magog can be found in the Dead Sea Scrolls (1QM 11:16; 4QpIs^a[4Q161] 3.21). John observes that the "number" of this army is like the sand of the sea (20:8; cf. Josh 11:4; 1 Sam 13:5; 1 Macc 11:1). In 9:16 John observed that the "number" of the mounted armies was twice ten thousand times ten thousand.

John now turns to the "war" itself, drawing upon the general picture set forth in Zech 14:2: "I will gather all the nations against Jerusalem to battle" (cf. *Sibylline Oracles* 3.663-68). First, the nations marched up "over the broad earth" (20:9: *epi to platos tes ges*). John echoes Habakkuk, who speaks of the Babylonian armies marching "over the broad earth" (Hab 1:6 LXX: *epi ta plate tes ges*). Then the nations "surrounded the camp of the saints"— i.e. ("and" is epexegetic) "the beloved city" (20:9), a normal strategy of ancient warfare. "Camp," found only here in the book, is typically used as a military term—an encampment of troops (e.g., 1 Macc 3:15, 23, 27; 4:34; 1QM 3.4-5; 7.1, 3, 7), and reminds the reader of the armies of heaven in 19:14. The "beloved" city recalls 1:5 (cf. 3:1), where Jesus is characterized as "him who loves us." It also reminds the reader of the Bride of the Lamb (19:7), which will be identified as the "holy city" in 21:2, 9-10. In addition, in Ezek 38:16 Gog of Magog advances to attack "my people Israel" (Ezek 38:16), over whom God is "the LORD their God" (Ezek 39:22, 28). That this is an attack upon "the saints" recalls 13:7 (cf. 14:12). Given all of the above, as well as the theme developed from the outset that the Church is the true Israel, to identify the camp, the beloved city, as the Church (as opposed to, e.g., physical Jerusalem) is the only understanding that makes sense in the book. As in 19:11-21, the description of the war itself is brief, with the focus on the end result, the destruction of the enemies (cf. 19:21): "fire came down from heaven and consumed them" (20:9; cf. 1 Kgs 1:10, 12; Ps 11:6). The language is strikingly similar to 11:5, where "fire" comes from the mouths of the two witnesses and "consumes" their foes; indeed, anyone who seeks to "harm" the two witnesses "is doomed" to be killed in this manner. In 20:9 the reader finds the fulfillment of that ominous prediction.

Finally, John comes to the real point of the scene: Satan is thrown into the lake of fire and sulfur (20:10). John ensures that the reader makes the connection with 19:20 by adding the phrase "where the beast and the false prophet were" (20:10). It is significant that John uses no verb (RSV adds "were"). Hence, the judgments of Satan and of the beast and the false prophet are not necessarily connected chronologically. The reader must not assume that just because she *reads* chapter 20 after reading chapter 19, then the events narrated in chapter 20 must *take place* at some point in history after the events narrated in chapter 19. What John *does* affirm is the certainty that Satan receives the same judgment as the beast and the false prophet. The interchange of Satan and the devil (20:7, 10; cf. 20:2) is once again reminiscent of chapter 12 (12:9), as is the use of the passive aorist "was thrown," which was used four times with reference to Satan in chapter 12 (12:9, 9, 10, 13). In chapter 12 Satan is thrown down from heaven to earth; here he is thrown into the lake of fire and sulfur.

John concludes that "they"—the dragon, the beast, and the false prophet—"will be tormented day and night for ever and ever" (20:10). The language recalls 14:10-11, which describes the punishment that awaits the followers of the beast: they will be tormented with fire and sulfur in the presence of the holy angels and of the Lamb, the smoke of their torment goes up for ever and ever, and they have no rest, day or night. The verb "torment" suggests a conscious punishment elsewhere in the book (e.g., 9:5; 11:10; 12:2). The one who would accuse Christians "day and night" (12:10) will find himself tormented "day and night," in stark contrast to those who have washed their robes in the blood of the Lamb, who will serve God in his temple "day and night" (7:15; cf. 4:8).

Once again the mention of people gathering for "the war" (20:8: *ho polemos*) links this section with "the war" in 19:11-21 and "the war" in 16:14, 16. The allusions to Ezek 38–39 (20:8-9; cf. 19:17-18, 20) confirm this connection. The battles of Armageddon (16:16), the rider on the white horse (19:11-21), and Gog and Magog (20:8-9) are one and the same "war."

Why is John given two visions of the same war (19:11-21 and 20:7-10)? First, the visions provide different perspectives on the war. On the one hand, it is a confrontation between the rider on the white horse (and his armies) and the beast (and his armies). On the other hand, it is a confrontation between the nations and the Church. This dual perspective—the role of Jesus and the role of Christians—has been a running theme throughout the book. Second, the visions set forth, one at a time, the fate of the two primary enemies of Jesus (and the Church): the beast (along with the false prophet) and Satan. Separating the sections in which each is thrown into the lake of fire completes the dramatic buildup of the defeat of the enemies: first Babylon, then the beast (and the false prophet), then the ancient serpent himself. But drama is not chronology. The point is not so much the *when* of the enemies' defeat, but the certainty *that* the defeat will take place. In typical Jewish (and early Christian) fashion, all of it will take place at the End. To try to find some specific chronology in the order of these events is to miss John's point.

"Then I saw a great white throne and him who sat upon it": The judgment of the dead and the opening of the Lamb's book
Revelation 20:11-15

The primary non-human enemies of God and of the Church—Babylon, the beast (and the false prophet), and the dragon—have all been destroyed. It is finally time for the Judgment to be rendered in the heavenly Throne Hall, an event anticipated since chapter 4. Drawing once again on Daniel 7, John records his vision of a great white throne and describes the judgment that takes place there (20:11-15).

Jews and early Christians looked forward to the final judgment of the dead. This book is no different. But in its literary context, the starkness of this scene is stunning. It consists of two parts of unequal length, each introduced with "And I saw" (20:11: RSV "Then"; 20:12). The first part focuses on the Judge, the second on the judgment.

John sees "a great white throne and him who sat upon it" (20:11). Apart from the mention of the details "great" and "white," the language is similar to 4:2, the first mention in the book of a throne with someone seated on it (cf. 7:15). There is no reason to believe this is a different throne; the additional details simply heighten the drama. The one seated upon the throne is presumably God-and-the-Lamb (cf. 4:6; 7:9). Though it is not mentioned explicitly, one assumes that the Church is also participating here (see on 20:4). John notes further that "from his presence [lit., face: *prosopon*] earth and sky [cf. 5:3, 13; 10:6; 14:7; 21:1, 1] fled away" (20:11). The reader recalls the sixth seal, where startling natural phenomena strike the sky and the earth and terrified people long to hide from the "face" (*prosopon*) of the one who is seated on the throne and from the wrath of the Lamb (6:12-17). John notes that no place was found for earth and sky (20:11; cf. 12:8; Dan 2:35 Theodotion). The Day of Judgment, anticipated in 6:17 as "the great day of their [God's and the Lamb's] wrath" has come, and there is nowhere to hide. *All* must stand before the throne.

Second, John witnesses the judgment itself. He describes those being judged in three ways. First, they are "the dead" (20:12). Five of the eight references to "the dead" in the book occur in this chapter, four of them in this scene (20:12 [twice], 13 [twice]). The reader remembers that in 11:18 the twenty-four elders say the time has come for judging "the dead" and that in 20:5 John notes that the rest of "the dead" did not come to life until the 1.000 years were completed. It is the time for judgment. The 1,000 years have passed. But how can "the dead" be gathered before the throne at all? The answer is given in 20:13: the sea and Death and Hades "gave up the dead in them." Death and Hades have been juxtaposed previously in 1:18 and 6:8. The sea is probably singled out because those who die at sea do not receive proper burials. Although John does not designate it as such, he probably understands this to be the "second" resurrection (cf. 20:5). Certainly the idea of a general resurrection of the dead at the Day of Judgment is found in both Judaism and early Christianity (e.g., Dan 12:2; *1 Enoch* 51:1; *Pseudo-Philo* 3:10; John 5:28-29). What is surprising is not that the dead have been raised to life for judgment, but that another "resurrection" has preceded this one. Second, John describes those being judged as "great and small" (20:12; cf. 11:18; 13:16; 19:5, 18). Third, he says they are "standing" before the throne, which recalls two key passages. The first is 6:17, where the description of the events following the opening of the sixth seal closes with terrified people asking, "Who can stand [before God and the Lamb on the great day of their wrath]?" This passage makes it clear that all *must* stand before them, even if they will stand only briefly before receiving their punishment (20:15). The second passage is 7:9, where John sees the Great Multitude "standing" before the throne. But this group is not awaiting judgment. They have washed their robes and made them white in the blood of the Lamb (7:14). Hence, they are praising God (7:9-10). They have nothing to fear.

John also describes the manner in which the judgment is carried out. In typical Jewish fashion (see on 2:23), John observes (twice!) that the dead are being judged "by what they had done" (20:12, 13). John notes that their deeds have been written in books (20:12) that are now opened (aorist passive of *anoigo*), presumably by God. The whole scene is strongly reminiscent of Dan 7:9-10 LXX, where the Ancient of Days takes his seat upon his throne: "the court sat in judgment and the books were opened [aorist passive of *anoigo*]." Other Jewish writers also understood the deeds of people to be recorded in books to be opened at the judgment (e.g., *1 Enoch* 47:3; 81:2; 89:61-77; 90:17; *Jubilees* 39:6). But John notes that another book is opened, a book he mentions twice: the book of life (20:12, 15). Noteworthy is that he calls this book both *biblion* (20:12) and *biblos* (20:15). Indeed, he has earlier spoken of the *biblion* of life (13:8; 17:8; 21:27) and the *biblos* of life (3:5); there is no difference. Although having one's name written in the book of life is an important Jewish concept (see on 3:6), its presence at the judgment scene is unexpected and is probably due to the influence of Dan 12:1: "But at that time your people shall be delivered, every one whose name shall be found written in the book." Indeed, the presence of the book of life at the judgment provides a *second* criterion for judgment. Not only are the dead judged according to their deeds but also according to whether or not their names are found in the book of life (20:15). In fact, it is only the latter that is mentioned explicitly in connection with the punishment the dead receive (20:15). At last the book of life—the scroll in the hand of the one seated upon the throne in 5:1, that was transferred to the Lamb in 5:7, whose seals were broken in 6:1-17 and 8:1—is open!

Once again, John's focus is on the final result: Death and Hades "were thrown into the lake of fire" (20:14; cf. 19:20; 20:10; cf. Isa 25:8). Similarly, "if any one's name was not found in the book of life, he was thrown into the lake of fire" (20:15; cf. 14:10; 21:8). John's identification of the lake of fire with the second death (20:14) brings together the two main symbols he has used previously to characterize judgment. On the one hand, the second death will not hurt the conqueror (2:11), and it has no authority over the "beheaded" (20:6). On the other hand, the beast and the false prophet (19:20) and Satan himself (20:10) have been thrown into the lake of fire. Finally, the mention of the lake of fire three times in 20:14-15 underscores the dramatic—not chronological—destruction of all of the enemies of God's people. The beast and the false prophet (19:20), Satan (20:10), Death and Hades (20:14), and those whose names are not found in the book of life (20:15) all meet the same end. "The destroyers of the earth" have now been destroyed (11:18)!

With its startling juxtaposition of two criteria for judgment, the final judgment scene ultimately permits the reader to solve some of the most basic questions that have been left unanswered to this point in the book. In Judaism the dead are judged according to their deeds. This remains true in this book—to a point. Since the dead are judged according to their deeds, and since their deeds are necessarily lacking because they follow the beast (13:3, 8), then the Day of Judgment is something of which people are terrified (6:15-16). Who can stand before the One who sits upon the throne at the judgment (6:17)? No one. All will be punished. The books recording their deeds (20:12-13) do not lie. All will be raised from the dead to stand before the Judge (20:12-13), where Satan will fulfill his role by accusing them (cf. 12:10). All who follow the beast will share his fate (19:20; 20:14). But the Judge also has another book (5:1): the book of life. Those whose names are written in it will not share the fate of the beast and his followers (20:15). Why? Because the Lamb, who was slain, has received the book of life from the Judge (5:7). Hence, it is now the *Lamb's* book of life (13:8; 21:27). He and he alone has the right to receive the book of life (5:2-5) because by his death he has ransomed people for God (5:6-10)—i.e., he has delivered them from the destruction that awaits the rest of humanity. These people and these alone are able to stand before the Judge (7:9) because they have received the benefits of the Lamb's death (7:14). Satan will *not* be able to rightly accuse them at the Judgment because he has lost all standing to do so (12:7-11). In fact, unlike "the rest of the dead," who await resurrection to Judgment (20:5), these people have *already* been raised from the dead and reign even now with Christ (20:4-6). Finally, the Lamb has joined the Judge on the throne (5:6; 7:9; 20:11) to ensure that at the Judgment the book that he alone can open will, in fact, be opened (5:2-6; 20:12) in order to take those whose names are written in it as his Bride (19:7)—i.e., the new Jerusalem (21:1–22:6a).

The judgment of the dead is over. It is time for the reward (cf. 11:18): the marriage of the Lamb (cf. 19:6-9).

"The Bride, the wife of the Lamb"

Revelation 21:1–22:6a

Armageddon is over. The judgment is complete. Babylon, the beast, the false prophet, Satan, and even Death and Hades have been destroyed. Those whose names are not written in the Lamb's book of life have received their due. But what about those who have been ransomed by the Lamb, who have held faithfully to the word of God and the testimony to Jesus—who have "conquered?" What about the Bride of the Lamb? What about the good stuff?

John's fourth "in the Spirit" experience, the shortest of them all, focuses on "the good stuff." Following an opening vision of a new heaven and a new earth (21:1-8), John is taken to a great, high mountain to see the Bride, the wife of the Lamb (21:9-10). There he sees the new Jerusalem, coming down out of heaven from God (21:10). The vision of the new Jerusalem, which takes up the rest of the section (21:11–22:6a) is breathtaking in its beauty and provides a magnificent climax to the entire book.

"Behold, I make all things new":
The announcement of the dwelling of God with his people
Revelation 21:1-8

The introduction to John's fourth "in the Spirit" experience is the longest of the four. It consists of two sections. In the first section (21:1-4) John is the subject of the main verbs: "I saw (21:1) . . . I saw (21:2) . . . I heard (21:3) . . . ." In addition, the reference to something as having "passed away"—the "first" (*protos*) heaven and the "first" (*prote*) earth (21:1) and the "first things" (*prota*: 21:4)—forms an inclusion linking these verses together. In the second section (21:5-8) the one sitting upon the throne is the subject of the main verbs, and he speaks to John three times (21:5 [twice], 6).

The imagery in this section is based largely upon Isa 65:17-19 (cf. Isa 66:22):

For behold, I create new heavens and a new earth;
and the former things shall not be remembered
or come to mind.
But be glad and rejoice for ever in that which I create;
for behold, I create Jerusalem a rejoicing
and her people a joy.
I will rejoice in Jerusalem,
and be glad in my people
no more shall be heard in it the sound of weeping
and the cry of distress.

The creation of the new heaven and the new earth is bound inextricably to the creation of a (new) Jerusalem. Indeed, John will quickly shift his focus from the new heaven and the new earth, mentioned only in 21:1 in the entire book, to the new Jerusalem (21:2–22:6). They are one and the same.

John sees "a new heaven [*ouranos*] and a new earth" (21:1). His observation in 21:1 that the first heaven and the first earth had passed away, repeated essentially in 21:4, is reminiscent of 20:11, where earth and sky (*ouranos* means both "heaven" and "sky") were said to have fled from the presence of the one sitting upon the great white throne. He adds that the sea "is [RSV "was"] no more" (21:1). Like Death and Hades the sea had been a repository for the dead (20:13). Unlike Death and Hades there was no mention of the sea being thrown into the lake of fire (20:14); the sea is not an enemy as such. But its connection with death does align the sea with those things that have no place in the new heaven and the new earth. Hence, just as the sea "is no more" (*ouk estin eti*), so also death "shall be no more" (21:4: *ouk estai eti*), and there "shall be" neither mourning nor crying nor pain "any more" (21:4: *ouk estai eti*).

John also sees the holy city, the new Jerusalem (21:2). The holy city was mentioned in 11:2 and will be mentioned again without further identification (cf. Neh 11:18) in 22:19. The new Jerusalem (cf. *Testament of Dan* 5:12) was mentioned in 3:12. Only here and in 21:10 ("the holy city Jerusalem") are the two brought together (cf. Isa 52:1; Neh 11:1). John characterizes the new Jerusalem with two participles. First, it is "coming down out of heaven from God" (21:2; cf. 21:10; 3:12). Second, the new Jerusalem is "prepared as a bride adorned [cf. 21:19] for her husband" (21:2). In 19:7 John is told that the Bride has prepared (aorist active) herself; here he comments that the Bride has been prepared (perfect passive). This apparent identification of the new Jerusalem with the Bride will be confirmed in 21:9-10.

John then hears a loud voice from the throne (cf. 16:17; 19:5), which affirms that "the dwelling of God is with men" (21:3). The use of the noun "dwelling" (*skene*), along with the verb form in the first of the six promises that follow (21:3: *skenoo*) recalls the promise to the Great Multitude in 7:15 that God "will shelter them [*skenoo*] with his presence." The image is based upon God's promise to Israel in Lev 26:11-12, which is picked up and modified slightly in Ezek 37:27: "My dwelling place [*kataskenosis*] will be with them; I will be their God, and they will be my people" (cf. Jer 24:7; 31:33; 32:28). Next comes a series of promises, all firmly rooted in Old Testament language. The first three are based upon God's promises to Israel in Lev 26:11-12/Ezek 37:27 (cf. Ps 95:7; Jer 31:1; Ezek 11:20): first, God "will dwell with them"; second, "they shall be his people" (cf. 18:4); and third, "God himself will be with them" (21:3). The promises that God "will wipe every tear from their eyes," found almost verbatim in 7:17, and that "death shall be no more" (21:4) reflect Isa 25:8. The promise that "neither shall there be mourning nor crying nor pain any more" (21:4) recalls the new heaven and new earth passage in Isa 65:19 (cf. Isa 35:10; 51:11), along with the picture of the glorified Jerusalem in Isa 60:19, 23, which will be a key passage underlying the portrait of the new Jerusalem that will follow in 21:10–22:5. The promise of the demise of Death has been vividly depicted in 20:14 with Death being thrown into the lake of fire. The voice concludes with the affirmation that "the former things have passed away" (21:4). As noted above, the affirmation (cf. Isa 42:9) forms an inclusion with 21:1 and, hence, refers to the passing away of the first heaven and the first earth.

The key to understanding 21:1-4 is the affirmation in 21:3: "Behold, the dwelling of God is with people." First, it explains the vision of the new heaven and new earth/new Jerusalem. Second, the five promises that follow are simply commentary on it. Once again, this central, defining affirmation is nothing less than the reaffirmation of a central, defining affirmation to Israel (Lev 26:11-12). The Bride of Christ—not ethnic Israel—is the true Israel.

The one who sat upon the throne now speaks three times. First, he says, "Behold, I make all things new" (21:5). The language is almost identical to Isa 43:19 (LXX; cf. Isa 42:9), including the use of the present tense. The statement serves as an explanation of 21:1-4. Second, he says, "Write this, for these words [cf. 17:17] are trustworthy [*pistos*] and true" (21:5). These words are repeated almost verbatim at the close of the vision of the new Jerusalem in 22:6a. Jesus was called "faithful [*pistos*] and true" in 3:14 and 19:11. This is only the third time since the letters to the seven churches that John has been commanded to write something (cf. 14:13; 19:9).

The third time the one who sat upon the throne speaks he directs his words specifically to John (21:6: "to me"). He also speaks at greater length (21:6-8). He begins with a statement of fact: "It is done!" (21:6: *ginomai*). At first glance, that the plural perfect is used here without a subject (*gegonan*) might seem odd. The singular perfect, found in 16:17 (*gegonen*) to refer to the act of pouring out the seven bowls, might seem more natural. But the use of the plural may well be intended as an allusion back to 1:1 and 19, which speak of "the things" (*ha*; RSV "what") that must take place (*ginomai*), an expression that will be repeated at the end of this very section (22:6a).

The one who sat upon the throne next makes two statements of self-revelation. First, he says, "I am the Alpha and the Omega, the beginning and the end" (21:6). The first phrase was found in 1:8; both will be repeated in 22:13. He then adds a promise: "To the thirsty I will give from the fountain of the water of life without payment" (21:6; cf. Ps 36:9; Jer 2:18; Zech 14:8). This is an allusion back to 7:16-17, which says that those who have washed their robes and made them white in the blood of the Lamb will not "thirst any more" but will be guided by the Lamb "to fountains [RSV "springs"; cf 8:10; 14:7; 16:4] of the water of life [RSV "living water"]." An invitation to the thirsty to come and drink from the water of life "without payment" (RSV "without price") will be extended in 22:17.

The one who sat upon the throne concludes with two promises to him "who conquers" (21:7) and an observation about those who do not (21:8). The reference to the conqueror takes the reader back to the letters to the seven churches, each of which ended with a promise to "him who conquers" (2:7, 11, 17, 26; 3:5, 12, 21). Indeed, the theme of "conquering" (always the verb *nikao*) provides a loose, chiastic structure to the book overall:

A. promises to him who conquers (2:1–3:22)
    B. the Lamb has conquered (5:5; cf. 6:2)
        C. the beast will conquer the two witnesses (11:7)
            D. the Lamb's followers conquered the beast (12:11)
        C'. the beast is allowed to conquer the saints (13:7; cf. 15:2)
    B'. the Lamb will conquer the ten kings (17:14)
A'. promise to him who conquers (21:7)

The center of the entire chiasm (D), the heavenly commentary on the dramatic war in heaven that results in the dragon losing his position as accuser, is precisely what defines what it means for the Lamb's followers to "conquer" and therefore provides the rationale for the promises at the beginning and the end of the chiasm (A, A'). The ability of the Lamb's followers to "conquer" is itself rooted in the Lamb's own conquering (B, B'). Given all of this, the beast's attempt to "conquer" the followers of the Lamb (C, C') is ultimately doomed to failure.

The promise that the conqueror "shall have this heritage" (21:7) undoubtedly refers back to the promises in 21:1-4. The second promise—"I will be his God and he shall be my son" (21:7; cf. 21:3)—draws upon the language of 2 Sam 7:14: "I will be his father, and he shall be my son" (cf. 1 Chr 22:10; 28:6; *Jubilees* 1:24).

The stark contrast between the blessings that come to the conqueror and the "lot" (21:8) of others indicates that these "others" are to be identified primarily in terms of what they are not—i.e., they are not conquerors. Specifically, eight groups are named. Five of them—murderers, fornicators, sorcerers (cf. 9:21), idolaters, and liars (cf. 14:5) will be found again in 22:15 (cf. 21:27: lit., "the one doing a lie"). The three that are mentioned only here—the cowardly, the faithless (*apistos*), and the polluted (*bdelussomai*; cf. 21:27: lit., "the one doing abomination" [*bdelugma*])—are placed first. The third reminds the reader of the great harlot's "abominations" (*bdelugma*: 17:4, 5) and the second contrasts with the "faithfulness" (*pistos*) of those with the Lamb (17:14; cf. 2:10, 13). "Cowardly" certainly contrasts with the bravery required of the Lamb's followers when faced with the opposition of the dragon and the beast (e.g., 14:12). To view these eight categories as specific "sins" to be avoided (cf. Rom 1:29-31; 1 Cor 6:9-10; Gal 5:19-21; 1 Pet 4:3; *Didache* 2:2-3; *Epistle of Barnabas* 20:1-2) is to miss the point. They are different ways of talking about those who choose to follow the beast. The choice throughout the book is always between following the Lamb and following the beast. The "lot" of these people "shall be in the lake that burns with fire and sulfur, which is the second death" (21:8). On the first clause, see on 19:10; on the second, see on 20:6 (cf. 2:11). They were previously brought together in 20:14.

The introduction to John's fourth "in the Spirit" experience is now over. Yet even though a magnificent vision is about the follow, John has already oriented the reader as to how to understand the vision: it is the fulfillment of a host of Old Testament passages about God dwelling, personally and intimately, with his people.

"He . . . showed me the holy city": John's vision of the new Jerusalem

Revelation 21:9–22:6a

The vision of the new Jerusalem is the climax of the book of Revelation. As in the case of those occasional television shows that are presented "without commercial interruption," one is tempted to say to the reader, "Just read it!" Any attempt to comment on it can only lessen its beauty and power . . . but that could easily be said about the entire book!

On the other hand, one problem the reader encounters in this section is that some of its images—e.g., "pearly" gates, streets of gold—have become stock images in Western culture, even for people who know little about the Bible. The very familiarity of these images can lead the reader into a false sense of security, assuming as self-evident that this section is simply a picture of "heaven." Nothing could be further from the truth.

The beginning of the section is strikingly similar to that of the third "in the Spirit" experience. Indeed, both begin with same twelve Greek words: *kai elthen heis ek ton hepta aggelon ton echonton tas hepta philias* (17:1; 21:9: lit., "And came one of the angels who had the seven bowls"). These are the only two references after chapter 16 to an angel who had one of the seven bowls. In 21:9 John adds, presumably for emphasis, "full of the last seven plagues" (cf. 15:1). Then once again there is a verbatim agreement, this time of eight more Greek words: *kai elalesen met' emou legon, Deuro, deixo soi* (17:1; 21:9: lit., "and he spoke with me, saying, 'Come, I will show you'"; cf. 4:1). What is shown to John is, of course, different, but afterward the angel carries John away (*apenegken me*) in the Spirit (*en pneumati*) (17:3; 21:10). Without doubt the opening of the fourth "in the Spirit" experience is intended to recall the opening of the third, though it will become clear that the point of comparison is one of stark contrast. In the third experience John is carried to a wilderness to see a gaudy harlot; in the fourth he will be carried to a great, high mountain to see a beautiful Bride.

21:9–22:6a contains a loose structure consisting of the opening encounter with the angel (21:9-10), an initial description of the city (21:11-14), a scene in which the angel measures the city, its gates, and its walls (21:15-21), another description of the city (21:22-27), a description of the river of the water of life (22:1-2), and a final description of the city (22:3-6a).

That John is conducted through this vision by "one of the seven angels who had the seven bowls full of the seven last plagues" (21:9) is, at first glance, somewhat surprising. Those angels were associated with God's wrath, while the vision John is about to receive is a thing of beauty. But that is precisely the point: judgment involves both punishment and reward (cf. 11:18). There are those who are terrified at the thought of standing before God at the judgment (cf. 6:15-17), and there are those who stand before him shouting, "Salvation!" (cf. 7:9-10). This angel will be identified further in 22:6b.

The angel promises to show John "the Bride, the wife of the Lamb" (21:9). The reader has been waiting for the marriage of the Lamb since 19:7-9. Surely now it is about to take place! That the angel takes John to "a great, high mountain" (21:10) is an allusion to Ezek 40:2 ("and he set me down upon a very high mountain"), which marks the beginning of Ezekiel's final vision of the restored Temple and land (Ezek 40–48), a vision that will have a significant influence in this section. (For high mountains as places of revelation, see, e.g., Deut 19:1-25; *1 Enoch* 17:2; *Testament of Levi* 2:5; 4Q213 frag. 1 2.17-18; Mark 9:1.) But instead of seeing the Bride, John, like Ezekiel, sees a city (21:10; cf. Ezek 40:2): "the holy city Jerusalem coming down out of heaven from God" (21:10). One final time in the book John hears one thing and sees another. Like the conquering Lion who is really a slain Lamb (cf. 5:5-6); like the 144,000 "Jews" who are really a Great Multitude from every nation, tribe, people, and tongue (7:4-9); like the marriage supper of the Lamb that is really a feast for scavenging birds (19:9, 17-21); so the Bride of the Lamb is really the new Jerusalem, an identification that has already been made—if only briefly—in 21:2. And so the Bride of the Lamb abruptly vanishes from the book, and all attention becomes focused on the new Jerusalem. This is the third reference (cf. 3:12; 21:2) to the new Jerusalem in the book (though without the explicit "new" only here). In all three passages the new Jerusalem is said to be "coming down [present participle; 3:12 with the definite article: RSV "which comes down"] out of heaven from [3:12 adds "my"] God." Here and in 21:2 the new Jerusalem is called "the holy city" (cf. 3:12: "the city of my God"). The "holy city" is also mentioned in 11:2 and 22:19 (cf. 20:9).

That the book of Revelation climaxes in a picture of the glorified Jerusalem should not be surprising. The future glorification of Jerusalem is a common theme in the Old Testament prophets (e.g., Isa 54:11-12; 60:1-22; Jer 31:38-39 ; Ezek 40–48; Mic 4:1-2; Zech 8:1-23; 14:10-11) and in Second Temple Jewish literature (e.g., Tob 13:16-17; Bar 5:1-3; *Psalms of Solomon* 17:30-31; 11QTemple 30-45; the "new Jerusalem" texts from Qumran [2Q24, 4Q554-555, 5Q15, 11Q18]). Indeed, some New Testament writings, as well as some Jewish writings that are roughly contemporary with Revelation, even speak of a heavenly Jerusalem that is to come (cf. Gal 4:26; Heb 11:16; 12:22; 13:14; *4 Ezra* 13:35-36; *2 Baruch* 4:3;

4 Baruch 5:35). It is only appropriate that the climactic vision in John's book, steeped in Jewish tradition as it is, should be of the glorified Jerusalem.

The rest of the vision is taken up with John's description of the new Jerusalem. Sometimes he comments on things he sees (e.g., a gold street [21:21]), while other times he comments on things that are *not* part of the actual vision (e.g., "There shall no more be anything accursed" [22:3]). As always, John has had time to reflect on his actual visionary experience and adds his own commentary throughout. At one point the angel uses a "measuring rod" to measure "the city and its gates and its walls" (21:15-17), a motif drawn once again from the beginning of Ezekiel's great closing vision (cf. Zech 2:1-2). After being taken in a vision to a very high mountain, from which Ezekiel sees a city, he sees "a man whose appearance was like bronze, with a line of flax and a measuring reed in this hand" (Ezek 40:3). The man proceeds to take extensive measurements of the Temple area (Ezek 40:4–42:20), as well as of the length of the river that issues from the Temple and flows east (47:1-6). John's angel does far less measuring. That his measuring rod is of "gold" is consistent with the various items made of gold that John has already seen in heaven (crowns [4:4; 14:14], bowls [5:8; 15:7], a gold censer [8:3], the gold altar [8:3; 9:13], belts [15:6]). The passage is reminiscent of 11:1-2, where John is given a measuring rod and is told to measure certain features relating to the Temple of God.

Consistent with the use of symbolic numbers in the book, the reader will encounter frequent references to the number twelve throughout the description of the new Jerusalem, as well as to multiples of twelve: twelve gates (21:12, 21); twelve angels (21:12); twelve tribes of the sons of Israel (21:12); twelve foundations (21:14); twelve names of the twelve apostles of the Lamb (21:14); 12,000 (= 12 x 1,000) stadia (21:16); 144 (= 12 x 12) cubits (21:17); twelve pearls (21:21); and twelve kinds of fruit (22:2). The number twelve is, of course, the symbolic number for Israel (see on 7:4-8).

John's initial response to the appearance of the new Jerusalem is to say that it has "the glory of God" (21:11; cf. 21:23; 15:8; Isa 58:8; 60:1-2; Ezek 43:2, 4-5). Indeed, just as he described earlier the one seated on the throne in terms of precious stones (4:3), so also he compares the city's "radiance" to that of "a most rare jewel, like a jasper, clear as crystal" (21:11). Babylon may have been adorned with jewels (*lithos timios*—17:4; 18:16), but the new Jerusalem has the appearance of *precious* jewels (*lithos timiotatos*). "Jasper" recalls the appearance of the one seated upon the throne in 4:3 (cf. 21:18); similarly, "clear as crystal [*krustallizo*]" recalls the "sea of glass, like crystal [*krustallos*]" that was before the throne (4:6). In 21:18 John adds one final detail about the general appearance of the city: it was "pure gold, clear as glass" (cf. 21:21).

John's detailed observations about the construction of the new Jerusalem reflect the way in which ancient cities were built. Ancient cities were surrounded by walls for defense against attacking armies. The stability of a city's wall began with its foundation. Foundation stones or blocks were typically the largest in the wall (cf. 1 Kgs 5:17; 7:10); one of the foundation stones of Herod's wall that enclosed the Temple mount, for example, is 40 feet long, 10 feet high, and 13 feet thick, and weighs about 400 tons. While John does not comment on the size of the foundation stones in the wall, he does note that there are twelve such stones and that on them are "the twelve names of the twelve apostles [cf. Matt 10:2] of the Lamb" (21:14). Whether the twelve names are on each stone, or whether there is a different name for each stone (which seems more likely; see on the angels in 21:12 and the pearls in 21:21 below), John does not say. He is more interested in the symbolism of the twelve apostles (cf. 21:12-13). The thought is similar to Eph 3:20, which speaks of the Church being built "upon the foundation of the apostles and prophets." John's particular interest is in the appearance of the foundation stones: "the foundations of the wall of the city were adorned [cf. 21:2] with every jewel" (21:19). He goes on to list the specific jewels for all twelve foundation stones (21:19-20). On the glorified Jerusalem being built with jewels, see Isa 54:11-12 and Tob 13:16-17 (cf. Ezek 28:13, 17-20). By listing twelve precious stones here John echoes Exod 28:15-21, which lists twelve jewels, one for each of the tribes of Israel, to be set in the breastplate of the high priest (though the jewels listed here are not identical with those in Exodus). Three of the jewels are found elsewhere in Revelation: jasper (4:3; 21:11), jacinth (9:17), and carnelian (4:3).

The height and thickness of a city wall, as well as the material from which it was constructed, played a significant role in its ability to withstand the various military stratagems used in a siege (e.g., battering rams, ladders, and siege engines). John observes that the wall is "great and high" (21:12) and that it measures 144 cubits (roughly 240 feet). John's observation that the measurement reflects "a man's measure, that is, an angel's" (21:17), reflects Deut 3:11 ("by the cubit of a man"; RSV "the common cubit") and is probably intended to indicate that the angel was of a normal, human size, rather than a gigantic one (cf. 10:2, 5; *2 Enoch* 1:4; 18:1). Whether the measurement is of the height or the thickness of the wall John does not say. In any event, the specific distance is not the issue; the number is symbolic (see on 7:4). John further observes that the wall "was built of jasper" (21:18;

cf. 4:3; 21:11, 19). Once again, John is concerned with appearance, not practicality.

In order for people to get in and out of a city, there were gates in the wall that could be opened and shut. John pays particular attention to the gates in the wall of the new Jerusalem. Like Ezekiel (cf. Ezek 48:30-34), he notes that there are twelve gates, three on each side of the city (21:12-13) and observes that "on the gates the names of the twelve tribes of the sons of Israel were inscribed" (21:12). Yet there are differences between the two visions. While Ezekiel moves around the city clockwise, from north to east to south to west (11QTemple 39.12-13 also moves clockwise, starting with the east [cf. 11QTemple 40.9-12; 4Q364-365 frag. 28 2.1-4], while 5Q554 2.12-3.9 moves clockwise, starting with the south), John takes a different order: east, north, south, and west. The reason for this peculiar order is not clear. In addition, while Ezekiel associates one gate with each tribe (cf. 11QTemple 39.12-13; 40.13-41.11; 4Q463-465 frag. 28 2.1-4), John does not. Though John likely understands that there is one gate per tribe (see on the angels in 21:12 and the pearls in 21:21 below), he is more interested in the symbolism of the twelve tribes here than he is with the individual tribes as such (cf. 7:4-8; 21:14).

John also notes that there are twelve angels at the gates (21:12), presumably one per gate. This is probably a reflection of the practice of having gatekeepers at the Temple (cf. 1 Chr 23:5; 26:12-18). As in the case of the wall itself, John also comments on the material out of which the gates are constructed: "the twelve gates were twelve pearls, each of the gates made of a single pearl" (21:21). Here John clearly allots a specific pearl to each gate. As the doomed harlot Babylon bedecked herself with pearls (cf. 17:4; 18:16), so also pearls will characterize the new Jerusalem. As always, the focus is on appearance, not typical construction practices. Finally, John observes that the gates "shall never [emphatic *ou me*] be shut by day [cf. 3:7] for [*gar*: RSV "and"] there shall be no night there" (21:25). The words echo Isa 60:11: "Your gates shall be open continually;/ day and night they shall not be shut." Since the purpose of shutting the gates of a city is for protection, especially under the cover of darkness, this feature of the new Jerusalem underscores the absolute security of the city; cf. Zech 14:11: "Jerusalem shall dwell in security."

John comments also on the layout of the city. Specifically, he observes that it will be a cube: "its length and breadth and height are equal" (21:16). This is clearly an allusion to the shape of the holy of holies, which was 20 cubits long, 20 cubits wide, and 20 cubits high (cf. 1 Kgs 6:20). The entire city is a holy of holies! The place into which only the high priest could enter, and then on only one day a year (see on 11:19), now takes up the whole city. What symbolized God's presence with Israel—but always separated by a barrier—encompasses everyone in the city. There could hardly be a more striking image to underscore the promise made in 21:3: "Behold, the dwelling of God is with men." John gives the dimensions of each side of the cube as 12,000 stadia (about 1,400 miles). Such dimensions impress upon the reader the enormity of the new Jerusalem, though they are not to be pressed literally. Ezekiel also observes the rebuilt Jerusalem to be a square, though he does not comment on its height: 4,500 cubits (about 7,500 feet) along each side (Ezek 48:15-16, 30-35; cf. 11QTemple 39.13-16; 40.12-41.11). On the symbolic use of the number 12,000, see on 7:5-8.

Every major city in the Roman world had its *cardo maximus*—its great street leading through the main part of the city. John observes that, like the city itself (21:18), the "street of the city was pure gold, transparent as glass" (21:21). John will mention the street again in 22:2.

John observes that several things are missing from the city. First, there is "no temple" (21:22). Temples were staples of ancient cities. Large cities in the Roman empire typically had numerous temples devoted to various gods, and Jerusalem, of course, had its Temple dedicated to God. John comments that the reason the new Jerusalem has no Temple is because "its temple is the Lord God the Almighty [see on 1:8] and the Lamb" (21:22). The thought is similar to Jer 3:16-17: "In those days, says the LORD, they shall no more say, 'The ark of the covenant of the LORD' . . . . At that time Jerusalem shall be called the throne of the LORD" (cf. Zech 2:4-5; *Testament of Dan* 5:13; 4Q511 frag. 35 3). Indeed, though he sees a Temple in the glorified Jerusalem, Ezekiel concludes his great final vision as follows: "And the name of the city henceforth shall be, The LORD is there" (Ezek 48:35; cf. 43:4). Two observations need to be made here. First, once again John underscores the essential identity between God and the Lamb (cf., e.g., 5:13; 6:16; 7:10; 14:4; 15:3). Second, that the presence of God and the Lamb vitiates the need for a Temple once more highlights the fact that in the new Jerusalem, God (and the Lamb) dwells directly and intimately with his people (cf. 21:3-4, 16, 23).

Second, "the city has no need of sun or moon to shine upon it" (21:23). This is a surprising statement, to be sure; what city can exist without light? But John's answer is simple: "the glory of God [cf. 21:11] is its light, and its lamp is the Lamb" (21:23). Once again John echoes Isaiah's vision of the glorified Jerusalem (cf. Isa 24:23; Zech 14:7):

> The sun shall be no more
> your light by day,
> nor for brightness shall the moon
> give light to you by night;
> but the LORD will be your everlasting light,
> and your God will be your glory.
> Your sun shall no more go down,
> nor your moon withdraw itself;
> for the LORD will be your everlasting light,
> and your days of mourning shall be ended. (Isa 60:19-20)

And once more John connects, this time through synonymous parallelism, God and the Lamb. Indeed, this thought will be repeated in 22:5, where John will simply say that "the Lord God will be their light." The Lord God and the Lamb are one.

Although the focus in 21:23 is on the light that comes from the moon (and the sun), the obvious inference to be drawn from the lack of the need for the moon is that "there shall be no night there" (21:25), a phrase repeated with a slight variation in 22:5: "night shall be no more." John has picked up half of Zech 14:7: "It will be a unique time, without daytime or nighttime."

In 21:24-27 John comments on who will and will not be permitted to enter the new Jerusalem. John observes that by the light of the city (cf. Isa 60:3) "shall the nations walk; and the kings of the earth shall bring their glory to it" (21:24). Again he writes, "they shall bring into it the glory and honor of the nations" (21:26). Once again John is drawing upon the passage from Isa 60:11 quoted above in connection with 21:23, which continues as follows: "that men may bring to you the wealth of the nations, / with their kings led in procession." John echoes one of the most widespread expressions of hope in the Old Testament and in Second Temple Judaism—that the nations will stream to the glorified Jerusalem (cf., e.g., Ps 72:10-11; Isa 2:2-3; Jer 3:17; Dan 7:14; Mic 4:1-2; Zeph 3:9; Zech 8:20-22; Tob 14:6-7; *1 Enoch* 10:21; *Sibylline Oracles* 3.772-774; *Testament of Zebulon* 9:8; *Psalms of Solomon* 17:30-31; 4Q504 4.8-11).

On the other hand, John observes, echoing the language of Isa 35:8 (cf. Isa 52:1), "nothing unclean shall enter it, nor any one who practices abomination or falsehood" (21:27). As in 21:25, John uses an emphatic negative (*ou me*). The Greek word John uses here (*koinon*: lit., "common") is a synonym of the one he uses in 18:2 to denote "unclean" (*akathartos*) spirits, birds, and animals. The idea is the same: John is talking about things that are regarded as ritually impure in the Law, presumably people who fall into the

ritually unclean categories (e.g., having touched a corpse) as defined by the
Law (e.g., Lev 13–15; Num 19:11-22). The reference to those practicing
abomination (cf. 17:4, 5) and falsehood (cf. 14:5; 22:15) reminds the reader
of two of the eight "categories" of people whose lot is said to be the lake of
fire in 21:8. As was implied in that verse, such expressions characterize
people not in terms of their specific sins but as followers of the beast. Here
they are specifically contrasted with "those who are written in the Lamb's
book of life" (21:27; see on 20:15), who are permitted to enter the city.

There is a minor break ("Then he showed me . . ."; cf. 21:10) in 22:1.
The reader wonders what is left to see. But John immediately follows with an
elaboration of an image only recently introduced into the book but that will
serve as a key symbol in the epilogue (22:1-2) and then wraps up his description of the new Jerusalem (22:3-6a).

The angel shows John "the river of the water of life" (22:1). In 21:8 the
one who sat upon the throne promised that he would give to the thirsty the
fountain of the water of life, something hitherto unmentioned in the book.
Now John explains it further. He draws upon Ezek 47:1-12, where Ezekiel is
shown water issuing from beneath the Temple (cf. Joel 3:18; Zech 14:8) that
becomes a deep river as it flows eastward all the way to the Dead Sea, which
will be made fresh, to be inhabited once again by fish. Along both sides of
the river Ezekiel sees trees, which, he is informed, bear fruit monthly; their
fruit will be for food and their leaves for healing (Ezek 47:7, 12). John sees
the river "flowing from the throne of God and of the Lamb" (22:1). The
throne of God has been a major motif throughout the book. In the new
Jerusalem it is the throne of both God and the Lamb, a statement he will
repeat in 22:3 (cf. 7:9; Jer 3:17). John also observes that the river is "bright
[see on 19:8] as crystal" (22:1). The "sea of glass, like crystal" that stood
before the throne (4:3) has been replaced by the river of the water of life that
flows *from* the throne. John observes that the river flows "through the middle
of the street [cf. 21:21] of the city" (22:2) but, unlike Ezekiel, does not
follow its course any farther.

Instead of trees on both sides of the river, as in Ezekiel, John sees a single
tree—"the tree of life" (21:2). Introduced by John in conjunction with the
very first promise to the conqueror (see on 2:7), the tree of life returns to the
book here, to be mentioned again twice in the epilogue (22:14, 19). Like the
trees in Ezekiel, the tree of life bears fruit monthly (22:2), but unlike those
trees it bears "twelve kinds of fruit" (22:2). John does not say whether each
month the tree yields a different kind of fruit, or whether each month it
yields all twelve. The former is more likely, but, as elsewhere in this vision,
John is more interested in the symbolism of the number twelve than with

such specifics (cf. 21:12, 14, 21). As in Ezekiel, the leaves of the tree are for healing (22:2), though John adds "of the nations" (see on 21:24), which is not in Ezekiel.

John observes that "there will no more be any curse" (22:3; RSV "There shall no more be anything accursed"). To what *kind* of curse is John referring? The answer lies in Zech 14:11. Speaking of the whole land, Zechariah says, "It shall be inhabited, for there shall be no more curse; Jerusalem shall dwell in security." The "curse" clearly refers to the curse of the threat of desolation (so Zech 5:3; Mal 4:6; cf. Gen 3:14, 17; Isa 24:6). In the new Jerusalem, there will no longer be any such threat. After all, "the throne of God and of the Lamb shall be in it" (22:3).

John brings the vision of the new Jerusalem to a close with four observations about the "citizens" of the city—the "servants" (cf. 1:1; 2:20; 7:3; 10:7; 11:18; 19:2, 5; 22:6) of God and of the Lamb—that are interrupted by a final comment about God that repeats a detail from 21:23.

First, they "shall worship him" (22:3). The reader remembers the description of the Great Multitude in 7:15: "Therefore are they before the throne of God, and worship [RSV "serve"] him day and night within his temple." Second, "they shall see his face" (22:4). The idea of "seeing" God's face, a hope expressed in both the Old Testament (cf. Job 42:5; Ps 17:15) and the New Testament (cf. Matt 5:8; Heb 12:14; 1 John 3:2), underscores the intimacy of God's dwelling with this people that was promised in 21:3-4. It also adds to the irony of the fears of those who sought to hide themselves from the "face" of him who is seated on the throne after the opening of the sixth seal (6:16). They had every reason to fear the face of God; God's servants need have no fear at all. Third, "his name is [no explicit verb: RSV "shall be"] on their foreheads" (22:4; cf. 7:3; 9:4; 14:1; 20:4). One final time there is a contrast with the followers of the beast (cf. 13:16; 14:9).

At this point (22:5) John interrupts his observations about God's servants in order to repeat his previous comments about the absence of the night and the sun, to which he adds a light or a lamp, in the new Jerusalem (cf. 21:22, 25). But instead of mentioning both God and the Lamb here, he speaks of "the Lord God" (cf. 18:8) as their light. The two have finally been merged into one expression.

Finally, John observes that God's servants "shall reign for ever and ever" (22:5). Using the language of Dan 7:18, 27 that the saints will receive an eternal kingdom, John concludes his vision of the new Jerusalem by bringing to completion a theme he has been developing throughout the book. By virtue of the Lamb's death, his followers have received a kingship that will last not merely 1,000 years, but for ever and ever (1:6; 5:9-10; 20:4).

The angel (cf. 21:9) speaks again to John: "These words are trustworthy and true" (22:6a). The angel's words form an inclusion with 21:5, thus bringing the section on the new Jerusalem (21:5–22:6a) to its conclusion.

A number of questions might arise in the reader's mind as she attempts to make sense of John's vision of the new Jerusalem. How can a city be 1,400 miles long on each of four sides? Even more, how can a city be 1,400 miles high? And is not a 240-foot high wall a bit out of proportion for a 1,400-mile high city? How can the kings of the earth bring their glory into the city when they have already been killed by the sword of the rider on the white horse and devoured by birds (19:19, 21)? or the nations walk by the light of the city—or be healed by the leaves of the tree of life—when they have already been thrown into the lake of fire (20:8, 10)? Speaking of the tree of life, how can a single tree grow on *both* sides of a river? In what kinds of houses do people live in the new Jerusalem? Are they all the same? One could go on with similar questions, but the point is clear: if one attempts to view Revelation as a progression of "events" that take place successively in history, or take all of the details of the vision of the new Jerusalem literally, one is going to have serious problems. What is worse, one is going to misread the book and the vision.

The vision of the new Jerusalem plays a crucial role in the book. For one thing, the new Jerusalem provides the perfect counterpart to the great harlot Babylon. One might say that the book of Revelation is indeed "A Tale of Two Cities." For another thing, the vision of a new Jerusalem is precisely what one would expect to find from someone as steeped in the Old Testament and Jewish tradition as John is. Finally, the vision of the new Jerusalem provides a fitting climax to the book.

First, that John contrasts two cities should not be surprising. Even in the Roman empire, cities were the center of everyday life—and indeed a source of pride—for most people. Competition between cities could be fierce. For John to speak of two major figures in the book in terms of cities and to describe them as such—whether in terms of products or of walls, gates, and streets—is only natural. The reader who attempts to find some specific meaning in all of the various details that are presented about the cities misses the point.

Second, as has been pointed out, the hope of a glorified Jerusalem was strong in Judaism. As he does with the fall of Babylon, John mines the Old Testament for appropriate passages that he then weaves into his own seamless garment. Numerous images—from the holy of holies to kings bringing their glory to a flowing river—come together in a vision that unites a variety of symbols of hope into a single portrait. The reader who misses the plethora of

Old Testament allusions and tries to take the vision "literally" misses the powerful fulfillment of Jewish expectation that the vision presents.

Finally, several major themes come together in the vision of the new Jerusalem. First, John's deliberate, sustained identification of the Lamb with God reaches its peak with references to God and the Lamb in 21:22, 23; 22:1, 3 culminating in the simple—but telling—reference to "the Lord God" in 22:5. Similarly, John's deliberate, sustained identification of the Church with Israel reaches its peak with the identification of the Church with the new Jerusalem.

And it is this latter point that brings the reader face to face with what is perhaps the most surprising feature of all concerning the vision of the new Jerusalem. Despite popular perception that 21:10–22:5 is a picture of "heaven," it is in fact nothing of the sort. The new Jerusalem is, of course, none other than the Bride of the Lamb (21:2, 9-10). Christians do not "go to" the new Jerusalem; Christians *are* the new Jerusalem!

One final word is necessary. Each time John mentions the new Jerusalem in the book, he uses the present tense: "coming down out of heaven." Given what Jesus has *already* accomplished for his followers—they are *already* priests and a kingdom (1:6)—it follows that Christians *already* make up the new Jerusalem. That does not mean the new Jerusalem has been fully revealed yet. The dwelling of God with his people has begun, but it has not yet reached its culmination. The dragon still seeks revenge on the offspring of the woman, and that will not cease until he is thrown into the lake of fire. The Final Judgment is still future, and the final revelation of the new Jerusalem will take place only after that Judgment, when God makes all things new.

John's fourth "in the Spirit" experience is finished. The Bride of the Lamb—the new Jerusalem, the Church—has been described in all of her beauty. Those who conquer for the Lamb now know what has been prepared for them by the One who himself conquered by giving his very life for them.

"Behold, I am coming soon"

Revelation 22:6b-21

John's four "in the Spirit" experiences are over. The book ends with a series of brief, seemingly disjointed units that serve to bring the reader back to the opening verses of the book while also bringing the book to a close. The epilogue, which, along with the prologue (1:1-8), frames John's visionary experience, consists of John speaking (22:6b), God/Jesus speaking (22:7), further interaction between John and the angel (22:8-11), Jesus speaking again (22:12-13), an oracle about those who wash their robes and those on the outside (22:14-15), Jesus speaking again (22:16), miscellaneous oracles and exhortations (22:17), a warning (22:18-19), Jesus speaking again and John's response (22:20), and a closing benediction (22:21).

It is customary to view 22:6 as a single sentence spoken by a single individual (so the RSV), resulting in the angel rather awkwardly speaking of himself in the third person in the latter part of the verse ("sent his angel"). The reader needs to understand that Greek contains neither punctuation marks nor quotation marks. As already noted, 22:6a functions as the conclusion to the larger unit that begins in 21:5. On the other hand, 22:6b echoes 1:1 almost verbatim. The "and" at the beginning of 22:6b need not connect it integrally with the preceding clause. Indeed, "and" (*kai*) in Revelation frequently introduces new sentences and even new paragraphs. Such is the case here. The angel has finished his revelation of the new Jerusalem (22:6a); now John returns to the beginning of the book (22:6b). Thus, the reader should place a period, with closing quotation marks, after 22:6a and understand 22:6b, with no quotation marks, as the beginning of a new paragraph on the order of 1:1. The words are not those of the angel, but of John, who has returned to where he began: God sent his angel to show his servants what must soon take place. In other words, this book is a revelation from God.

The mention of the angel clears up once and for all one of the issues left unspecified in the opening of the book. In 1:1 John says Jesus sent "his angel" to John to "show" his servants what must soon take place, but in the verses that follow the angel is nowhere mentioned, appearing only late in the book (19:9-10). Instead, John's visionary experience begins immediately with an encounter with the risen Jesus himself (1:10-18). Now, at the end of the book, John speaks of the angel "who showed" him the things he had seen and heard (22:8), and Jesus speaks directly of having sent "my angel" to John (22:16). The reader now realizes that this angel must be the same angel who was speaking with John in 22:6 and who had shown him the new Jerusalem—i.e., one of the angels who had the seven bowls full of the seven last plagues (21:9) and who had also shown John the punishment of the great prostitute (17:1). We learn in this last section, therefore, that the angel whom Jesus sent to John with the revelation is one of the seven angels with the seven bowls. Indeed, apart from Jesus in 4:1, this angel is the only one in the book who "shows" John anything (17:1; 21:9, 10; 22:1). Does the fact that this angel is introduced only in 17:1 and 21:9 indicate that while the whole book contains the revelation (John's reference in 22:8 to himself as the one who "heard and saw these things" recalls, e.g., 1:10, 12, 19), the most salient points of the revelation have to do with the destruction of Babylon and the coming of the new Jerusalem?

Two more items in this section serve to round off the transmission process. First, John is instructed not to "seal up" the words of the prophecy of this book (22:10). To "seal up" something has the connotation of keeping it hidden (cf. 10:4). The expression is drawn from Dan 12:4 (cf. Dan 12:9), where Daniel is told to seal up the message he has received because it refers to the distant future ("the time of the end")—i.e., it is not relevant to his readers' immediate situation (ostensibly the sixth century BC). John, on the other hand, is not to seal up the revelation given to him because it refers to the *near* future (cf. 1:3) and, hence, is directly relevant to the seven churches of Asia.

Second, John gives a warning to "everyone who hears the words of the prophecy of this book": the hearer is charged neither to add to, nor take away from, its words (22:18-19). The language is drawn from Deut 4:2 and 12:32, where Moses instructs the Israelites neither to add to nor take away from the commands he is giving them, commands he in turn has received from God (cf. Deut 4:5, 14; 6:1) as a covenant that elaborates upon the one given at Sinai (Deut 29:1). The future of the Israelites will depend upon whether they follow the covenant, which will distinguish them from the other nations, or whether they, in fact, follow the practices of those nations. One will bring God's blessings, the other God's curses (e.g., Deut 28). But in addition to the enticements of the other nations themselves, there will always be the threat that some of the Israelites will encourage others to depart from the covenant (e.g., Deut 13).

The analogy to John's situation is readily apparent. Pressures to accommodate to Roman culture come from both outside the church and inside (e.g., Jezebel, the Nicolaitans). The revelation John has received has set out in stark contrast the radically different fates of those who follow the Lamb, on the one hand, and those who follow the beast, on the other. Thus, a warning couched in Deuteronomic terms is entirely appropriate for the seven churches of Asia. To view this warning as having to do with the process of copying the book of Revelation or with the canonization of the New Testament (or the Bible) is to miss its point entirely. John's delineation of the consequences of failing to follow the warning is a creative, ironic expansion upon Deut 29:19-21, which says that "all the curses written in this book" will fall upon the Israelite who willfully departs from the covenant (cf. *Letter of Aristeas* 311). John warns that the one who "adds" anything to the book will have the plagues described in it added to him, while the one who "takes away" words will have his share in the tree of life and in the holy city taken away from him (cf. 22:14). Given the traditional language John uses, it is doubtful whether he intends any difference between the two warnings—i.e., that having things taken away from a person is not as bad as having all of the plagues heaped upon him, and, hence, that it is somehow worse to take things away from the book than to add things to it. The second part of the warning is an innovation that must surely be understood in terms of the false apostles and prophets who are deceiving the seven churches. John's warning is not just for outsiders. Even (and especially!) those within the church should beware of leading the church astray. Such action will merit the severest of consequences.

A number of other elements connect this final section with the opening of the book: "I am coming soon" (22:7, 12, 20; cf. 1:7, 8); a blessing upon the one who "keeps" the words of the prophecy of this book (22:7, 9; cf. 1:3); the characterization of the book as "prophecy" (22:7, 10, 18, 19; cf. 1:3) and its readers as those who "hear" it (22:18; cf. 1:3); John's identification of himself by name (22:8; cf. 1:1, 4, 9) and his mention of having heard and seen these things (22:8; cf. 1:2, 10); "the time is near" (22:10; cf. 1:3); "I am the Alpha and the Omega" (22:13; cf. 1:8); Jesus having sent his angel with this "testimony" (22:16, 20; cf. 1:1-2); and the mention of the "Spirit" (22:17; cf. 1:10). These elements serve the literary function of inclusion, connecting this section with the beginning of the book and, hence, alerting the reader that the book is drawing to a close.

But it is important to note that such echoes of the beginning of the book are more that just literary markers. The intervening visions have cast the opening of the book in a new light.

The opening of the epilogue also takes the reader back to the transition between the fall of Babylon and the destruction of the beast and the false prophet (19:1-10). At the close of that section there was an odd exchange between the angel and John, in which the angel intervened when John fell down to worship him (19:10). A similar incident takes place in 22:8-9. This time, however, John explains the reason for his action: the angel showed "these things"—the revelation—to John (22:8; cf. 1:1). Once again the angel, identifying himself as "a fellow servant with you and your brethren," insists that John stop, directing John instead, as in 19:10, to "worship God" (22:9). But rather than characterizing John and his brethren as those "who hold the testimony of Jesus" (19:10), the angel characterizes them as "the prophets and . . . those who keep the words of this book" (22:9). It is diffi-cult to draw any inference other than that those who hold the testimony of Jesus, the prophets, and those who keep the words of John's book are one and the same (cf. 11:18; 18:20). John rounded out the incident in 19:10 with an observation on the spirit of prophecy. Here he has preceded the inci-dent with a similar comment in 22:6b, where he identifies the Lord as "the God of the spirits of the prophets" (cf. 1 Cor 14:32; Num 27:16). It is God who inspires both John *and* his readers.

The epilogue brings together a number of themes John has developed throughout the book. Already in 1:5-7 John describes Jesus in terms used in the Old Testament for God. Throughout the book he continues to develop the notion that Jesus is God. Now he brings this theme to its completion. Perhaps the clearest statement of the identification of Jesus with God is found in 22:13. In 1:8 God identifies himself as the Alpha and the Omega. In 21:6 he repeats this self-characterization, adding to it that he is the begin-ning and the end. Jesus, on the other hand, has twice identified himself as the first and the last (1:17; 2:8). Now the three self-designations are brought together without distinction: first the Alpha and the Omega (God), then the first and the last (Jesus), and finally the beginning and the end (God). One final and climactic time John identifies Jesus as God.

Jesus further identifies himself in 22:16 in three ways. The first expres-sion, "the root . . . of David," is found earlier in the book (5:5) just prior to the dramatic scene where the slain Lamb takes the scroll from the one seated on the throne (5:7). To return to it here reminds the reader of both the royal Davidic status of Jesus and the fact that this status is integrally connected with Jesus' death. The second expression, "the offspring of David," is found only here. It underscores Jesus' royal status over against the Roman emperor. Finally, "the bright morning star" is found, without the adjective, in one of the promises to the conqueror (2:28). It also seems to represent a polemic against the Roman emperor (see comment on 2:28).

Finally, because of the status that he has attained, Jesus has the authority to execute judgment on all, which he will do when he comes (22:12). He will bring his "reward" (RSV "recompense"; cf. Isa 40:10; 62:11), which echoes 11:18, and will "repay [cf. 18:6] every one for what he has done" (see on 2:23; cf. 20:13, 15).

The epilogue places a strong emphasis on the "coming" of Jesus. Three times Jesus says, "I am coming soon [*tachu*]" (22:7, 12, 20 [the last time quoted by John]; cf. 16:15). The expression recalls Jesus' words to the churches at Pergamum (2:16) and Philadelphia (3:11) and is similar to that found in 1:3 and 22:6b (*en tachei*). The Spirit (cf. 2:7, 11, 17, 29; 3:6, 13, 22; 14:13) and the Bride (19:7-8; 21:2, 9) say, "Come," and both the one who hears and the one who is thirsty are encouraged to say, "Come" (22:17).

The epilogue also contains the sixth and seventh beatitudes in the book (cf. 1:3; 14:13; 16:15; 19:9; 20:6). The sixth beatitude, like the third (16:15), is prefaced with "I am coming . . ." (22:7). Its content is similar to the first beatitude (1:3) insofar as it pronounces a blessing upon the one "who keeps the words of the prophecy of this book." That the similarity of content would provide a literary inclusion and, hence, would be a nice way to wrap up the beatitudes only serves to emphasize the importance of the fact that there is, to the surprise of the reader, one more beatitude—the seventh (22:14). The seventh beatitude draws together the most striking images John has used for faithful Christians: they are those who wash their robes in the blood of the Lamb (cf. 7:14) that they might have access both to the tree of life (2:7; 22:2; cf. 22:19) and to the city (the new Jerusalem; cf. 21:27; Ps 118:19-20).

Following the final beatitude is a most vivid continuation of the description of the city, or, to be more precise, what lies outside of it (22:15). After an initial mention of "the dogs," five groups of people are listed, all of which were previously mentioned, along with some other groups, in 21:8 (cf. 9:21). "Dogs," mentioned only here in the book, provides a fitting characterization of these groups, since they are "unclean" (see on 21:27). The "and" after "dogs" is therefore epexegetic, meaning the reader should replace the "and" with a colon. But what does it mean to say that these groups are "outside" the city? Have they not all been destroyed at the judgment (19:21; 20:15) before the new Jerusalem came down out of heaven (21:10)? As in the case of the "nations" and "the kings of the earth" in 21:24, the language is intended not chronologically but pictorially. Since scavenging dogs would commonly be found in cities throughout the Roman world, to mention dogs is appropriate for the new Jerusalem as well. The point is not that these five groups are somehow still in existence after the Judgment—that the condemned will be living just outside the city walls. Rather, the point is that these groups will have no place in the new Jerusalem (cf. 21:27; 4QMMT[394-399] 61-65).

The four exhortations in 22:11 (third person imperatives in Greek: hence, the form, "Let A do B") might seem a bit odd at first. To be sure, encouraging people to do right and to be holy makes sense. But why exhort people to do wrong and be vile? Would it not make better sense to call such people to repentance? The answer to these questions lies in recognizing that John has patterned the exhortation after Ezek 3:27: "he that will hear, let him hear; and he that will refuse to hear, let him refuse; for they are a rebellious house" (cf. Isa 6:9-10; Dan 12:10). As in 22:11, the "exhortation" in Ezekiel follows a statement concerning prophecy. The point is not that people are *commanded* to do something, but that the word of God will inevitably meet with two diametrically opposed responses from its hearers. Some will listen to it, do right, and be holy (cf. 20:6), while others will refuse to listen, do evil, and be filthy. Or, to put it differently, some will follow the Lamb, and some will follow the beast. John's prophecy is not to be sealed up, because the time is near; hence, it will elicit both kinds of response from its hearers.

There are three more third person imperatives in 22:17, this time all of a positive nature. The recipient of the imperative is described as the one who hears (cf. 22:18; 1:3; 2:7, 11, 17, 20; 3:6,13, 22; 13:9), the one who is thirsty (cf. 7:16; 21:6), and the one who desires (only used here in the book as an intransitive verb). The first imperative, to say "Come," aligns the hearer with the Spirit and the Bride (cf. 19:7-8; 21:2, 9), who say "Come" in the preceding sentence. Taken together, the second and third imperatives are essentially identical with the promise given in 21:6: the thirsty one is invited to take "the water of life without price." The language is drawn from Isa 55:1: "Ho, every one who thirsts, come to the waters" (cf. *1 Enoch* 48:1). But what is striking is that the promise in 21:6 is cast in the future ("I *will* give"), while in this verse the individual is invited to take the water of life *now*. Once again there is a blurring of promises that seem to be both future and available in the present. Even now the Christian can begin to partake of the promises that will reach their fullness in the new Jerusalem.

Following John's warning in 22:18-19, "he who testifies to these things"—Jesus (cf. 1:1)—repeats one last time that he is coming soon (22:20). John's response is one of affirmation: "Amen [cf. 1:6, 7; 3:14; 5:14;

7:12; 19:4; 22:21]. Come, Lord Jesus" (22:20; cf. 1 Cor 16:22). John then closes his book with a simple benediction: "The grace of the Lord Jesus be with all the saints" (22:21; cf. 1 Cor 16:3; 2 Cor 13:14; Gal 6:18; Phil 4:23; 1 Thess 5:28; 2 Thess 3:18; Philem 25).

John's book is complete. The reader understands by now that Jesus indeed is "coming soon." Though the reader does not know precisely when that coming will take place, she now has a more complete understanding of how that coming will bring punishment and reward. And she realizes that whether Jesus' coming stands, for her, as a promise or a threat is based upon whether she has chosen to follow the Lamb or the beast. And she understands that the only appropriate response to the revelation is to "worship God"—as he is now understood in his intimate connection with the Lamb who was slain.

Select Bibliography

General Commentaries

Harrington, Wilfrid J. *Revelation*. Sacra Pagina. Collegeville MN: Liturgical Press, 1993.

Mounce, Robert H. *The Book of Revelation*. Revised edition. New International Commentary. Grand Rapids: Eerdmans, 1998.

Talbert, Charles H, *The Apocalypse: A Reading of the Revelation of John*. Louisville: Westminster John Knox, 1994.

Advanced Commentaries

Aune, David. *Revelation*. 3 volumes. Word Biblical Commentaries. Dallas: Word, 1997–1999.

Beale, G. K. *The Book of Revelation*. The New International Greek Testament Commentary. Grand Rapids: Eerdmans, 1999.

Osborne, Grant R. *Revelation*. Baker Exegetical Commentary on the New Testament. Grand Rapids: Baker, 2002.

Reddish, Mitchell. *Revelation*. Smyth & Helwys Bible Commentary. Macon: Smyth & Helwys, 2001.

Other Studies

Bauckham, Richard. *The Theology of the Book of Revelation*. New Testament Theology. Cambridge: Cambridge University Press, 1993.

Duff, Paul B. *Who Rides the Beast?: Prophetic Rivalry and the Rhetoric of Crisis in the Churches of the Apocalypse*. New York: Oxford University Press, 2001.

Friesen, Steven J. *Imperial Cults and the Apocalypse of John: Reading Revelation in the Ruins* New York: Oxford University Press, 2001.

Metzger, Bruce M. *Breaking the Code: Understanding the Book of Revelation*. Nashville: Abingdon, 1993.

Michaels, J. Ramsey. *Interpreting the Book of Revelation*. Guides to New Testament Exegesis 7. Grand Rapids: Eerdmans, 1992.

Thompson, Leonard L. *The Book of Revelation: Apocalypse and Empire.* New York: Oxford
    University Press, 1990.

Turner, William. *Making Sense of Revelation.* Macon: Smyth & Helwys, 2000.

Worth, Ronald H., Jr. *The Seven Cities of the Apocalypse and Greco-Asian Culture.* New York:
    Paulist Press, 1999.

————. *The Seven Cities of the Apocalypse and Roman Culture.* New York: Paulist Press,
    1999.

THE SMYTH & HELWYS
BIBLE
COMMENTARY

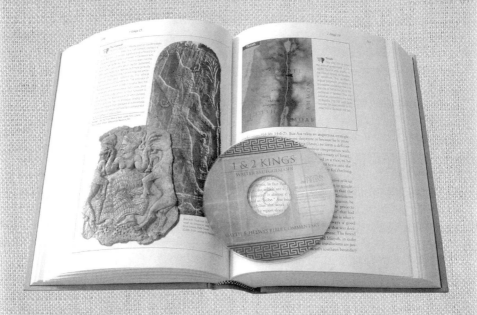

Far too many Bible commentaries fall short of bridging the gap between insights of biblical scholars and the needs of students of Scripture. In an unprecedented way, the *Smyth & Helwys Bible Commentary* is visually stimulating, user-friendly, and written to make available quality Bible study in an accessible format.

Using a revolutionary format, the *Smyth & Helwys Bible Commentary* offers a wealth of visual information. Each volume includes artwork from across the centuries, photography, archaeological artifacts, maps, and much more.

View additional sample pages and find out more about hyperlinks online.

www.helwys.com/commentary